FAMILY MEDIATION HANDBOOK

SECOND EDITION

FAMILY MEDIATION HANDBOOK

SECOND EDITION

Barbara Landau
Ph.D., LL.B., LL.M.
Psychologist and Member of the Ontario Bar

Mario Bartoletti
M.A., Ed.D.
Marriage and Family Counsellor

Ruth Mesbur
B.A., LL.B.
Member of the Ontario Bar

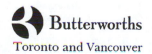 Butterworths
Toronto and Vancouver

Family Mediation Handbook

© Butterworths Canada Ltd. 1997
January 1997

The Butterworth Group of Companies

Canada:
75 Clegg Road, MARKHAM, Ontario L6G 1A1
and
1721-808 Nelson St., Box 12148, VANCOUVER, B.C. V6Z 2H2

Australia:
Butterworths Pty Ltd., SYDNEY

Ireland:
Butterworth (Ireland) Ltd., DUBLIN

Malaysia:
Malayan Law Journal Sdn Bhd, KUALA LUMPUR

New Zealand:
Butterworths of New Zealand Ltd., WELLINGTON

Singapore:
Butterworths Asia, SINGAPORE

South Africa:
Butterworth Publishers (Pty.) Ltd., DURBAN

United Kingdom:
Butterworth & Co. (Publishers) Ltd., LONDON

United States:
Michie, CHARLOTTESVILLE, Virginia

Canadian Cataloguing in Publication Data

Landau, Barbara
 Family mediation handbook

2nd ed.
Includes bibliographical references and index.
ISBN 0-433-39809-4

1. Family mediation – Canada.   2. Divorce mediation –
Canada.   3. Domestic relations – Canada.   4. Domestic
relations – Ontario.   I. Bartoletti, Mario Dante,
1933 –   .   II. Mesbur, Ruth,   III. Title.

HQ838.L36 1997   306.89   C96-932525-8

Printed and bound in Canada.

Preface to the Second Edition

A decade has swept by since the first edition, and family mediation has gone through a period of examination and professional growth. Three areas of discussion have been most influential and have prompted this second edition.

First, the entire legal system has been called into question as a system that is too expensive, too slow and cumbersome, and too adversarial for relationship disputes. Alternative dispute resolution mechanisms have increasingly been employed in North America, and in fact around the world, as a way of resolving disputes more expeditiously, often at less cost, and with a greater emphasis on cooperative problem solving. Many jurisdictions now require that clients be informed about, and in appropriate cases, attempt mediation before they proceed to litigation. The hope is that the courts will be reserved for those disputes that cannot be resolved in other ways or that are not appropriate for mediation.

Second, family mediation in particular has had its methodology and some of its basic assumptions called into question by women's advocates. They asked: how could there be an assumption of equality of bargaining power between a woman and her husband or common law partner in relationships where abuse was a factor? How could mediators protect victims of abuse (most often women) if a central tenet of mediation was the neutrality of the mediator? How could a mediator possibly mediate an agreement that was fair to both parties and that would reasonably protect children if they did not ask questions about the past history of the relationship, particularly questions about abuse and control? In addition, women's advocates questioned the process followed by many mediators of only seeing the couple together and not screening each party individually before deciding whether they were able to negotiate as equals. Their questioning was the catalyst for the most significant changes in mediation over the past decade. We are grateful for their concern and wisdom.

Third, the field of family law has gone through several important developments. Many questions have been raised on several different levels. On the most philosophical level, Madame Justice Rosalie Abella asked a number of questions in her paper, delivered to the Family Law Section of the Canadian Bar Association — Ontario Division on January 25, 1996, from which I will quote at length. Justice Abella, reflecting on the views of separating couples, asks rhetorically;

> Then why are so many people feeling frustrated? Perhaps because in our zeal to reform, we have spent too much time tinkering with the edges of the law, and not enough examining what its central premises should be now

that preventing divorce and punishing marital offences are no longer the guiding philosophies. What is it that family law is supposed to resolve? That, for me, presents an ironic anomaly: the law of the family is not, in fact, about the family at all; the law of the family is about the family when it seeks no longer to be a family. The law of the family is really about the law of the *former* family, and the post-modern law of the family is really the post-modern law of the post-family.

Historically, the only thing the state used to be interested in was making sure the law kept families together, so the only thing the law regulated was exits. If they stayed together, the law respected their privacy. If they did not, the law was all over them. Is the post-modern law really so different in its preoccupations?

What happens inside a family while it is a family, aside from child welfare and spousal assault protection, is something in which the law interests itself very little. Family law has never been concerned with the actual workings of the family, with the happiness or fulfilment or economic realities of its individual members, only with what happens when members want to cancel their membership. It only invades the privacy of the home when someone seeks permanently to walk out the front door. One has to wonder why.

What is there about the decision of an adult no longer to remain with another adult that gives a state, and through it a court, the right to say what happens to that adult and anyone he or she leaves behind, when the state has said nothing about how the very same people were to treat each other while they were together? If there is no state interest in the relationship while it is ongoing, what is there about a desire to end it that triggers it? Do we have a clear understanding of where the right to privacy ends and the right of the state to intervene begins? Why is there a gap between the flexibility we offer people when they live together and the scrutiny we impose when this is no longer the case?

Is the gap a sensible one, or does it help explain why some people who confront the system find it so frustrating and unresponsive to the realities they have just come from.

· · · · ·

The *substance* of family law should be nourishing and expeditiously available; the *process* should be lean and fair. To the extent that procedural reliance unduly delays legitimate entitlements and arbitrarily blocks access to them, it ought not to be tolerated by the system.

Are we entitled to be confident that the over-judicialization and justiciability of family law is producing greater fairness to those who are between families? What we should be thinking about instead is how to minimize the possibility that family disagreements find their way into a courtroom at all, and help former families get on with their lives. It would be interesting to interview persons at the end of multi-year disputes to see whether their satisfaction increases with the amount of procedure they have been exposed to, or whether it varies with the result.

Everyone wants their days in court, not their years. We have lost the punitive substantive approach in family law which sought to prevent departures by penalizing the wayfarer, but we have replaced it with a punitive procedural approach which penalizes everyone.

If the law is going to be truly responsive to social realities, then it should be more responsive to the reality that most people cannot afford to go through a civil trial, and that many people who require the assistance of the law will be unable to avail themselves of its benefit because the complications and ambiguities and procedural hurdles make the possibility of access to a resolution unattainable.[*]

In addition, a number of court decisions and federal government policies have been issued which will have a considerable impact on clients' expectations about custody and support issues and therefore will directly affect the practice of family mediation.

These decisions resolved questions such as, "When a custodial parent chooses to move to another jurisdiction with a child, is the only test 'what is in the child's best interests?' or does the custodial parent have the right to make this decision as part of his or her rights as a custodial parent? If the test is the child's best interests, are there any criteria the court should rely on to evaluate 'best interests'?"

Also, with respect to support, the government was faced with a court challenge to the fairness of taxing women (recipients of child support) while giving their partners a tax break. Furthermore there was the ongoing reality that the majority of those obligated to pay support either do not pay on time or pay less than they should. The government was faced with the question of how best to ensure that children are adequately supported?

These questions peel back the onion-like layers of legislative objectives, substantive provisions, and procedural options. The social-political context, the concerns about gender issues, the welfare of children, the locus of control over family decisions when families no longer want to be families, all impact on the substance of this book.

The authors feel that the answer is to offer a greater number of alternatives so that parents can select the process that most closely suits their situation. The direction is towards greater control by parents and less intrusiveness by the legal system, unless there are concerns about abuse, intimidation, or serious inequality of bargaining power. Hence the increasing interest in family mediation as a cooperative, empowering, and expeditious choice for families who seek no longer to be families.

---

[*] Abella, R., now reported in a fuller version in "The Law of the Family in the Year of the Family" (1994), 26 *Ottawa L. Rev.*, 533-49. Reproduced with permission.

Preface to the First Edition

Over the past decade, judges, lawyers, mental health professionals, and disputing spouses have all become disillusioned with the adversarial approach to resolving family disputes. Conflicts among family members are different than most other legal challenges in that the relationship between the warring parties does not end with the judge's decision. Unlike other civil litigation cases in which the disputants go their separate ways after an adversarial court battle, parents must continue to cooperate in the interests of their children for years following the court proceeding. Recent research has shown that children are the real victims of family breakdown, and the more intense the parental conflict following separation, the more likely it is that the children will be torn apart by a conflict of loyalties over their parents. Also, the more adversarial the struggle to end the marriage, the more difficult it is for parents to work cooperatively in the future.

Mediation is a method of dispute resolution that has as its objective a cooperative, voluntary, and equitable outcome to a dispute. Agreement is reached by the parties themselves with the assistance of an impartial professional. The emphasis on improved communication and cooperation between the parties is attractive to the legal profession, the mental health profession, and parents, because a mediated solution is more likely to be honoured, tension between the parties usually diminishes, and the children often benefit from a more meaningful relationship with both parents. Over the past several years mediation has attracted considerable interest as an alternative to litigation, particularly for disputes involving children.

The *Family Mediation Handbook* is a comprehensive Canadian text that explains the process of mediation, distinguishes mediation from other forms of dispute resolution such as litigation, counselling, or arbitration, and reviews the ethical issues that must be considered by all professionals involved in this field. This book covers the mediation of family law disputes involving property and support issues, as well as disputes with respect to custody of and access to children.

The *Family Mediation Handbook* is a handy reference tool for mental health professionals, lawyers, family doctors, and clergymen who intend to practise as mediators or who are in a position to refer clients for mediation services. This book could also be read by potential clients who wish to evaluate the alternatives of mediation, litigation, and other methods of dispute resolution.

The *Family Mediation Handbook* contains a great deal of practical advice and information as to the procedure followed in mediation, communication skills, methods of dispute resolution, ethical standards, and the effects on children of separation and divorce. In addition the book contains a detailed Appendix with samples of forms, agreements, and correspondence that will be particularly helpful to the beginning mediator.

The *Family Mediation Handbook* offers a summary of law in Canada, with special reference to the Province of Ontario. Mediation has been described by Professor Robert Mnookin[*] of Stanford University as a process of "bargaining in the shadow of the law", and therefore it is essential to include both the law and the clinical practice of mediation.

Finally, the *Family Mediation Handbook* is a useful reference for professionals who deal with either children or adults who are undergoing separation and divorce and who wish to be more sensitive to this process. For example, teachers, family physicians, and clergymen are often looked to for assistance during a marital crisis. This book provides an understanding of the mediation process so that these professionals can offer guidance to families experiencing a marriage breakdown.

Chapter 1

Provides the historical background to mediation from both a legal and a mental health perspective. Information is provided about the development of mediation services in both Canada and the United States up to the present.

Chapter 2

Examines alternative methods of dispute resolution, such as counselling, mediation, arbitration, litigation, and assessments as methods of resolving family law problems.

Chapter 3

Sets the stage for mediation by outlining the roles of referral sources, clients, and the mediator in the mediation process. Practical information is provided to assist in deciding who are appropriate candidates for mediation and in particular how to screen for abuse and power imbalances. For those who are appropriate, practice tips are included for initiating the mediation, arriving at interim arrangements, and terminating the mediation. The emphasis is on ethical issues that might arise at various points in the process.

---

[*] R. Mnookin and L. Kornhauser, "Bargaining in the Shadow of the Law: The Case of Divorce" (1979), 88 *Yale Law Journal* 950.

Chapter 4

Focuses on the principles and steps underlying an interest-based bargaining model. The mediation procedure for family cases is set out in detail, including the objectives for meetings with counsel, the parties, children, and other significant individuals during the course of mediation. Particular emphasis is given to the development of a "parenting plan" which is central to custody and access issues. It is expected that there will be differences in procedure between mediators depending on the nature and complexity of the problems as well as the experience of the mediator.

Chapter 5

Examines the clinical skills associated with mediation. In this chapter the mediator is seen as an educator, a fact gatherer, and a communicator. The chapter offers considerable information as to the responses of children to separation and divorce, the key factors affecting children's post-separation adjustment, as well as specific suggestions for information gathering. In addition, the chapter contains practical ideas for dealing with communication problems or serious power imbalances that surface during the mediation process. This chapter will be of interest to both mediators and non-mediators, as it provides extensive background material for anyone dealing with families who are experiencing marital difficulties.

Chapters 6 and 7

Chapters 6 and 7 set out the relevant family law in Canada and, more specifically, in Ontario with respect to custody and access (Chapter 6) and property and support (Chapter 7). These chapters will be of particular interest to non-lawyers who are looking for a clear, concise, and readable outline of the most important features of family law for the purpose of mediating matrimonial disputes. Of particular interest are the recent Supreme Court of Canada decisions with respect to mobility and spousal support and the federal government's proposed child support guidelines. Although non-lawyers cannot give legal advice, it is important for the mental health professional who is acting as a mediator to understand the legal context relevant to the issues in dispute.

Chapter 8

Discusses in some detail the rules of professional conduct that have been adopted by the Ontario Association for Family Mediation. In addition this chapter explores the areas of conflict between mental health professionals and lawyers, as well as within the legal profession, with respect to lawyers acting as mediators. This chapter demonstrates the direction mediation is taking in its efforts to become a recognized profession. All

mediators and those referring to mediators need to be aware of the ethical code of conduct expected from those who practise.

Chapter 9

Contains practical information with respect to preparing memoranda of
understanding, minutes of settlement, or reports in cases where the parties have arrived at a full agreement, a partial agreement, or in some
cases no agreement at all. This chapter clarifies the differences in reporting requirements for mediators depending on whether the mediation is a
closed or open process.

Chapter 10

Compares the procedure in custody assessments with that of mediation of
custody and access disputes. This chapter explores the purpose of a custody assessment, the differences between mediation and assessments, and
the procedure to be followed. In addition, specific information is given as
to the contents of an acceptable custody assessment report.

Chapter 11

Sets out specific, detailed information with respect to the role of the
mediator/assessor as expert witness. The difference between privilege and
confidentiality is discussed, and the guidelines for giving testimony in
court, including the qualifications of an expert witness, are explored in
some detail. Practical suggestions are given for those mental health professionals who are to appear as an expert witness and for the lawyer who
requires the services of an expert witness in a family law trial.

Each chapter contains an annotated bibliography, a handy reference
for the reader who may wish to explore particular subjects in more detail.
In addition, precedent material is provided for all steps in the mediation
process, and will be particularly helpful for those who are new to mediation. Copies of the standards of professional conduct adopted by Family
Mediation Canada, the Ontario Association for Family Mediation, the
Law Society of Upper Canada, and the American Bar Association are
included. This information will be useful for mediators in other jurisdictions who are presently developing a code of conduct for practising mediators.

The *Family Mediation Handbook* clearly sets out the purpose of mediation, the procedure followed, and all of the material necessary to inform
clients about mediation services or carry out these services as part of a
professional practice. The format adopted can be easily used for lectures,
quick reference, or a practical guide. It covers both custody and access
mediation as well as comprehensive financial mediation, and will be of
interest to a variety of audiences.

Acknowledgements

The authors wish to express their gratitude to the many parents and children who have helped us understand the process of separation and divorce. We have benefitted greatly from hearing their stories, listening to their pain, observing their growth, and assessing what seemed to be helpful.

Of particular importance to this edition is the contribution made by women's advocates from a broad spectrum of cultural, racial, and economic groups from across North America. Their input served as the catalyst for the most significant changes in family mediation in a decade, and they have enlightened us all. In particular, Barbara Landau would like to thank Trudy Don, Barbara Hart, Mary Lou Fassel, and Sheila Kuehl for their friendship and their wisdom.

We have also learned from the students who participated actively in our mediation training programs, and have been enriched by a growing number of colleagues who share our enthusiasm for finding more effective, constructive, safe, and empowering processes for assisting adults and children through the bumpy terrain of marriage breakdown.

Special thanks are due to Niki Landau for her patience and careful preparation of the manuscript for this second edition. Her diligence and ability to focus kept the project on track, and her helpful suggestions improved the quality of the book. We also appreciate the time, patience, and creative suggestions of Joni Fisher, our lawyer and an enthusiastic supporter of this project.

The authors dedicate this edition to their spouses and children, whose support and encouragement is the prime inspiration for our efforts in working with families.

January 1997

Barbara Landau
Mario Bartoletti
Ruth Mesbur

Table of Contents

Chapter One

Historical Overview of Mediation

A. LEGAL ASPECTS: THE EVOLUTION OF NON-ADVERSARIAL DISPUTE RESOLUTION IN FAMILY LAW AND OTHER LEGAL AREAS

Until recently, because of the very serious consequences of divorce, both in the courts and in terms of society's reaction, family law cases were handled in an intensely adversarial manner. The objective of each lawyer was to present his or her client as morally pure and blameless while alleging immoral conduct by the other spouse. This resulted in highly polarized morality plays that were staged in the courtroom and were usually emotionally destructive to both participants.

Present-day family laws reflect a change in social attitudes to marriage breakdown. In the first place, the law no longer provides strong protection for marriage or a bulwark against divorce, but rather reflects the concept that adults should be free to choose whether or not to remain in the marital union. Fault is no longer a necessary ingredient for being granted a divorce, and support and custody are no longer used as part of the social sanction against divorce.

Over the past two decades, the legislation affecting separation and divorce has become far less arbitrary and reflects such concepts of equity and fairness as marriage is a social and economic partnership. That means the product of the marriage should be shared between the spouses at the time of breakdown. Custody laws are now tied to the needs or best interests of children, and economic support is determined on the basis of financial need and ability to pay, with conduct explicitly excluded as a criterion (unless this conduct is directly relevant to parenting, for example, domestic violence or substance abuse).

Family law is extremely susceptible to pendulum shifts as social and moral values change. Where the 1980's catered to the individualism of the "me generation", the 1990's have seen the pendulum shift back to a concern about "family values" and the disintegration of our traditional moral structure. Divorce, which was initially seen as an opportunity for a second chance at adult happiness, has brought with it such unanticipated costs as the emotional and financial burden on children, the disappointment and disruption of extended family and friendship ties, and, most ironically, the recognition that where there are children, parental ties last forever.

All of these changes have resulted in important shifts in the way our legal system approaches separation and divorce. Increasingly there has been an emphasis on negotiation, pretrial conferences, mediation of matrimonial disputes, the use of expert assessment reports, and other techniques designed to assist couples in reaching an early resolution of the issues in dispute, particularly where children are involved. When those efforts fail to produce practical parenting arrangements, a custody/access evaluation is frequently ordered by the court as a means of obtaining an impartial professional report with recommendations for carrying out parenting responsibilities and caring for the children. Such action reflects the increasing awareness by legislators and judges that while the spousal relationship may come to an end, there is a need to continue a cooperative framework for the sake of children. While adversarial procedures lead to bitterness and hostility between the parents, research has consistently demonstrated that the ones who suffer the most as a result of an adversarial divorce are those who are least at fault — namely the children.

Clinical research has not only demonstrated the need for parents to cooperate in the interests of their children, it has also demonstrated that divorce is a complex experience, with many individuals going through stages that are somewhat similar to a grieving process. The research of Drs. Wallerstein and Kelly[1] that followed 60 families over a ten-year period documents the long-term emotional repercussions for both parents and children. A number of studies have shown that litigation exacerbates and prolongs the emotional strain on all parties, and therefore non-adversarial alternatives are being encouraged to limit the harmful emotional consequences.

Further impetus for changing the procedure in family law cases comes from the tremendous increase in the number of divorces in recent years, the backlog of cases in the courts, the great expense of family law litigation, and the tremendous increase in the number of children affected by marriage breakdown. Although there are recent statistics that show a slight levelling off in the rate of marital breakdowns, it is still estimated that each year approximately 1.5 million children in the United States and an additional 150,000 children in Canada experience separation. To deal with the problem, a number of jurisdictions in the United States have reduced trial lists by requiring couples to attend at least one mandatory meeting with a mediator prior to litigating custody and access issues. For example, California requires mandatory mediation in their conciliation court. In Canada, mediation can only be ordered or arranged on consent in most provinces. However, in Quebec, Winnipeg, Saskatchewan, Edmonton and New Brunswick, couples can be ordered to attend at least one meeting with a mediator, but only after they have been screened for domestic violence.

---

[1]   J.S. Wallerstein and J.B. Kelly, *Surviving the Breakup: How Children and Parents Cope with Divorce* (New York: Basic Books Inc., 1980).

In recent years several factors have slowed the growth of mediation as an option for divorcing couples. An unexpected development affecting financial support for family mediation (and custody assessments) has been the recent economic recession. Due to massive cutbacks in spending impacting on government and private business, less public and private funding is available for mediation and assessments, or for legal aid services for family law clients. Already, the reduced funding is resulting in the need for more volunteer time to handle the caseloads, plus the development of more expeditious mediative and assessment procedures (such as arbitration). As the recessionary pressures produce tighter economic realities, there has been fiercer competition for family law work within the legal profession, and fewer referrals of separating clients to mediation. Unfortunately this leaves many couples with fewer options for resolving matters in a non-adversarial way with the assistance of a trained mediator.

Another issue that has emerged strongly over the past few years has been resistance to mediation by certain women's groups. Underlying this opposition is a concern about domestic violence and the belief that spousal abuse can place a woman at a distinct disadvantage when she is negotiating in a mediation session with an abusive partner. One result of these concerns has been increased training for mediators in screening for domestic violence and the development of professional standards of practice or criteria for determining the appropriateness of mediation with each family.

It is too early to predict the overall impact that such developments may have on family mediation. However, it is obvious that mediation cannot be viewed as a panacea — and the rapid growth which the profession has experienced during the past two decades may not continue until these issues have been adequately addressed.

It is important to note that mediation has been used to resolve matters other than family law problems and was used in other cultures prior to its use in North America. For example:

- Non-westernized cultures such as those in Asia and Africa have long traditions of using mediation and conciliation as preferred methods of resolving neighbourhood disputes.
- In many cultures, respected elder members of the extended family have acted as mediators for resolving conflicts within the family.
- Religious leaders, priests, ministers, and rabbis have often served as mediators in family disputes. They encourage family members to use religious principles to resolve conflicts rather than take family problems to court.

One of the first areas of law to use mediation for the resolution of disputes was labour law. Mediation has been used largely to resolve labour-management conflicts, such as disputes with respect to working conditions, pay scales, hiring and firing practices, and employee benefits. More recently, it has been applied to harassment issues and human rights concerns.

Family law and labour law share an important common feature that lends itself to mediation, as opposed to an adversarial method of dispute resolution. That is, both in labour-management conflicts and in family conflicts, individuals are usually in a relationship that will continue in some form following the resolution of the dispute. Unlike criminal cases or other civil matters where the parties may have no further contact after one party is declared the "winner" and the other the "loser", in family law and labour law cases the parties usually have to be able to cooperate with each other on an ongoing basis. The need for continuing cooperation between the parties makes mediation a more suitable process for dispute resolution than an adversarial method.

In mediation, an experienced, impartial professional helps the parties reach a voluntary settlement that has been designed by them. Ideally the settlement is a fair and reasonable resolution of their competing needs and interests such that neither party is a complete winner and neither party suffers a humiliating loss. Because the settlement is reached voluntarily by the parties themselves, it is more likely to be carried out without the need for external enforcement or further litigation. The non-adversarial nature of the process and the emphasis on cooperation are likely to reduce tension and encourage future cooperative behaviour. This is an important objective where children are involved.

The success of non-adversarial techniques, such as mediation and pre-trial conferences, in addition to the continuing shift in philosophy away from fault and toward a more cooperative approach to family law problems, has stimulated the recent reforms of family law, both federally and in many provinces and states.

1. Family Law: The Evolution of Mediation from Reforms in Family Law

(A) FEDERAL LEGISLATION — THE *DIVORCE ACT*

The present *Divorce Act*[2] encourages a no-fault approach to divorce by stating that the sole ground for a divorce is "marriage breakdown". A divorce can now be obtained after a one-year separation (rather than the three- or five-year separation period required under the previous *Divorce Act*)[3] or more quickly if one spouse alleges adultery or cruelty as the basis for the marriage breakdown.

This Act requires lawyers to advise their clients to consider mediating any issues in dispute (including custody and child and spousal support)

---

[2]   R.S.C. 1985, c. 3 (2nd Supp.), s. 8.
[3]   R.S.C. 1970, c. D-8.

prior to litigating these issues. Section 9(1)(*b*) also requires lawyers to inform their clients about mediation services that are available in the community. In addition, lawyers are obligated to try to resolve matrimonial issues through negotiation rather than litigation.

The "best interests of children" is the sole criterion for determining custody of and access to children. Any person can apply for custody of or access to children; that is, persons other than biological parents or relatives can apply if they have a meaningful relationship with the child.

Joint custody is an option for judges to consider in custody awards. The principle of encouraging maximum contact between the child and both parents, consistent with the child's best interests, is set out in the legislation. The judge must consider which parent will facilitate maximum contact with the other parent when determining who will be awarded custody. Conduct, except ability to parent, is not considered when determining custody and access.

Need and ability to pay are the sole criteria for determining awards for spousal maintenance. Fault and matrimonial misconduct are expressly excluded in determining entitlement to and quantum of support.

(B) PROVINCIAL LEGISLATION

The Ontario Children's Law Reform Act and The Ontario Family Law Act, 1990

In Ontario, on the consent of the parties, the court can order mediation with respect to custody and access under s. 31 of the *Children's Law Reform Act*,[4] as well as for child and spousal support and the division of assets under s. 3 of the *Family Law Act*.[5]

The Manitoba Court of Queen's Bench Act

In Manitoba, under the *Court of Queen's Bench Act*,[6] the court can make a referral to a conciliation officer to resolve any matter without a formal trial. The judge or Master can make this order at any stage of the proceedings and can appoint either a conciliation officer or any other person on the consent of the parties. In practice, the Provincial Court of Manitoba (Family Division) in Winnipeg requires that every couple attend at least one mediation session in cases where there is an application for custody of or access to children. That is, the couple must attend at least one mandatory mediation session before they will be permitted to litigate custody and access issues.

---

[4]   R.S.O. 1990, c. C.12.
[5]   R.S.O. 1990, c. F.3.
[6]   S.M. 1988-89, c. 4 [also C.C.S.M., c. C-280].

The British Columbia Family Relations Act

The *Family Relations Act*[7] of British Columbia permits the court to appoint a family court counsellor to assist in the resolution of family law matters. This is not restricted to custody and access issues.

In addition, in most provinces:

- The "best interests of children" is the sole criterion for determining custody of and access to children.
- Need and ability to pay are the criteria for determining child and spousal support.
- Matrimonial misconduct is specifically excluded from determinations of custody, access, and support.
- The value of all assets acquired during the course of the marriage (with certain exceptions, such as gifts or inheritances from third parties) is divided equally at the end of the marriage, based on the philosophy of marriage as an economic and social partnership. The trend is toward sharing all assets with very limited judicial discretion to vary the 50-50 split. Limiting judicial discretion reduces the likelihood of an adversarial battle, because the more accurately the parties can predict the outcome in court, the easier it is to arrange a settlement.

The trend in family law is toward less adversarial procedures that encourage early settlement on a cooperative basis, with the assistance of an impartial professional, as well as independent legal advice. The legislation, by moving away from fault and toward more consistent, predictable, and objective criteria, is highly compatible with a more cooperative approach to dispute resolution in family law cases.

B. MENTAL HEALTH ASPECTS: THE EVOLUTION OF MEDIATION FROM MODELS OF CLINICAL INTERVENTION

Mediation bills and procedures have evolved from clinical psychology, as well as from labour negotiations. It is important to review the clinical roots of mediation to understand the similarities and differences between mediation and other forms of clinical intervention. Initially, clinical psychology focused on the intrapsychic needs of individuals, then on interpersonal relationships, particularly between parent and child, then broadening to include the entire family system, and finally on group counselling strategies.

---

[7]   R.S.B.C. 1979, c. 121.

1. Freudian Theories

Modern interpersonal psychology as a mental health discipline has its origins in the theories of Sigmund Freud. An understanding of the significance of his psychological concepts is important for seeing their relation to the evolution of mediation.

Freud's concept of a human unconscious, his hypotheses about infant sexuality, and his division of mental functioning into three distinct yet interrelating parts have all had a significant impact on the field of human relations. According to Freud:

- Human functioning is not entirely a rational, conscious process. There are areas of mental functioning that become overladen with fear and guilt, and become lodged in the unconscious because they are too painful to be confronted. Nevertheless, they affect personal decision making and behaviour.
- Infant sexuality is a powerful force in the emerging personality. It is important to understand this aspect of childhood development and its role in adult emotions.
- The human mind can be conceived as a tripartite construct of the id (instinctual impulses), the ego (the self as distinguished from the environment), and the super-ego (the conscience or counterbalance to the id). Functionally, the ego is the mediator between primal drives and society's expectations.

As part of his study of human behaviour, Freud developed clinical means for assisting emotionally disturbed persons:

- free association, whereby the unstructured verbal ramblings of an individual begin to assume some cohesion and relevance;
- individual psychotherapy, often extending over many months of confidential, regular visits, wherein a trusting and accepting relationship with the counsellor is developed.

The clinical treatment Freud developed is termed "psychoanalysis". It produced several important contributions to the understanding of human behaviour.

One of the more significant contributions is a development of a theory of the processes by which the human mind defends itself against painful confrontations. Collectively they are described as defence mechanisms, being the psychological armour that individuals use to protect themselves from rejection, real or imagined:

- *projection* — a process wherein the individual unconsciously attributes to another person his or her own thoughts and feelings;
- *repression* — a process wherein there is an unconscious denial of painful or traumatic experiences; and
- *suppression* — a process wherein the individual consciously denies

experiences that cause him or her pain.

These defence mechanisms are often evident at times of serious stress, such as separation or divorce. For example, adults, to reduce the painful sense of personal responsibility for marriage breakdown, often project blame on others and deny their own role in the marital failure.

2. Neo-Freudian Theories

Later, there were significant departures from Freud's theories. In particular, the neo-Freudians represented a strong rejection of his focus on instinctual and intrapsychic functioning.

The neo-Freudians placed much greater emphasis on interpersonal behaviour, specifically parent-child interactions. These theories have yielded valuable insights for understanding relationship issues and the needs of children. For example:

- *Harry Stack Sullivan* emphasized that personality is made manifest through interpersonal relations.
- *Alfred Adler* postulated that the child becomes emotionally "stuck" at an infantile stage as the result of an overbearing parental focus on discipline and punishment. He emphasized the need for nurturing parental behaviours.
- *Eric Fromm* developed the concept of "social character", a core of social behaviours resulting from parental influence during childhood.

Concurrent with the work of the neo-Freudians, *Carl Rogers* was independently pursuing careful research into counselling methodology:

- He took the position that counselling should focus more on healthy drives within the individual than on negative instinctual impulses.
- He placed greater emphasis on the present than on past experiences.
- He developed a positive, supportive "client-centred" approach to psychotherapy that tended to shift some responsibility from the counsellor to the individual.

Family mediation can trace its roots to this shift toward building on strengths and focusing on present and future relationships.

A further theoretical shift of power from the counsellor to the client occurred with the development of *group therapy*. The focus then changed from primarily intrapersonal issues to interpersonal relationships, with an added emphasis on problem solving in the present.

Group therapy was first used by *Jacob Moreno* as a means of dealing with large numbers of patients in institutional settings. He soon came to recognize that groups provided several advantages over one-to-one counselling, namely:

- Group therapy provides the opportunity for peer input and more closely approximates the real world.
- Personal conflicts are often dealt with more quickly through group interaction than in individual counselling.
- The members of the group function as a support system and also as models for each other in attempting to resolve current conflicts both within and outside the group. This has relevance to the familial, social, and community support that influences adult decisions at the time of separation.

3. Conjoint Family Therapy

The next major theoretical advance was an increased emphasis on the family unit, not only as a key factor in personality development, but also as an important element in counselling intervention. The counselling process became known as "conjoint family therapy".

There were rapid strides in the study of the family unit and its method of communication. A number of innovative people from a variety of professional backgrounds helped develop new approaches to the family unit as a means to understanding and changing behaviour:

- *Virginia Satir* demonstrated the importance of involving every family member when dealing with the behaviour of one family member.
- *Jay Haley* provided important mechanisms for assessing the non-verbal and verbal behaviour of all family members as part of the process of changing the family system.
- *Nathan Ackerman* helped family members understand how individual dysfunction is tied closely to family dysfunction.
- *Salvador Minuchin* was instrumental in developing the "enmeshed-disengaged" continuum for explaining the preferred transactional style of a particular family.

The majority of researchers and practitioners in family therapy have integrated the concept of the normative family. It is important that family counsellors recognize that most families have strengths and areas of healthy functioning despite the problems and crises that bring them into counselling. Often, one of the most important services the counsellor can provide is to help the family members identify and apply those strengths.

- *Don Jackson* integrated the work of Satir, Haley, and Ackerman, and used family systems as a means to improve family therapy.
- *Carl Whitaker* explored how the therapist's "use of self" can help the family take more responsibility for therapeutic change.

4. Family Mediation

Family mediation can be represented best as the flip-side of the professional coin to family therapy. Both share the historical antecedents described earlier; however, each has a very different theoretical objective. Whereas family therapy is a process to assist families working to remain together, family mediation is a process to assist families where there has been a decision to separate and/or divorce.

- *James Coogler*, a lawyer, was one of the first professionals to question the advisability of using the traditional legal/judicial process for handling marital and family conflict during separation and divorce. He became active in advocating that family law lawyers apply non-adversarial or mediative techniques rather than adversarial techniques. He advocated a system of comprehensive mediation for resolving all issues in dispute, such as support, property division, and custody of and access to children.
- *Howard Irving* and *John Haynes* were also among the early researchers and proponents of family mediation as an effective alternative to litigation.
- At about the same time, other mediators were focusing on the effect of separation and divorce on parents and children. Their work had important implications for the resolution of custody and access issues. The work of *Judith Wallerstein* and *Joan Kelly* confirmed the value of regular involvement by both parents in the lives of their children after separation.
- *Donald Saposnek's* work has supported the value of resolving parent-child disputes outside the courts, confirming the earlier work of *Meyer Elkin* and *Hugh McIsaac* at the Conciliation Court program in Los Angeles.
- A more recent development has been the "Special Masters" approach of *Philip Stahl* and *Margaret Lee*, wherein the mediator is appointed by the court (or hired by the parents) to make decisions affecting the children when the parents cannot reach a resolution. The objective is to avoid the resumption of litigation and a return to court.

As mediation continues to develop, integrative work is being done that is blending family therapy objectives with family mediation. The awareness that there really is no such thing as a "single parent family", in the sense that both parents from broken marriages continue to function in important ways in the lives of their children, has resulted in continued innovative approaches. A useful approach that provides mediation of all issues combined with a separation contract that includes ongoing monitoring and support of all family members after the separation is now being applied across North America, Europe, Australia, and New Zealand, and is being developed in Israel, South Africa, and South America.

5. Summary

The historical sequence of events, from Freud's focus on the individual's intra-psychic processes, through the interpersonal and parent-child theories of the neo-Freudians, to the increasing interest in and involvement of the whole family in both counselling and mediation, has been briefly chronicled in this section. Of particular importance for mediation are the following facts:

- Mental health professionals have been moving toward techniques that encourage clients to take more personal responsibility for decision making.
- Resolutions worked out in a cooperative atmosphere by family members produce the most stable and long-lasting results.
- Means for avoiding court and encouraging constructive problem solving continue to be developed to reduce the potentially destructive impact of separation and divorce on family members.

Following this paragraph is a chart containing some of the significant developments in family mediation in North America, with particular emphasis on Canadian initiatives. The list is not exhaustive, but does include a number of important events in the relatively brief history of family mediation. Today, all provinces have developed provincial mediation associations. There is also a national association, Family Mediation Canada, which was established in 1984. It works cooperatively with all the provincial associations and co-sponsors a national mediation conference annually.

C. CHRONOLOGICAL DEVELOPMENT OF FAMILY MEDIATION IN NORTH AMERICA

Table 1

Organization	Developers	Year
1. Conciliation Court Los Angeles County	Meyer Elkin Hugh McIsaac	1961
The first court-based mediation service in North America.		
2. Association of Family and Conciliation Courts	Judge R.A. Pfaff Meyer Elkin	1963
The first international association of family mediators. Initially directed at court-based services, more recently it has included private mediation as well.		
3. Divorce Counselling Unit Health and Welfare Ottawa, Ontario	Gerry Gaughan	1969
The first initiative by the Canadian government, following the enactment in 1968 of the *Divorce Act*, S.C. 1967-68, c. 24, to encourage established counselling services to offer conciliation services to divorcing couples.		

Table 1 — cont'd

Organization	Developers	Year
4. Supportive Separation System Family Life Centre Markham, Ontario	Mario Bartoletti Judge T. Moore	1971
The first non-court-based family counselling agency in Canada offering family mediation and custody evaluation services to separating couples. Referrals were accepted from the community as well as from the county court.		
5. Conciliation Services Family Court Edmonton, Alberta	Judge M. Bowker	1972
The first court-based conciliation service in Canada.		
6. Conciliation Counselling Family Court Hamilton, Ontario	Judge David Steinberg	1973
The first court-based conciliation service in Ontario.		
7. Conciliation Project Provincial Court, Family Division Toronto, Ontario	Howard Irving Judge H.T. Andrews	1973
A three-year demonstration research project, funded by Health and Welfare Canada, examining the effectiveness of family conciliation services.		
8. Family Mediation Association Bethesda, Maryland	O.J. Coogler	1973
The first mediation association focused on private mediation.		
9. Frontenac Family Referral Services, Family Court Kingston, Ontario	Judge G. Thomson Molly Knowles	1973
The first court-based, comprehensive mediation service in Ontario, offering assistance with such issues as custody, access, property, and financial support.		

Table 1 — cont'd

Organization	Developers	Year
10. Conciliation Service Unified Family Court Hamilton, Ontario	Judge J. VanDuzer	1977
The first federal-provincial venture establishing a court-based conciliation project.		
11. Academy of Family Mediators Claremont, California	John Haynes	1978
An international association of family mediators that encourages a more clinical approach to mediation. Membership consists primarily of mediators in private practice.		
12. Family Conciliation Service, Superior Court Montreal, Quebec	Chief Justice Jules Deschenes	1981
The first court-based conciliation service in Quebec offering comprehensive mediation.		
13. Ontario Association for Family Mediation Toronto, Ontario	John Goodwin Mario Bartoletti Ellen Macdonald	1982
The first provincial family mediation association in Canada (OAFM).		
14. Family Mediation Services of Ontario Toronto, Ontario	Philip Epstein Helen Goudge James MacDonald	1982
The first court-based conciliation service in Ontario, established specifically for the Supreme Court.		
15. The Family Mediation Project: Law Society of Upper Canada Legal Aid; Sub-Committee on Mediation and Assessments	Fran Kitely Barbara Landau Craig Perkins	1984
The first research project to evaluate the cost-effectiveness and social benefits of mediation services for legally aided clients.		

Table 1 — cont'd

Organization	Developers	Year
16. Family Mediation Canada Toronto, Ontario	Howard Irving Audrey Devlin	1984
The first national mediation association in Canada, with representatives from every province. Established by the Department of Justice.		

17. Code of Professional
    Conduct
    Ontario Association for
    Family Mediation
	Barbara Irving**	1986

The first code of conduct for family mediators established in Canada.		
18. Professional Academy of Custody Evaluators (PACE)	Barry Bricklin Gail Elliot	1992
The first national association in the United States of custody accessors and evaluators. It is focused upon establishing competency standards and educational opportunities for professional evaluators.		

19. Policy on Mediation in cases
    of Domestic Violence:
    Ontario Association for
    Family Mediation &
    Academy of Family
    Mediators
	Barbara Landau***	1994

The first policy on mediation in cases of domestic violence established in Canada.		

20. Ontario Interdisciplinary
    Association of Custody/
    Access Assessors
	Barbara Anderson
	Mario Bartoletti
	Barbara Chisholm
	Barbara Landau
		1994

The first association in Canada of custody assessors and evaluators. The primary objective is to establish competent standards of practice that will be supported by all relevant mental health and legal professional organizations, provincial government agencies, and the courts.		

Note: The dates cited are the authors' best estimates of when significant developments in mediation occurred. The list does not presume to be complete, but rather is a list of highlights in family mediation across North America.

*   S.C. 1967-68, c. 24.
**   Chairperson, Standards and Ethics Committee (OAFM).
*** Chairperson, Committee on Domestic Violence (OAFM & AFM).

D. PROVINCIAL MEDIATION ASSOCIATIONS IN CANADA

Table 2

Organization	Developers	Year
1. Ontario Association for Family Mediation (OAFM) Toronto, Ontario	John Goodwin Mario Bartoletti Ellen Macdonald	1982
2. Alberta Arbitration and Mediation Society Edmonton, Alberta	David G. Elliott William Geddes Nanette Moreau	1982
3. Alberta Family Mediation Society Edmonton, Alberta	Renee Cochard Kent Taylor	1983
4. Mediation Association of British Columbia Victoria, B.C.	Catherine Scambler Andrew Pirie Dinah Stanley Jerry McHale	1985
5. Family Mediation Association of New Brunswick Moncton, N.B.	Louis Richard	1985
6. Ass'n de Mediation Familiale de Quebec	Linda Berube Audrey Wise Andre Murray	1985
7. Nova Scotia Association for Divorce and Family Mediation	Susannah Starnes	1986
8. Yukon Public Legal Education Association Mediation Committee	Steven Smyth Lynn Gaudet Trish Archibald	1986
9. Family Mediation Newfoundland and Labrador	Rick Morris Rick Browning Dennis McKay	1987
10. Family Mediation Manitoba	Justice A.C. Hamilton Shirley Smith Marta Smith	1987
11. Family Mediation Saskatchewan	Daniel L. Hamoline Francine D'Aoust Elaine Lund	1986

ANNOTATED BIBLIOGRAPHY

Abella, Judge R. "Procedural Aspects of Arrangements for Children Upon Divorce". (1983), 61 *Canadian Bar Review* 443. This article examines the present adversarial system and recommends non-adversarial refinements to the present process, such as pre-trials, mediation, expert assessments, and independent legal representation for children for the adjudication of custody and access disputes.

Bartoletti, M.D., "Separation: Perspectives on the Couple, the Counsellor and the Lawyer". (1974), 17 *The Single Parent Journal* 4. This paper describes the procedure developed for helping separating couples to mediate all issues and arrive at an interim separation agreement.

Brown, D. "Divorce in Family Mediation: A History, Review, Future Directions". (1982), 20 *Conciliation Courts Review* 1. This article outlines the history of the divorce mediation movement and discusses significant issues in the mediation process.

Camozzi, D. "Divorce Mediation: A Perspective From Quebec". (1985), 11 *Therapy Now* 20. This article looks at the history of mediation in Quebec.

Chalke, D. "Family Mediation in British Columbia: A Struggle to Get Out of the Starting Gate". (1985), 11 *Therapy Now* 22. This article examines the history of mediation of family disputes in British Columbia.

Coogler, O. J. *Structured Mediation and Divorce Settlement: A Handbook for Marital Mediators*. Toronto: D.C. Heath & Co., 1978. This was the first major textbook on family mediation and outlines the author's procedure known as *structured mediation*.

Folberg, J. "A Mediation Overview: History and Dimensions of Practice". (1983), 1 *Mediation Quarterly* 1. This article sets out the evolution of mediation and its use as a tool for resolving neighbourhood and intra-family disputes in different cultural groups.

Folberg, J., and Taylor, A. *Mediation: A Comprehensive Guide to Resolving Conflicts Without Litigation*. San Francisco: Jossey-Bass Publishers, 1984. The first chapter of this excellent book on mediation contains a discussion of the development of mediation, what mediation means, and what the objectives of the mediation process are.

Haynes, J. M. *Divorce Mediation: A Practical Guide for Therapists and Counsellors*. New York: Springer Publishing Co., 1981. This is one of the early texts in mediation.

Irving, H. *Divorce Mediation*. Toronto: Personal Library, 1980. The first text on mediation published in Canada. It presents the results of a court-related mediation project directed by the author.

Irving, H. "Family Mediation — Coming of Age". (1985), 11 *Therapy Now* 7. The author explores the history of family mediation in Canada.

Mclsaac, H. "Mandatory Conciliation, Custody/Visitation Matters". (1981), 19 *Conciliation Courts Review* 73. This is an in-depth review of the development of California's mandatory mediation law and how the Los Angeles Conciliation Court functioned within that legislation.

McWhinney, R. "Family Mediation in Ontario: Origins and Development". (1985), 11 *Therapy Now* 18. This article traces the history of family mediation in Ontario.

Mnookin, R., and Kornhauser, L. "Bargaining in the Shadow of the Law: The Case of Divorce". (1979), 88 *Yale Law Journal* 950. This thought-provoking article discusses the role of law in the private settlement of legal disputes and presents the arguments in favour of "private ordering" of dispute resolution over the results of litigation for family law matters.

Payne, J. "Aspects of Mediation: Mediation in Canada and the United States". (1985), 11 *Therapy Now* 4. This article examines the evolution of conciliation and mediation as methods of dispute resolution in both Canada and the United States.

Saposnek, D. *Mediating Child Custody Disputes*. San Francisco: Jossey-Bass Publishers, 1983. This book is a practical and comprehensive approach to the resolution of child custody disputes.

Statistics Canada. *Divorce: Law and the Family in Canada*. (February 1983). This book chronicles the changes in Canada to the structure of the family, the divorce rate, the outcome of divorce, and family laws from 1800 to the 1980's.

Chapter Two

Dispute Resolution:
Alternative Methods

A. NON-ADVERSARIAL METHODS OF DISPUTE RESOLUTION

There are many methods for resolving conflict. Some methods are distinguished by their non-adversarial nature. Clients may be involved with more than one method; therefore, it is important to understand the range of options available for non-adversarial dispute resolution. This information is helpful in advising clients about the most appropriate method(s) for their particular situation.

1. Counselling

Counselling is a process whereby clients are assisted in dealing with their personal and interpersonal emotional conflicts. The approach used will depend upon the theoretical orientation of the counsellor. It may be brief or long-term, depending upon the severity of the problem and the commitment of the client. Counselling is intended to assist clients in learning and applying improved problem-solving techniques.

- *Individual counselling* is a process whereby the client is seen alone for one or more of a variety of problems.
- *Marital counselling* is a process whereby a couple is seen together, in most instances. The emphasis is usually on communication and relationship difficulties between the two partners.
- *Reconciliation counselling* is a process whereby the counsellor sees the couple together, although some individual sessions may be needed. The emphasis is on helping them to re-establish communication and trust after an intense conflict. Often, separation has been either contemplated or attempted for a brief period.
- *Separation counselling* is a process whereby the partners may be seen individually, together, or both. The emphasis is on helping each person through a repositioning process from living together to living apart. The sessions identify the partner initiating separation and the partner responding to that initiative, and then provide appropriate supportive intervention. Provision of information about mediation is usually made available during separation counselling.

2. Conciliation

Conciliation is a process whereby separating partners are helped to deal with their issues in a non-adversarial manner. Conciliation is a term that was often used to refer to a court-based service. However, today, both public and private conciliation services tend to offer mediation to clients.

3. Mediation

Mediation is a process whereby an impartial third party is retained to effect a resolution of issues between two or more disputants. There are several important elements in mediation:

- It is a voluntary process. If the parties reach an agreement, the mediator will draft a Memorandum of Understanding outlining the terms of the agreement reached by the parties.
- All agreements in mediation arise from the parties to mediation themselves. To ensure that the agreement is reached voluntarily by informed parties, the mediator encourages the parties to obtain independent legal advice before mediation begins and certainly before any agreement is finalized.
- If the parties fail to reach an agreement, then this will be so stated by the mediator.

With specific reference to separation and divorce, family mediation is a voluntary procedure that offers four major advantages to the couple:

- The whole decision-making process remains in the hands of the two parties, who best know their needs and resources and those of their children.
- The parties can avoid the trial process, which is often traumatic to both the parents and their children, as well as their extended family.
- Mediated settlements generally work better and are more stable than court-ordered dispositions.
- Parties who have succeeded in reaching resolutions once are more likely to deal successfully with differences that develop later.

(A) "CLOSED" AND "OPEN" MEDIATION

There are two basic forms of family mediation that separating partners may choose, *closed* or *open*. There are some essential differences between the two:

With *closed mediation*:

- The mediator's report includes only the issues that the parties themselves have resolved.
- If the parties fail to obtain a resolution on one or more issues, the mediator's report will contain a description of any agreement

reached, as well as a statement specifying which issues remain unresolved.

- All other information disclosed to the mediator remains confidential and unreported (with the exception of child abuse data).

With *open mediation*:

- The mediator's report may include any information that is considered relevant to the issues being mediated.
- If there is a resolution of the issues, the report will usually be restricted to a description of the agreement reached.

In choosing between open and closed mediation, the parties will want to consider the following factors:

- Some mediators restrict their practice to either open or closed mediation.
- With closed mediation, there is an assumption that the total confidentiality of the process may make the parties less apprehensive about disclosing personal information. (That impression is not supported by research at the present time.)
- With open mediation, if the process breaks down the mediator may prepare a report outlining the differences in the parties' positions.
- Any information acquired during the mediation can be used in the report.
- If requested by one or both parties, the mediator may make recommendations as to how the unresolved issues might be resolved.
- For this reason it is important to select a mediator with sufficient expertise to make a recommendation about the issues in dispute.
- Open mediation eliminates the need to commence a new process from the beginning, which is a saving of time, money, and effort.
- Also, the parties and their children can avoid further intrusions on their privacy by another professional, in those cases where the judge is seeking a professional opinion.

(B) REFERRALS

There are several common ways in which parties are referred to mediation. The following is a listing of the more frequent sources of referral:

- *Self-referral* is a process whereby a couple comes voluntarily into mediation, usually as the result of recommendations by family or friends, or in response to the media. It is not uncommon for the couple to be assisted through a resolution of all the issues pertaining to their separation.
- *Referral by lawyer(s)* is a process whereby both lawyers and their clients agree on mediation to resolve specific issues. Most often, those issues are the custody of, residency of, and access to the couple's children, but financial and property issues may also be mediated.

- *Referral by mental health professional(s)* is a process whereby family physicians, psychiatrists, social workers, or family counsellors recommend a couple into mediation to resolve any issues related to a decision to separate or divorce.
- *The marriage or family counsellor* may refer the couple to another professional for mediation or, if the counsellor is a trained mediator, may ask both parties if they wish to continue with the counsellor as the mediator. The advantage of this option is that the parties remain with the same professional throughout the whole process of marriage counselling, separation counselling and mediation, thus facilitating the emotional transitions being experienced by both parties. There are cautions that need to be considered, however. This process should be undertaken only if the parties have discussed the option of mediation at the outset with the counsellor and confirm in writing that they accept the change in professional role. It is inappropriate for the mediator to provide personal counselling to either partner during or after mediation.

4. Arbitration

Arbitration is a process whereby a neutral third party who is agreeable to both sides functions in a quasi-judicial capacity. It differs from mediation in that decisions will be made by the neutral party on behalf of the disputants. In binding arbitration, the decisions and recommendations of the arbitrator are final and cannot be appealed.

B. ADVERSARIAL METHODS OF DISPUTE RESOLUTION

There are also adversarial methods for resolving conflict that are supported and practised in society:

1. Litigation

Litigation is a process whereby a judge arrives at a legal resolution of the differences between the opposing parties (or litigants). In family law, litigation is used as a last resort, especially for resolving custody and access disputes. Recent legislation and court procedure encourages the use of alternative dispute resolution, including mediation, for family matters.

2. Custody-Access Assessment

Custody-access assessment is a process whereby a trained professional prepares a report about the parenting arrangements that may best meet the child's needs, given the capabilities of the parents. Information is obtained through a variety of sources, and recommendations are then made for a parenting plan that is seen to be in the best interests of the child. If the parties and both counsel agree, the assessor should adopt a mediative approach, that is, he or she should encourage input from the parents in designing the parenting plan. Whatever the parents agree on is usually incorporated into the assessor's recommendations and is more likely to be followed by the parents in the future.

3. Negotiation

Negotiation is a bargaining process that can be utilized in any of the non-adversarial or adversarial methods of conflict resolution. It basically involves the exchange of something by one of the parties in return for something else by the other party, which both perceive to be fair and equitable. Negotiation can occur between the parties or between their counsel, with or without the assistance of an intermediary. It may occur face to face, by letter, or by telephone, and is frequently applied to resolve a broad range of deadlocks.

C. COURT-ORDERED METHODS OF DISPUTE RESOLUTION

Either party may apply to the court for an order appointing a mediator or an assessor.

1. Court-Ordered Mediation

(A) ONTARIO CHILDREN'S LAW REFORM ACT

Legislation in Ontario provides for court-ordered mediation upon the consent of the parties.

Mediation with respect to custody and access disputes can be ordered under s. 31 of the *Children's Law Reform Act*[1] *which provides as follows:*

> 31(1) Upon an application for custody of or access to a child, the court, at the request of the parties, by order may appoint a person selected by the parties to mediate any matter specified in the order.

The mediator must consent to being appointed and must agree to file a report with the court within a time period specified by the court.[2] The mediator shall file his or her report with the clerk or registrar of the court, and the clerk or registrar shall give a copy of the report to each of the parties and to any counsel representing the child.[3]

Before beginning the mediation, the parties must decide whether they wish open mediation or closed mediation.[4] If the parties have agreed to

---

[1]   R.S.O. 1990, c. C.12.
[2]   *Ibid.*, s. 31(2).
[3]   *Ibid.*, s. 31(5), (6).
[4]   *Ibid.*, s. 31(4).

closed mediation, then evidence of anything said or of any admission or communication made in the course of the mediation is not admissible in any proceeding except with the consent of all parties to the proceeding in which the mediation order was made.[5]

The court shall require the parties to pay the fees and expenses of the mediator and shall set out in the order the proportions to be paid by each party.[6]

(B) ONTARIO *FAMILY LAW ACT*

Section 3 of the *Family Law Act*[7] permits the court in Ontario to order mediation on the consent of the parties for resolving disputes involving property division, and child and spousal support. The provisions of this statute are similar to the court-ordered mediation under s. 31 of the *Children's Law Reform Act*, as described above. That is, mediation is only ordered on the consent of the parties and when the parties agree on a mediator.

(C) MANITOBA *COURT OF QUEEN'S BENCH ACT*[8]

The rules of the Provincial Court of Manitoba (Family Division) permit the court to order mandatory mediation with respect to any of the issues in dispute. Section 47(1) of the Act states as follows:

> 47(1) Where a judge or master is of the opinion that an effort should be made to resolve an issue otherwise than at a formal trial, the judge or master may, at any stage of the proceeding, refer the issue to a mediator.

Section 47(2) sets out the duties of the conciliation officer, namely:

> 47(2) A mediator to whom an issue is referred under subsection (1) shall attempt to resolve the issue.

In Manitoba, the legislation provides for closed mediation, unless the parties otherwise consent. Section 48 states:

> 48. Unless the parties otherwise agree,
>
> (*a*)   a mediator who renders services
>
> > (i)   under section 47, or
> > (ii)   at the request of the parties; or
>
> (*b*)   a party to a mediation;
> is not competent to give evidence in respect of
> (*c*)   a written or oral statement made by a party during the mediation, or
> (*d*)   knowledge or information acquired during the mediation by a person under clauses (*a*) or (*b*).

---

[5]   *Ibid.*, s. 31(7).
[6]   *Ibid.*, s. 31(8), (9).
[7]   R.S.O. 1990, c. F.3.
[8]   S.M. 1988-89, c. 4 [also C.C.S.M., c. C280].

It would appear that legislation in Manitoba does not even permit the conciliation officer to submit a report if a settlement is reached, unless the parties consent to such a report being prepared and submitted to the court.

There is no provision in the legislation with respect to an order for payment of the mediator's services.

(D) BRITISH COLUMBIA *FAMILY RELATIONS ACT*

The *Family Relations Act*[9] of British Columbia permits the court to appoint a family court counsellor for the purpose of resolving family law issues that are in dispute. The family court counsellor is authorized under the legislation to offer the parties to the dispute any advice and guidance that he or she believes will assist in resolving the dispute.[10]

The *Family Relations Act* protects information from disclosure in mediation cases unless the parties consent otherwise. Section 3(3) states:

> 3(3) Subject to the law of Canada, where
>
> (a)   a family court counsellor receives under subsection (2) evidence, information or a communication in confidence from a person who is a party to the proceeding, or from a child; and
> (b)   the person who gave the evidence, information or communication to the family court counsellor under subsection (2) does not consent to the family court counsellor disclosing the evidence, information or communication,

the family court counsellor shall not disclose the evidence, information or communication in a proceeding in a court or tribunal, and no person shall examine him for the purpose of compelling him to disclose that evidence, information or communication.

The *Family Relations Act* does not provide for an order for payment of fees, and a report cannot be prepared, even if a settlement has been reached, unless the parties consent.

2. Court-Ordered Assessments

(A) ONTARIO *CHILDREN'S LAW REFORM ACT*

In cases where either the parties themselves or the court wishes an assessment in relation to custody of or access to children, the court may order a custody assessment pursuant to s. 30 of the *Children's Law Reform Act*. The parties may agree that the assessor can attempt to reach an agreement between them with respect to a parenting plan, provided the plan is in the best interests of the children.

Section 30 provides as follows:

> 30(1) The court before which an application is brought in respect of custody of or access to a child, by order, may appoint a person who has techni-

---

[9]   R.S.B.C. 1979, c. 121.
[10]   *Ibid.*, s. 3(1), (2).

cal or professional skill to assess and report to the court on the needs of the child and the ability and willingness of the parties or any of them to satisfy the needs of the child.

Where possible, the court will appoint a person who is agreed upon by the parties, but if the parties are not able to agree on an assessor, the court will choose and appoint a qualified person. The assessor must consent to carry out the assessment and to report to the court within a specified time period.[11]

The court has the power to order the parties, the child, and any other person who has been given notice of the order for assessment to participate in the assessment. In the event that one or more of the persons who have been ordered to participate in the assessment refuses to participate, the court may draw a negative inference with respect to the ability and willingness of any person to satisfy the needs of the child. That is, a judge may order an assessment to be performed without the consent of one or both parties.[12]

In suitable cases, particularly those that do not involve allegations of abuse or neglect, the assessor may attempt to involve the parties in designing their parenting plan. It is not necessary to have a court order to incorporate a mediative approach into the assessment process. It is the practice of many assessors to give the parties an opportunity to reach a mediated solution, that is, one that the parties agree to voluntarily, before preparing an assessment report with their own recommendations. Of course, the assessor has the responsibility of reporting to the court what he or she believes would be best for the children, but whenever a plan is arrived at through consensus it is more likely to be implemented and adhered to in a cooperative spirit.

The assessor is required to file his or her report with the clerk or registrar of the court and the clerk or registrar must give a copy of the report to each of the parties and to any counsel representing the child. The assessor's report is admissible as evidence on the application.[13]

Any of the parties and counsel representing the child may require the assessor to attend as a witness at the hearing of the application.[14]

The court will require the parties to pay the fees and expenses of the assessor and will specify the proportion of the assessor's fees and expenses to be paid by each party.[15]

(B) MANITOBA *COURT OF QUEEN'S BENCH ACT*

The legislation in Manitoba permits a judge to order a family investigation with respect to the issues of custody, access, or other family-related matters. In this case, the family investigator must submit a report to court.

---

[11] *Children's Law Reform Act, supra*, note 1, s. 30(3), (4).
[12] *Ibid.*, s. 30(5), (6).
[13] *Ibid.*, s. 30(7), (8), (9).
[14] *Ibid.*, s. 30(10).
[15] *Ibid.*, s. 30(12).

Section 49 of the Act sets out the court's jurisdiction as follows:

49(1) Where a judge or master is of the opinion that a report of a family evaluator is required at a hearing with respect to custody, access or a related family matter, the judge or master may by order appoint a family evaluator.

(2) A family evaluator appointed under subsection (1) shall interview the parties and such other persons as may be appropriate and shall provide to the court a report containing information and opinion relevant to custody, access or a related family matter that is in issue in the proceeding.

D. OPEN MEDIATION, CLOSED MEDIATION, AND CUSTODY ASSESSMENTS

There has been considerable confusion about the essential differences between open and closed mediation and custody assessments. The following chart sets out the similarities and differences between the three procedures.

Closed Mediation	Open Mediation	Assessment
This is a *non-adversarial* method of dispute resolution that parties participate in voluntarily in the hope of avoiding an adversarial court proceeding.	This is a *non-adversarial* method of dispute resolution that parties participate in voluntarily in the hope of avoiding an adversarial court proceeding.	This is an *adversarial process*, in that it contemplates adversarial court proceedings and may be entered into voluntarily or by court order.
The parties in dispute meet with the *mediator.*	The parties in dispute meet with the *mediator.*	The parties in dispute usually meet with the *assessor.**
Discussions are *confidential* and it is agreed that the parties will *not* subpoena the mediator to court.	Discussions are *not* confidential, and it is agreed that the mediator can be *subpoenaed* by the parties to court.	Discussions are *not* confidential, and it is agreed that the assessor can be *subpoenaed* by the parties to court.
Usually *no* conclusions or recommendations are made by the mediator to the court.	Usually *no* conclusions or recommendations are made by the mediator to the court.	The assessor makes *recommendations* and arrives at a *conclusion* that may be communicated to the court.

Closed Mediation	Open Mediation	Assessment
All *agreements* arise from the parties themselves on a voluntary basis.	All *agreements* arise from the parties themselves on a voluntary basis.	There is *no* requirement that the parties reach an agreement.
Only the terms of an agreement or the fact that there is no agreement is disclosed.	The terms of the agreement, or the fact that there is no agreement, is disclosed, and the mediator may report on the mediation process and, if requested, may make recommendations about issues in dispute. This presumes that the mediator has sufficient expertise to make a recommendation.	The assessor puts forward recommendations for a court-ordered agreement.
The parties, and usually the children, are seen by the mediator in a combination of individual and group sessions for the purpose of assisting the parties to arrive at a mediated agreement on the parenting arrangement that is in the best interests of the children.	The parties, and usually the children, are seen by the mediator in a combination of individual and group sessions for the purpose of assisting the parties to arrive at a mediated agreement on the parenting arrangement that is in the best interests of the children.	The parties and the children are seen by the assessor in a combination of individual and group sessions. In addition, extensive investigations are carried out and information is collected from collateral sources, *e.g.*, visits and discussions with teachers, family doctors, other relevant professionals, *etc.* This information is used for the purpose of evaluating parenting capacity and helping the assessor to arrive at a recommendation.

* Some mediators prefer to begin the mediation process by meeting with each party individually prior to a joint meeting. This is particularly likely in cases of alleged abuse or intimidation.

ANNOTATED BIBLIOGRAPHY

Cochrane, M. *The Everyday Guide to Canadian Family Law*. Toronto: Prentice-Hall Canada Inc., 1991. This is a helpful book for parents going through a separation. It gives an overview of Canadian family law on a wide range of topics including the emotional stages of marriage breakdown, domestic violence, and alternatives to going to court (mediation and arbitration).

Haley, J. *Problem-Solving Therapy*. San Francisco: Jossey-Bass Publishers, 1976. This book explores the systems approach to family therapy and contains many helpful suggestions for interviewing family members.

Minuchin, S. *Families and Family Therapy*. Massachusetts: Harvard University Press, 1974

and

Minuchin, S., and Fishman, C.H. *Family Therapy Techniques*. Massachusetts: Harvard University Press, 1981. These two books describe a number of strategies for dealing with families from a family systems approach.

Ross, N. "Should Court Mediation Be Mandated?" (1995), 29 *Gazette* (The Law Society of Upper Canada) 3-4, 283-92.

Shipley, A. "Custody Law Reform in Ontario: The Children's Law Reform Act". In B. Landau, ed., *Children's Rights in the Practice of Family Law*. Toronto: Carswell Publishing Co., 1986. This chapter contains a detailed discussion of the Ontario *Children's Law Reform Act*.

Stitt, A., ed. *Alternative Dispute Resolution Practice Manual*. Toronto: CCH Canadian Ltd., 1996. This manual discusses ADR applications in a wide range of subject areas including family, school, environmental, commercial, landlord and tenant, public policy disputes, *etc*. It includes descriptions of a wide range of dispute resolution strategies including mediation, arbitration, negotiation, judicial mini-trials, pre-trial conferences, and others, in both the private and public sector. This valuable practice manual is updated quarterly.

Taylor, A., and Bing, H. "Settlement by Evaluation and Arbitration: A New Approach for Custody and Visitation Disputes". (1994), 32 *Family and Conciliation Courts Review* 4, 432-44.

Wiseman, J. M. *Mediation Therapy: Short Term Decision-Making For Couples and Families in Crisis*. Massachusetts/Toronto: Lexington Books, 1990.

Zibbell, R. "The Mental Health Professional as Arbitrator in Post-Divorce, Child-Oriented Conflict". (1995), 33 *Family and Conciliation Courts Review* 4, 462-71.

Chapter Three

Mediation in Practice: Issues

A. EXPECTATIONS OF REFERRAL SOURCES

Referrals for mediation come from a variety of sources. The expectations of the referral sources are not the same. Therefore, the response of the mediator must be specific to the referral source. Also, the mediator needs to review the appropriateness of the couple for mediation with the person who is making the referral to mediation. The following guidelines will assist the mediator in establishing a more useful and practical relationship with the referral sources:

Referral Source	Expectations
Judge	— Confirmation from the mediator of readiness to proceed with mediation.
	— Agreement as to date when the mediator's report can be expected. (If additional time is required, the mediator will make a request in writing to the court for an extension.)
	— Receipt of the report by court and counsel at least two weeks prior to the date of the hearing.
Lawyer	— Agreement by both parties to enter into mediation. (If only one client is supporting mediation, it cannot proceed.)
	— Confirmation from the mediator of readiness to commence mediation of stated issues.
	— Clarification on fees regarding proportion to be paid by each party and when due.
	— Clarification regarding open or closed mediation.
	— Receipt of up-to-date copy of *curriculum vitae* from mediator.
Family physician	— Acknowledgement confirming referral.
	— Feedback by letter regarding whether mediation was successful or not.

Counsellor	— Acknowledgement confirming referral.
	— Clarification regarding any on-going professional involvement by the counsellor.
	— Feedback by letter regarding whether mediation was successful or not.
Family or friend	— Normally, contact from the mediator is neither required nor recommended. There may be an exception in cases of domestic violence.

Feedback to the referral source, within the guidelines suggested, is not only a professional courtesy, but also serves to educate other professionals about the mediative process. It also encourages a more cooperative approach with other professionals involved.

B. EXPECTATIONS OF CLIENTS

Expectations of the clients coming for mediation can vary greatly. There may be an expectation that:

- mediation has as its objective reconciliation;
- mediation is similar to personal and marital counselling;
- mediation will vindicate the position of one or the other partner through assignment of blame; or
- the mediator will decide the issues in dispute (particularly if the mediator is a solicitor).

It is very important that the mediator explain the purpose and function of mediation carefully to correct such misconceptions. The following issues should be covered with all clients contemplating mediation:

- The mediator is an impartial professional who will remain unaligned with either party. (There is often a tendency by the parties to want to convert the mediator into an ally.)
- Mediation is not the same as counselling; that is, discussions will be focused on reaching a settlement of the issues in dispute.
- Mediation is not a process for personal attack or blame by one party on the other, and such verbal attacks will be interrupted by the mediator.
- Mediation is not arbitration; that is, the parties, not the mediator, make the decisions.
- The time period for issues to be addressed in mediation is understood and agreed upon by both parties and their lawyers.
- The nature of the mediator's report will be determined by the issues under discussion and the type of mediation, open or closed, that has been chosen.

C. EXPECTATIONS OF MEDIATOR

The mediator will want assurances on the following factors prior to commencing mediation:

- Both parties and their lawyers are agreeable to proceeding with family mediation and are satisfied with the mediator selected.
- The parties are appropriate candidates for mediation; that is, they are capable of negotiating on their own behalf without fear of retaliation, intimidation, or duress.
- Responsibility for payment of the mediator's fee is agreed upon.
- A decision has been made as to whether the mediation will be open or closed, and the implications of both types of mediation are fully understood by the parties and their lawyers. The mediator will be provided with full disclosure of all information pertinent to the issues in dispute. For example, if financial or property issues are to be mediated, the parties and their counsel agree to provide full and frank disclosure.
- The parties will consider granting permission to contact or see any persons relevant to the issues addressed in mediation.
- A mediation contract integrating the foregoing will be signed by both parties (and their counsel) prior to commencing mediation.

D. SCREENING FOR APPROPRIATENESS

Before formally accepting the clients for mediation, both the lawyers and the mediator should screen the clients to be sure that they are appropriate candidates. In order to qualify, the parties to mediation must be able to negotiate safely, voluntarily, and competently in order to reach a fair agreement. That means the parties should enter mediation voluntarily (although some jurisdictions do mandate mediation), they should be informed about their legal rights and responsibilities, they should feel safe while negotiating face to face with the other party — that is, they should not be concerned about physical, psychological, or economic reprisals as a result of something they might say in mediation — and they should voluntarily reach an agreement that they believe to be fair. There are a number of factors that should be evaluated by both the lawyer and the mediator in order to decide whether to accept the clients as candidates for mediation.

1. Expectations of Counsel

Before referring a client to mediation, it is important for the lawyer to conduct his or her own screening interview. That is, the lawyer should determine whether:

- there has been a history of physical, psychological, economic, substance, or other abuse in the relationship;
- the client would be intimidated when negotiating face to face with the other party or in "shuttle mediation";
- the client would feel endangered either before, during, or after a mediation session;
- the clients are relatively equal in power (that is, would the client be able to assert his or her own point of view or would he or she be intimidated by the other person?);
- the client is able to articulate his/her own needs, separate and apart from those of the children and his/her spouse.

If the client is a suitable candidate for mediation, then a referral should be made.

2. The Mediator's Responsibility

Screening for Power Imbalances, Control, and Domestic Violence

The mediator can carry out the screening in a number of different ways:

- *Intake telephone calls* — This is a brief screening interview conducted by the mediator or by a trained intake worker or secretary.
- *Client questionnaire* — The clients could be asked to respond in writing to a questionnaire that is sent to each of them separately.
- *Individual meeting* — The mediator would screen each client separately before the mediation commences.

For a variety of reasons, individuals may be reluctant to admit to a history of abuse or control. For example, they may be ashamed to admit the abuse, blame themselves for what has occurred, be afraid of the consequences of divulging "family secrets", or not want to appear disloyal. Individuals from particular cultural or religious groups may find it even less acceptable to share this information, especially with someone from a different group. Also, the presence or absence of a family support system may make it easier or more difficult to report abuse. Therefore, it is helpful to use more than one method to screen clients, and to be alert to signs of abuse throughout the mediation process.

3. Objectives of Screening

The purpose of screening is to determine whether each party has the ability to negotiate on his or her own behalf, so that any agreement reached meets the prerequisites of a valid contract. That is, the mediators should determine that:

- both parties are participating voluntarily;
- both parties are informed as to their rights and obligations under the law;
- each believes that the other is negotiating in good faith; and
- any agreement reached is reached without duress or intimidation.

4. Type of Information Sought

During the screening, it is important to determine whether there are control issues, a serious imbalance in power, or domestic violence by asking questions about the following:

- why the marriage ended;
- how decisions were made in the marriage;
- how anger was expressed;
- any instances of physical or verbal abuse;
- any concerns with respect to drug or alcohol abuse;
- whether each party is comfortable negotiating in the same room as the other party; and
- any concerns about the safety of either party before, during, or after a joint mediation process.

If these questions are asked in person, then the intake person must listen for both what is said and what is not said. Silences or hesitations may indicate that there is a problem requiring further investigation.

5. Options Following Screening

At the end of the screening process, the mediator should decide, taking into account the view of the clients, whether the clients are:

- appropriate for mediation conducted in the usual way;
- possibly appropriate for mediation under specific circumstances; or
- not appropriate for mediation.

In each case, the mediator should do the following:

(a) *Where the parties are appropriate for mediation conducted in the usual way* — These are cases where the couple has a history of consultation or joint decision-making, they respect each other's point of view, including the right to hold different points of view, neither party feels afraid or intimidated, and both believe the other is acting in good faith. Therefore, mediation can proceed with primarily joint meetings.

(b) *Where the parties are possibly appropriate for mediation under specific circumstances* —In these cases, there may have been a history of some abuse, primarily verbal or psychological, or an isolated incident of physical abuse in the past, which the abuser has acknowledged, and the abuser has demonstrated a change in behaviour. The abuser may have participated in anger management counselling or be prepared to do that at the present time, and the abusive incidents can be discussed in the mediation (they are not a family secret). In these cases, the mediator should make it clear that violence and intimidation are unacceptable and will result in the mediation being terminated, should there be any further incidents.

Also, if the victim has had counselling, is removed from the situation without recent incidents, and feels confident about proceeding, the mediator should consider the victim's wishes carefully. It would be particularly important to ensure that both parties are in fact participating voluntarily and feel they can express their own point of view. The mediator would need to establish ground rules for communication and implement a safety plan, such as having the abuser arrive early for appointments and stay later, so that the victim of abuse can enter and leave the process without the fear of being followed. In these cases, it is essential that the parties have independent legal advice, and it is likely that most if not all of the sessions would be conducted individually. This is sometimes referred to as "shuttle mediation", that is, the mediator would relay proposals between the parties. If the parties meet jointly, each could be offered the option of bringing a support person if this would ease the tension. The mediator would need to be alert to the use of duress or intimidation in arriving at an agreement, and would want to monitor the clients to make sure there were no reprisals after the mediation. These changes have increased the range of participants who can benefit from mediation.

(c) *Where the parties are not appropriate for mediation* — These are clients who are unable to negotiate safely, are not participating voluntarily, and are unable to reach an agreement without threats to their physical safety, economic security, or psychological health. The task of the mediator in this case is to safely terminate the screening process so that the parties are directed to alternative means of resolving their family law problems and, to the extent possible, protected from further abuse.

6. Safe Termination Following Screening

The following are some "do's" and "do not's" for the mediator with respect to safe termination of the screening process:

(a) *Do's — Meeting with the victim individually* — The mediator should:

- discuss with the victim the mediator's concerns about mediation and alternatives that might better protect her and the children;
- ask the victim what would be a helpful approach for terminating safely; and

- tell the victim what the mediator will tell the abuser, and make a safety plan with respect to her and the children in case the abuser blames the victim.

(b) *Do's — Meeting with the abuser individually* — The mediator should:

- assist the abuser to see that mediation is unlikely to be suitable or productive or meet his needs (that is, it is not likely to succeed and therefore there will be added delay and cost);
- utilize the abuser's language, information, and rationale, if appropriate;
- state that the mediator has a "gut feeling", based on his or her experience that mediation is unlikely to succeed in this case, that is, take personal responsibility for termination;
- if guidelines are set and not adhered to where the couple is possibly appropriate for mediation, focus on this as the basis for termination; and
- tell the abuser that he is not ready for mediation, and suggest what needs to happen first (for example, counselling with respect to the effects of separation). They may be ready in the future.

(c) *Do Not's*

- If the abuse has not already been disclosed, the mediator should not reveal abuse to the abuser's solicitor or to court because this could endanger the victim.
- The mediator should not blame or put down the victim.

Note: As statistics reveal that most victims of domestic violence are women, the feminine pronoun is used here to denote the victim. Where this is not the case, the appropriate gender should be substituted.

7. Safety Planning

(a) *Questions to ask the victim* — It is important for the mediator to determine whether the victim is in danger, or will be in danger once the abuser learns the mediation is not proceeding. Therefore it is important to assist the victim to consider a safety plan. The following questions would be helpful:

- Are you worried about your safety now? How will he react to mediation being terminated?
- Do you feel safe in your present living arrangement? (especially if they are still living together). *If not*, have you talked to a woman's advocate or lawyer? (She should be encouraged to do this — give her names, addresses, and phone numbers, and help her to make contact).

- Do you know of any emergency shelters in case you need to find a place of safety for you and the children? (Give names and phone numbers).
- Do you have any other safe place to go? Do you have any money? Have you ever contacted the police?

(b) *Questions to ask the abuser* — The mediator has a responsibility to assist both parties, including the abuser, to find resources that are appropriate in their case. The following questions would be helpful:

- Do you have a lawyer? (He should be encouraged to get one. Give names, addresses and phone numbers).
- Do you have a counsellor? (He should be encouraged to get one and to enter a Batterer's Treatment Program if appropriate).

Even though clients may not be appropriate at the present time for mediation, if they take appropriate steps, and if the abuser changes his behaviour and the victim feels safer and more empowered, it may be possible for them to enter mediation at a later date. See "5.(b) Where the parties are possibly appropriate for mediation under specific circumstances" for some suggestions.

There are a number of reasons why the clients or the mediator may wish to terminate mediation, or the lawyers may advise such termination. One important reason has already been discussed, that is, concerns about domestic violence, which may make it impossible for clients to negotiate safely or to reach agreements voluntarily. For an additional discussion of the termination process, refer to Chapter 9.

E. ESTABLISHING MEDIATOR'S IMPARTIALITY

It is important for the mediator to be impartial, and for both parties and their solicitors to see the mediator as impartial, in order to accomplish the following objectives of the mediation process. The parties should feel that:

- any agreement reached was reached voluntarily, that is, without duress by either party or the mediator;
- they were the prime architects of any agreement, that is, the agreement reached was their agreement;
- the agreement was fair and reasonable;
- in cases where children are involved, the agreement was in the best interests of the children;
- the agreement was reached after each party had an opportunity to explain his or her views and after full disclosure of all relevant information had been made.

Agreements reached when the mediator is not seen as impartial are:

- less likely to be implemented following the mediation process;
- less likely to be followed voluntarily;

- more likely to be questioned in the future, either in a subsequent mediation process or in a court application.

For an agreement to last and to be carried out in a spirit of cooperation, both parties must feel that the procedure and the outcome are fair and reasonable.

In addition, for a court to enforce an agreement made outside of court, the agreement must be reached voluntarily, without coercion, with full disclosure and preferably with independent legal advice.

For these reasons, it is essential that the mediator establish his or her impartiality with both clients and solicitors from the outset.

Note: It is important for the mediator to clarify that where there are concerns about the safety of either client, the children, the mediator, or his or her staff, the mediator must take steps to address the safety concerns. *That is, the need to protect an individual's safety supersedes the duty to be impartial.*

1. Establishing Impartiality with Lawyers

If the initial contact for mediation is made by a lawyer for one party or if both parties are represented by solicitors from the outset, the mediator should contact both solicitors, by telephone or letter, and indicate that the mediator:

- will be acting as an impartial person as between the parties;
- will help the parties to focus on the best interests of their children, if custody of or access to children is being mediated;
- will require full financial disclosure from both parties as early as possible in the mediation process, if financial matters are being mediated.

2. Establishing Impartiality with Clients

In some cases the clients will contact the mediator directly. One or both parties may not as yet be represented by solicitors.

After screening the client to determine suitability for mediation, the mediator should indicate that he or she will be acting in an impartial manner as between the two parties. To ensure this impartiality the mediator should explain that:

- the mediator will act as a facilitator, that is, an impartial person who is helping the parties arrive at their own voluntary settlement of the issues in dispute. The mediator is not acting as a judge, but rather hopes that the parties will reach their own solution;
- the mediator will place a call to the other party following this initial telephone conversation;
- the mediator will call the solicitor for one or both of the parties if solicitors have been retained;

- apart from screening for domestic violence, the mediator will discourage any discussion of the client's position or any detailed description of the case until the initial interview (either held with the parties together or with the parties individually); and
- both parties will have an opportunity to explain their position to the mediator in either joint or individual sessions and will have an opportunity to respond to any allegations or issues raised by the other party.

It is important that the mediator maintain his or her impartiality and not mislead either client into believing that the mediator will be his or her ally. To ensure that the clients see the mediator as impartial, it may be desirable to meet with both clients together initially. Some mediators prefer to meet with the clients individually first, and if this is the case, the mediator should explain carefully to both clients that this does not suggest a preference for either client. The mediator could ask the parties to suggest which party should be seen first, in order to avoid the appearance of partiality.

Whether the parties are seen together initially or separately, if children are an issue, the mediator should help both parties to focus on the best interests of the children, rather than each party's individual interests.

If financial matters are an issue, then the mediator should encourage each party to give prompt and full financial disclosure to the other. Both parties should be encouraged to be fair and reasonable in their proposals with respect to support or division of property, on the basis that a fair settlement is more likely to last and to lead to less litigation in the future. The mediator should explain to both parties that:

- there will be open communication with both parties. The mediator will not have a confidential relationship with either of the parties and may in fact share whatever information the mediator feels is relevant with either party. If serious allegations are made that could affect the welfare of the children, this information will be shared with both parents and will likely be discussed with the child protection authorities. This is an example of the mediator's impartiality and underlines the mediator's concern for the best interests of the children. The parties should be told that the mediator has a statutory duty to report all cases of alleged child abuse to the appropriate child protection agency;
- he or she will be seeing both clients for approximately equal periods of time. If there is a valid reason why one party should be seen on more occasions than the other, this matter should be drawn to the attention of the other party, so that the mediator is not perceived as biased; and
- he or she will advise both clients to get independent legal advice before the mediation begins and certainly before signing an agreement on any of the issues resolved in mediation.

F. INTERIM ARRANGEMENTS

1. During Mediation

It is important that the status quo be maintained, to the extent possible, during the course of the mediation to ensure fairness to both parties. In order to achieve this goal, the following steps should be taken:

- In the first meeting with counsel and/or with the parties, the mediator should help the parties come to an agreement on the specific arrangements that will prevail during the course of mediation with respect to those issues that have been sent to mediation. That is, if custody of or access to children is an issue, an interim plan should be arrived at as soon as possible in order to offer the parties and children some stability. It should be clear that whatever arrangement is agreed upon on an interim basis will not necessarily be the final arrangement, and both parties should be assured that they will have an opportunity to obtain independent legal advice prior to agreeing to even an interim plan.

- If financial matters are an issue, then parties should agree not to change their wills or beneficiaries on their life insurance policies and not to close out or make substantial withdrawals from any bank accounts or otherwise dispose of assets. That is, the parties should not dissipate or remove assets during the course of mediation in a way that would prejudice the other party without prior consultation and agreement.

- If spousal or child support is an issue, an interim agreement should be reached, in consultation with the parties' solicitors. The parties should agree that these arrangements are "without prejudice" to any final agreement (see F(2), "Without Prejudice").

- If the parties are still living together but want to separate, an important issue to be decided in an initial meeting may be who will live in the matrimonial home. Should both parties remain in the matrimonial home? Should the home be put up for sale? Should one party be granted interim exclusive possession? Should both parties live in the home on some alternating basis? The determination of who has exclusive possession of the matrimonial home is often a significant factor in cases where custody of or access to children is an issue. Also, the matrimonial home may be the largest or only asset of the parties, and therefore its disposition is extremely important.

The mediator should determine from both counsel and the parties whether there is a particular urgency to arrive at an interim arrangement with respect to one or more issues. These issues should be given priority in order to:

- prevent litigation during the course of the mediation process;
- build the clients' confidence in the mediation process as a method of quickly, efficiently, and cooperatively dealing with issues of prime concern to the parties; and
- build the confidence of counsel in the mediation process. It is important that counsel be assured that the parties will be referred to them for independent legal advice before implementing any interim arrangements.

Interim arrangements are extremely useful in that they allow the parties and the mediator to try out and evaluate possible alternative arrangements. Parties often decide to try an interim arrangement and evaluate it with the assistance of the mediator before coming to a final agreement, particularly in cases where:

- the parties have not as yet separated or have separated only recently and therefore have not had experience with alternative solutions to their difficulties;
- the parties are highly suspicious of each other and do not trust each other enough to come to a final decision without some trial period; or
- one or more issues are in dispute and the resolution of one key issue affects the others. For example, if custody of and access to children, possession of the matrimonial home, support and division of property are all in issue, it may be essential to resolve the question of custody of and access to children before the other issues can be satisfactorily dealt with. In such a case, the parties may wish to try out one or more parenting plans before coming to a final decision on the other matters.

If an interim plan is being considered, the mediator and the parties should work out in advance the objective criteria that are going to be used to evaluate the arrangement. A time limit should also be set, at which point the arrangements should be reviewed.

In addition, the mediator and the parties should agree on the consequences in the event that one or both parties fail to live up to the terms of the interim agreement.

The parties should agree that either party can return the issue to mediation prior to the review date if he or she has some serious concerns.

2. Without Prejudice

The term "without prejudice" is usually used to refer to an agreement that is privileged or confidential. It also carries the implication that an agreement will not be detrimental to the rights of either party. It is important for the mediator to explain to both parties that it is not really possible to have a "without prejudice" agreement in mediation. That is, any interim arrangements that are arrived at by the parties will affect the parties' positions at the end of mediation, particularly if mediation fails and the matter is returned to court.

For example, if custody of or access to children is an issue and if the parties have not as yet separated, it may be determined that it is in the children's best interests and even the spouses' best interests for a separation to occur (for example, if there is continual bickering or physical violence in the home). However, if the children remain in the home, the spouse who leaves will be at a disadvantage with respect to custody of the children and exclusive possession of the matrimonial home. Any arrangement whereby one parent has *de facto* custody of the children and the other parent is absent from the matrimonial home is prejudicial to the absent parent, at least in a court of law. This would be particularly true if the *de facto* custody arrangement continued for some period of time, for example, during the mediation process, and then if mediation failed, until a court date could be arranged.

An arrangement concerning interim spousal support or interim child support could also be used to the detriment of the payor spouse in a later court proceeding. That is, it could be raised in evidence that one party did have sufficient funds to provide support or was willing at one point to provide support, and this might be used as a precedent for a subsequent order.

The important point is that the mediator should not mislead the parties by indicating that interim arrangements are really "without prejudice" in terms of their legal consequences. The mediator should recommend that the parties obtain independent legal advice on the likely effect of their proposed interim arrangements prior to entering into them. Also, any interim agreement should state that the specific terms are intended to be without prejudice to any subsequent agreement and will not be referred to in case of subsequent litigation.

In most cases, an important factor is the amount of time that an arrangement is in effect. For this reason, the mediator should attempt to deal with each mediation case as quickly as possible and should attempt to preserve the status quo on all issues to the extent that this is possible during the mediation process.

The mediator should ask both counsel and both parties to agree that there will be no further court proceeding during the course of mediation with respect to those issues that have been sent to mediation. The mediator in turn should assure counsel that if an urgent situation arises that would ordinarily be dealt with through litigation, the mediator will agree to meet immediately with both parties and, if necessary, the lawyers in order to deal with the particular crisis. If the crisis is not resolved through mediation, then the lawyers may have to take legal action. This may mean that mediation will be temporarily suspended or permanently ended.

G. RESPECTIVE RESPONSIBILITIES

With the strong emergence of family mediation as a viable alternative to court-imposed settlement during the past two decades, there has developed some corresponding confusion about the specific roles and responsibilities of the mediator, the lawyer, the clients, and others. The following guidelines clarify the responsibilities of each of the participants in the mediation process:

Participant	Responsibilities
The lawyer will:	— Describe the mediation process to the client.
	— Screen for appropriateness for mediation; *i.e.*, are there issues of violence, intimidation, substance abuse, mental illness, or other factors which would raise concerns about mediation?
	— If the case is appropriate, obtain consent of the client to proceed with mediation preparations.
	— Contact the lawyer of the other spouse to suggest mediation.
	— Ensure that both spouses are provided with a selection of qualified mediators, if the spouse's lawyer agrees to mediation. (Clients and lawyers both may suggest mediators for consideration.)
	— Arrange for the mediator to be contacted by one of the lawyers once a selection has been made. (A three-way meeting of both lawyers and the mediator is usually set up prior to the mediator's contact with the clients.)
	— Ensure that an up-to-date *curriculum vitae* is distributed to both lawyers prior to the commencement of mediation.
	— Clarify the parameters for mediation; *i.e.*, establish which issues are to be part of the mediation process and which are excluded.
	— Agree on a time limit for the mediation process, as well as the arrangements for the payment of the mediator's fee.
	— Monitor the progress of mediation with the client and mediator.
The court will:	— Ensure that both spouses are aware of the

option of mediation during pretrial procedures.

— Encourage mediation if it has not been attempted.

— Order open or closed mediation, if the parties agree, with a mediator who is selected on consent of both parties.

— Support mediated resolutions as drawn up in minutes of settlement.

— Make an order for the payment of fees.

The counsellor will: — Discuss mediation with any client(s) contemplating separation or divorce.

— Screen for appropriateness for mediation; *i.e.*, are there issues of violence, intimidation, substance abuse, mental illness, or other factors which would raise concerns about mediation?

— If the case is appropriate, provide client(s) with a list of qualified mediators to contact.

— Assist in the referral process to better ensure that the couple has at least an initial agreed-upon session with the mediator.

— Follow up with the couple to check on progress within first month. (If mediation has broken down, the counsellor will attempt a renewed effort with same or alternative mediator.)

The client will: — Commit to a specified mediator (acceptable to both spouses).

— Agree upon issues needing mediation and the payment of the mediator's fee.

— Work conscientiously to negotiate an agreement within the time period agreed upon.

— Attend scheduled mediation sessions.

— Remain task oriented.

— Avoid angry, disparaging remarks directed at the spouse.

— Avoid using intimidation, such as threats of violence, withdrawal of resources, or withdrawal of contact with the children.

— Put agreed-upon procedures into operation during the mediation process.

— Follow through with each spouse on resolutions, once the agreement has been signed.

— Agree to return to mediation in case of future disputes, rather than initiate litigation.

The mediator will:

— Contact both lawyers by telephone and arrange a conjoint meeting with them as soon as a preliminary screening for appropriateness has been done.

— If the case is appropriate, establish during the meeting the respective responsibilities of all professionals involved, the issues to be mediated, and the time limit agreeable to both parties.

— Provide up-to-date copies of *curriculum vitae* for lawyers, with extra copies for both parties.

— Contact the clients and arrange for the first appointment with the mediator.

— Meet with both clients (individually or conjointly) to confirm mediation contract; *i.e.*, including all factors previously agreed upon with both lawyers. (Copies of the signed contract should be given to both clients and both lawyers.)

— Establish regular mediation sessions convenient to both clients.

— Inform both lawyers of progress by telephone or letter.

— Contact lawyers immediately, should any difficulties develop that interrupt mediation.

— Submit a copy of the mediator's report (of issues resolved and unresolved) to both lawyers and both clients.

— Cooperate with both parties to draft minutes of settlement (if requested).

Mediation is an entirely different process from litigation in that the outcome is primarily the responsibility of the two parties rather than that of their respective lawyers or the judge. It is the couple who are in charge of the process as long as mediation is in progress. The following are some of the differences between mediation and litigation:

• Only the two parties themselves can decide to commence a family mediation and to continue the process until an agreement is reached.

• After the mediator, the lawyers, and the court have completed their work, the two parties have the ultimate responsibility for carrying out any agreement made between them and for avoiding future conflict. Therefore, it is essential that both the lawyers and the mediator permit and encourage the clients to take charge of making the decisions that will be affecting their lives and those of their children.

- The parties may have priorities that are not made apparent to the lawyer and that differ from legal entitlements. Therefore, in mediation the parties can reach an agreement that is very different from what a court might otherwise impose.
- The parties are more likely to follow through on settlements they have negotiated directly than on those imposed by the court.

H. RESPECTIVE CONCERNS

The issues of responsibility and power are directly related to a variety of concerns. Some of the more common concerns with respect to mediation are listed among the following:

Participant	Concerns
The lawyer(s)	— The mediator may fail to keep counsel informed of progress.
	— The client may be placed in a vulnerable position *vis-à-vis* the spouse.
	— The client may not be able to articulate his or her position as clearly and forcefully as the lawyer.
	— Agreeing not to litigate issues under mediation could reinforce the status quo.
	— The client may be induced to make too many concessions in the effort to reach resolution.
	— The time elapsed in mediation may prejudice the client in subsequent litigation.
	— The mediator may have unknown biases on issues relevant to the mediation.
	— The mediation process takes place in private and neither the process nor the outcome will be scrutinized by a judge.
	— In mediation there is no publicly reported outcome. Therefore, mediated cases do not provide precedents that can serve as helpful guidelines for subsequent cases.
The client	— The mediation process will not provide the protection provided by legal counsel.

	— The other spouse may use intimidation or violence to achieve an unfair result in mediation.
	— Dealing directly with the spouse may continue conflict and increase personal stress.
	— Mediating with the spouse may create false hopes about a possible reconciliation.

The mediator
— Litigating of other issues may impact negatively on mediation.
— Being pressured to achieve a resolution too quickly, or one that is unreasonable, could result in a less stable agreement.
— Losing the support of one of the lawyers would undermine the mediation process.
— Encountering parental sensitivities may block the effective involvement of the children or result in pressure on the children, or extended family members to take sides in the mediation process.
— The trust and cooperation built up between the parties during mediation may be weakened when they return to their lawyers for resolution of issues other than those in mediation.
— The resolutions may not function well over the long term.

I. TERMINATION

Mediation can be terminated by the clients (parties) or the mediator, but not by the lawyers. The lawyer may advise his or her client to terminate mediation or may raise concerns with the mediator. However, the actual decision to terminate rests with the client(s) or the mediator.

With court-ordered mediation, it would be necessary to return to court to have the original order withdrawn or terminated by the judge. (When mediation is terminated, the judge may decide to order an assessment or family investigation.)

There are a number of reasons why the clients or the mediator may wish to terminate mediation, or the lawyer(s) may advise such termination. Refer to Chapter 9 for a complete discussion of the termination process.

ANNOTATED BIBLIOGRAPHY

Barsky, A. "Issues in the Termination of Mediation Due to Abuse". (1995), 13 *Mediation Quarterly* 1. Barsky describes a strategic framework for analyzing ethical dilemmas when abuse is present.

Benjamin, M., and Irving, H. "Towards a Feminist-Informed Model of Therapeutic Family Mediation". (1992), 10 *Mediation Quarterly* 10(2), 129-53.

Ellis, D. *Family Mediation Pilot Project: Final Report*. Oakville, Ont., 1994. This research examined the cost effectiveness, client satisfaction, and incidence of domestic violence in mediation versus litigation clients.

Folberg, J., and Taylor, A. *Mediation: A Comprehensive Guide to Resolving Conflicts Without Litigation*. San Francisco: Jossey-Bass Publishers, 1984. See in particular Part Two, "Mediation Stages, Concepts and Skills," p. 38. This is an important early text which covers the theory and practice of mediation.

Freeman, R., Lambert, K., and Nosko, A. *Working Towards Eliminating Male Violence Against Women: A Group Intervention for Abusive Men: Pilot Project Outcome Report*. Toronto: Family Service Association of Metro Toronto, 1994.

Girdner, L. "Mediation Triage: Screening for Spouse Abuse in Divorce Mediation". (1990), 6 *Mediation Quarterly*, 365-76. This article provides a very useful guide for screening clients for domestic violence concerns. This screening is conducted with the clients separately and helps both the clients and the mediator decide whether mediation would be safe and appropriate in a particular case.

Girdner, L., ed. "Special Issue: Domestic Violence". (1990), 7 *Mediation Quarterly*.

Grillo, T. "The Mediation Alternative: Process Dangers for Women". (1991), 100 *Yale Law Review*, 1545-610.

Hart, B. *Mediation for Battered Women: Same Song, Second Verse, Little Bit Louder, Little Bit Worse*. New York: National Centre on Women and Family Law, 1984.

Jaffe, P., Wolfe, D., and Wilson, S. *Children of Battered Women, Volume 21*. Newbury Park, California: Sage Publications, 1990. This book summarizes the impact on children of witnessing violence directed at their mothers. It also reviews the literature on the number of children who are battered when their mothers are battered. Information is provided about the long-range consequence for these children and the likelihood that these children will become either batterers or victims of abuse.

Kelly, J., and Duryee, M. "Women's and Men's Views of Mediation in Voluntary and Mandatory Mediation Settings". (1992), 30 *Family and Conciliation Courts Review* 34-49. This article reports findings regarding women and mediation from a combined group of 184 persons who received mediation services from the Alameda County Superior Court Family Court Services or the Northern California Mediation Center. This empirical study refutes many of the feminist criticisms of mediation and demonstrates that women do feel empowered by the mediation process.

Landau, B. "Qualifications of Family Mediators: Listening to the Feminist Critique". In C. Morris and A. Pirie, eds. *Qualifications for Dispute Resolution: Perspectives on the Debate*. Victoria, B.C.: U. Vic. Institute for Dispute Resolution, 1994. This chapter summarizes the feminist critique of family mediation and makes suggestions for changes in family mediation practice and the training of mediators.

Landau, B. "Family Mediation: An Alternative Dispute Resolution Manual". In A. Stitt, ed. *Alternative Dispute Resolution Practice Manual*. Toronto: CCH Canadian Limited, 1996. This chapter contains an introduction to family mediation practice and highlights important policy issues.

Lemmon, J.A., ed. "Successful Techniques for Mediating Family Breakup". (1983), 2 *Mediation Quarterly*. This issue of the *Mediation Quarterly* contains a number of excellent articles with respect to the practice of mediation.

McIsaac, H., ed. "Special Issue: Domestic Violence". (1995), 33 *Family and Conciliation Courts Review*. This entire issue is devoted to articles on domestic violence.

McKie, D.C., Prentice, B., and Reed, P. *Divorce: Law and the Family in Canada*. Ottawa: Minister of Supply and Services, 1983. The authors provide a history of marriage and divorce in Canada, including a penetrating look at the social and legal aspects.

MacLeod, L., and Shin, M. *Isolated, Afraid and Forgotten: The Service Delivery Needs and Realities of Immigrant and Refugee Women Who Are Battered*.

Ottawa: National Clearinghouse on Family Violence, Health and Welfare Canada, 1990.

Mediation in Cases of Domestic Abuse: Helpful Option or Unacceptable Risk? The Final Report of the Domestic Abuse and Mediation Project. Coordinated by the Maine Court Mediation Service, 1992.

Pearson, J. *Divorce Mediation and Domestic Violence*. Denver: Center for Policy Research, 1996.

Perry, L. "Mediation and Wife Abuse: A Review of the Literature". (1994), 11 *Mediation Quarterly* 4, 313-27. This article reviews the concerns of those opposed to the use of mediation in such cases and outlines models of mediation, including screening procedures and special techniques, used by mediators to address the dynamics of violence.

Report from the Toronto Forum on Women Abuse and Mediation. Toronto: 1993. This important report was prepared by leading mediators and women's advocates working together to suggest standards of practice, policies, and protocols for the safe, fair, and specialized practice of mediation in cases involving abuse against women. Central to this report is the rebuttable presumption against the use of mediation in cases of domestic abuse. This report makes suggestions as to the education and training of family mediators with respect to abuse, techniques for pre-mediation screening, safety measures, and specialized mediation processes that should be considered, including techniques for safe termination and alternatives to mediation in those cases where mediation is inappropriate.

Samuels, M.D., and Shawn, J.A. "The Role of a Lawyer Outside the Mediation Process". In J.A. Lemmon, ed. "Successful Techniques for Mediating Family Breakups" (1983), 2 *Mediation Quarterly* 13. This article considers the role of the non-mediating attorney before, during, and after mediation. It provides specific guidelines for practice by mediators at each stage of the process.

Saposnek, D. *Mediating Child Custody Disputes*. San Francisco: Jossey-Bass Publishers Inc., 1983. See particularly Part H, "Structuring the Mediation Process", p. 44. This early text contains a number of concrete suggestions and case examples of mediation in practice.

Schaeffer, M. "Divorce Mediation: A Feminist Perspective". (1988), 46 *University of Toronto Faculty of Law Review* 1962-200.

Sinclair, D. *Understanding Wife Assault: A Training Manual for Counsellors and Advocates*. Toronto: Deborah Sinclair, 1985.

Chapter Four

Mediation in Practice: Procedures

A. OBJECTIVES OF MEDIATION

While mediators tend to have similar objectives and can usually agree on basic ethical standards, they may use different procedures in their mediation process. Despite differences in the procedure followed, each step should in some way further the overall objectives of mediation, namely:

- ensuring that both parties feel safe and comfortable expressing their needs and concerns and that any agreement is reached without duress or intimidation;
- fostering cooperation and trust between the parties, such that the parties will be able to share parenting tasks and significant information about their children and their financial needs;
- improving the parties' ability to communicate, such that they can understand each other's feelings about the marriage breakdown and share information and make necessary decisions together;
- providing an opportunity for parties to reassess their perceptions and assumptions about each other;
- ensuring that all relevant parties have an opportunity to have their views and needs heard, such that the parties gain an increasing sense of self-confidence, self-reliance and a feeling they have been dealt with fairly;
- reducing tension and conflict, particularly when children are involved, such that the children can continue to have a close relationship with both parents, free from intense conflicts of loyalty;
- obtaining full disclosure of all relevant facts, such that decisions are made on the basis of adequate information and after a consideration of alternative proposals for resolving the issues in dispute;
- encouraging private ordering and self-determination such that the parties arrive at their own, voluntary resolution of the issues in dispute;
- arriving at a fair and reasonable settlement, such that an adversarial court proceeding is avoided.

If an assessment rather than mediation has been requested, either by the court or by the parties or their counsel, many assessors follow a process that is similar to the mediation process. That is, with the consent of the parties, many assessors offer the parties the opportunity to mediate the issues in dispute, or at least narrow their differences, in the hope that they can arrive at their own resolution, without the need for an adversarial court proceeding.

However, an assessment should be distinguished from mediation in that there is an onus on the assessor to form an objective, independent evaluation of the parties in the event that the parties fail to reach an agreement. This may also be true of open mediation, where the mediator is required to prepare a report with recommendations.

Whenever the assessor or mediator must make recommendations, a more thorough process of information gathering is generally followed, and additional meetings are usually arranged with persons other than the parties themselves, such as with children, nannies, or other consistent caretakers, new partners, and extended family members in the case of custody disputes, or accountants or property evaluators in the case of financial disputes.

Before describing the steps of the mediation process, it is important to understand the principles underlying this process. These principles are based on the Harvard Negotiation Model and are adapted from the seminal book on the subject, *Getting to Yes,* by Roger Fisher and William Ury.[1] These principles are often referred to as *interest-based bargaining* and apply to negotiation as well as mediation.

B. INTEREST-BASED NEGOTIATION

Principled negotiation involves the following steps:

1. Separating the *people* from the problem.

The feelings the parties have about each other should be separated from the objective aspects of the problem. For example, in order to resolve a dispute about household contents, it is important to help the parties get past their anger at each other in order to divide the contents in a rational way, based on what each needs.

The parties should be helped to see themselves as working side by side in attacking the problem, rather than working in opposition and attacking each other. This can be accomplished using structural devices, such as having the parties actually sit side by side facing a flip chart, instead of glaring at each other across a table. Another powerful way to achieve this objective is to have the parties agree on a mutual problem statement. For example: *"How can we divide the household contents fairly so that we each get what we most need?"*

2. Focusing on *interests*, not positions.

A *position* is what a party wants or demands as his or her preferred outcome. A position, as opposed to an interest, is a specific solution put forward

---

[1]   R. Fisher and W. Ury, *Getting to Yes: Negotiating Agreements Without Giving In,* 2nd ed. (Markham, Ont.: Penguin Books, 1991).

by a party to settle the issues in dispute. This position is intended to meet the underlying needs or interests of one of the parties. A position represents the best outcome for that party and does not take into account the wants or needs of others. Often, that party cannot even visualize an alternative solution. For example: "*I want custody of the children.*" (As opposed to, "*I want to continue to play an important role in the lives of our children.*")

An *interest* is *why* a party has taken a particular position. Sometimes, interests are subconscious and even the party is not aware of them.

Interests may fall into three categories:

- *Substantive Interests* — These are quantifiable or objective needs such as the matrimonial home, spousal or child support, or custody of the children. A substantive interest might be described as follows:
  — General: "*I want a home to live in.*"
  — Specific: "*I want exclusive possession of the matrimonial home for at least 5 years.*"
- *Procedural Interests* — These are a party's expressed needs with respect to the dispute resolution process. For example: "*It is important that we use a non-adversarial approach for deciding on a parenting plan so that we minimize the conflict between us in the interests of our children.*"
- *Psychological Interests* — These are a party's emotional needs arising out of the behaviour of the other party. For example: "*It is important for me to know that I can trust the other person to keep a commitment both to me and to our children.*"

3. Creating a *mutual problem statement.*

Each party has a position, which is the result of a set of interests. In a conflict, the parties proceed as if their interests are necessarily in opposition.

An important task for the mediator is to assist the parties to reframe their conflict into a *mutual problem statement* that encompasses the important needs and interests of all parties. This is a key step in interest-based negotiation as it opens up the possibility that while interests may be different, they are often not in opposition.

A mutual problem statement is a statement of intention by the parties to achieve, to the extent possible, a *win/win* result based on meeting each of the parties' important interests. The format is often: "*How can we on the one hand...while at the same time...?*"

For example: "*How can we develop a parenting plan that gives the children the stability and predictability they need while at the same time ensuring that the children maintain a significant relationship with both parents and their extended family?*"

...ng options for *mutual gain*.

This is a creative process of generating a number of options, beyond each party's initial position, to be sure that the most satisfactory resolution for both parties is achieved. In the case of family mediation, it is important to ensure that the needs and interests of children, extended family members, and new partners are considered.

Too often, each party can see only a small number of alternatives for resolving the dispute. Since these alternatives tend to meet only one party's needs, a resolution is impossible.

Parties should generate as many options as possible, *without comment*, before any evaluation takes place. It is a good idea to record all of the options on a flip chart so that the parties can see both their own and the other parties' options. It is helpful to reassure parties that putting an option on the flip chart does not mean it has been accepted, it has just been put forward for consideration.

The parties should be encouraged to propose options that also meet the needs of the other party. This is especially important in order to build trust and good will in the process and to stimulate creative mutual problem solving.

It is often helpful to "fractionalize" the options, that is, propose options that address part of the problem, and build incrementally towards a whole solution. This is particularly helpful for complex or emotionally loaded issues.

In a win/win solution, the final agreement is usually constructed from a variety of options, without regard for who actually proposed them.

5. Using *objective criteria* for evaluating options.

Before evaluating the alternatives, the parties should agree on some fair and objective criteria or factors for discriminating between useful and non-useful options, for example, cost, convenience, age of the children, *etc*. Many of the criteria will derive from the *interests* of the parties. Rather than argue over options for personal reasons, it is helpful to use "objective" criteria.

It is important to avoid making decisions based on inadequate information, duress, or conflict avoidance. These decisions are often questioned later and may result in the agreement not being followed. The most durable agreements are those reached *voluntarily*, by *informed* participants, who are not under duress.

These principles form the basis for the interest-based negotiation and mediation model. This model is used for marriage breakdown and other family conflicts (including parent-child and multigenerational issues, child welfare concerns, adoption, small family business disputes, international disputes, workplace conflicts, victim-offender issues, as well as commercial, environmental, and other disputes). While the model is applied somewhat differently depending on the type of issue, the model itself consists of the following steps and objectives.

C. MEDIATION MODEL

1. Developing the Strategy — Prior to Mediation Session

The eventual success or failure of the conflict resolution process may depend on decisions made at this stage. Many of the issues may seem unimportant or obvious, but they are neither. It is important for the mediator to think strategically about each step of the process. The mediator should:

- contact both solicitors and/or parties by phone and/or letter;
- clarify who should participate in the process;
- explain the mediation process;
- determine whether the parties are willing to participate voluntarily;
- assess readiness to mediate: Are the parties aware of their rights and responsibilities? Are they able to negotiate on their own behalf with the other party?
- determine whether domestic violence, intimidation, emotional disturbance, drug or alcohol abuse are an issue. Assess appropriateness for mediation;
- clarify payment of fees; and
- set date, time, and place to meet.

2. Implementing the Strategy

At the mediation meetings, the parties should try to achieve the following goals:

- The mediator should introduce the process.
- The parties should
  — exchange positions
  — explore interests
  — define a mutual problem
  — generate options
  — establish criteria
  — reach agreement

(A) INTRODUCING THE PROCESS

The mediator should attempt to:

- Set a constructive tone: Welcome people and put them at ease.
- Establish a joint problem-solving climate.

- Explain the purpose: Make it clear why a process has been initiated, and why this one.
- Describe the process: What steps will be followed in solving the problem?
- Clarify roles: The mediator's and the parties'.
- Ask for the parties' explicit commitment to a *collaborative problem-solving process* with a goal of reaching a *mutually acceptable, win/win outcome*.
- Set guidelines for behaviour (respectful communication, no interruptions) and for the meeting process (time limits, opportunities to "caucus", breaks).

(B) EXCHANGING POSITIONS

- The participants exchange positions — Each participant makes an opening statement identifying the issue(s) and outlining what he/she hopes to accomplish in the mediation. This may include his/her preferred solution. The mediator should ensure that each participant hears and understands the other participant's position.
- Agreements and disagreements are noted — The mediator identifies the areas of agreement and disagreement.
- Issues are prioritized — The parties, with the assistance of the mediator, determine an order of priority for dealing with issues. They should start with those that are least difficult to reach an agreement on, or those that are most urgent.
- The participants develop an agenda — The parties agree on the agenda, including the sequence of items.

(C) EXPLORING INTERESTS

For each issue:

- The participants exchange interests — Each participant's underlying interests, concerns and needs are explored. The mediator should ensure that each participant hears and understands the other participant's interests, concerns, and needs.
- Mutual and non-competing interests are noted — Mutual interests are those that the parties share. Non-competing interests are those that are important to one party and do not interfere with the other party's interests.

Throughout the discussion:

- A collaborative atmosphere should be maintained — The mediator should reinforce a constructive sharing of views, and discourage intimidation, threats, or "bottom-lining".

(D) DEFINING A MUTUAL PROBLEM

This encourages the parties to "sit on the same side of the table", solving a mutual problem collaboratively, instead of fighting for their own positions.

- The parties should use mutual and non-competing interests to state a joint problem. For example: "*How can we (meet A's needs) while at the same time (meeting B's needs)?*"

(E) GENERATING OPTIONS

- The problem should be "fractionalized" — The participants should break the problem into smaller pieces and generate options for each piece.
- The parties brainstorm in individual, small group, or joint sessions — They should avoid criticizing each other's options.
- The pie must be expanded (where possible) so that there are increased benefits for all if a solution is reached — This is an *integrative orientation* (as opposed to a *distributive orientation*, which presumes that the pie is fixed, so that if one person gets a share, the others get less).

(F) ESTABLISHING CRITERIA

The parties develop objective criteria for evaluating options, following these steps:

- Start with the mutual problem statement — Each interest becomes one of the criteria.
- Add other criteria — Any other important factors, such as cost, deadlines, *etc.*
- Agree on weightings for criteria — Which criteria are essential in any solution, which are particularly important to a particular party, which are desirable, if there are sufficient resources, *etc.*

(G) REACHING AGREEMENT

- The options should be ranked according to objective criteria — win/win options first, versus win/lose options.
- Then trade-offs should be attempted — The parties should consider exchanging items that have a different level of priority for different participants. Where conflicts are over scarce resources and the pie cannot be expanded, the mediator should ask the participants to consider what they would trade off.
- An agreement should be formulated (preferably in writing) — The agreement reached should be specified in as much detail as possible. The mediator should clarify each participant's role in carrying out the agreement.

- Consideration should be given to what will happen if there are future impasses — The parties should develop a process for evaluating and reviewing progress, and for dealing with future disagreements. They should consider what could be done preventatively to avoid unwanted situations in the future.
- The mediator should evaluate and monitor the agreement — A review might be held, with specific objectives, at a future date.

The mediation model described above is put into practice in a series of meetings that will vary with the needs of the particular case and the style of the mediator. The following is an outline of some of the major meetings that might take place in a family mediation, including the objectives and the procedure followed.

D. MEDIATION MEETINGS

Note: Assume there has already been a screening for appropriateness using an individual telephone or face-to-face interview and/or a written questionnaire completed separately by each parent.

1. Meeting with Counsel

(A) OBJECTIVES

Where both parties are represented at the outset of mediation, it is desirable to hold a meeting with both counsel present, prior to beginning the mediation, to accomplish the following objectives:

- To establish that the mediator will act impartially as between the parties. One concern frequently raised is that the mediator may be biased in favour of the solicitor or client who recommended the mediator. One way of dealing with this spoken or unspoken concern is to have both solicitors meet with the mediator.
- To build trust between the mediator and counsel. Counsel may not have worked with a particular mediator previously and may have some questions and concerns about the mediator's experience and competence for dealing with a particular issue.
- To build confidence in the mediation process as a method for resolving the particular issues in dispute. Counsel need an opportunity to discuss the process their clients will follow, what will happen if one or more issues are not resolved, and how the mediation process will relate to other issues that are not referred to mediation.
- To clarify for counsel the contract with the clients. That is, what is expected of the mediator and what the mediator expects of the clients and counsel. For example, there should be clarification about whether the mediation is open or closed, what issues are to be

addressed and whether the mediator is being asked for recommendations in the event that the parties fail to reach an agreement on one or more issues.

- To establish how the mediator's fees are to be paid. It is usual for the clients to share the mediator's fees either equally or, if this is not possible, in proportion to their income. It is desirable to have some splitting of fees so that both parties see the mediator as impartial.

- To obtain from counsel a summary of the history of the case. Counsel should provide the mediator with any relevant documents, reports, or correspondence. Both counsel should have copies of all materials given to the mediator.

- To establish a cooperative atmosphere with counsel. This is necessary to encourage counsel to support a non-adversarial approach to resolving the issues in dispute.

(B) PROCEDURE FOR MEETING WITH COUNSEL

The meeting with counsel should be held in the mediator's office if possible, or if not possible, in some other neutral setting (rather than in the office of one or the other lawyer). A face-to-face meeting is preferred, but if this is not possible then a conference call could be used.

The clients are usually not invited to attend this initial meeting, because the lawyers are usually more relaxed, more willing to share information, and more direct in stating their concerns if the clients are not present.

During the course of the meeting, the mediator should:

- determine the issues to be resolved in the mediation process (for example, custody and access, child or spousal support, division of property, or exclusive possession of the matrimonial home);

- review with the lawyers the experience and qualifications of the mediator for dealing with the particular issues to be mediated;

- clarify what other issues are in dispute and how the lawyers intend to deal with them (for example, is litigation pending on any other issue, such as support, at the same time as custody and access are to be mediated?);

- clarify whether the mediation is to be open or closed;

- establish whether the mediator is to make recommendations in the event that a settlement is not reached on one or more issues;

- determine whether there are any concerns or questions with respect to the mediator's qualifications, competence, or biases. Invite discussion openly on these matters, because if they are not dealt with at this point, they could act as a hidden agenda later and result in the lawyers losing confidence in any potential settlement reached in the mediation process;

- clarify the procedure to be followed, that is, whether the parties are to be seen together or separately for the initial interview;
- determine whether there are other significant individuals who should be seen during the mediation process. For example, if the mediation concerns custody of or access to children, the mediator is strongly encouraged to meet with the children and determine their views, concerns, and preferences at some point during the mediation process;
- determine whether secondary sources should be contacted (for example, other mental health professionals, such as psychologists, psychiatrists, or social workers for information in relation to parenting capacity or the needs of the children, or an accountant with respect to financial status);
- determine the time frame for the mediation (for example, are there court dates pending? Is there a concern about the status quo in relation to either children or financial matters?);
- explain the need for disclosure of all information that is relevant to the issues in dispute. The mediator should indicate that he or she will determine what is relevant and will need the assistance and cooperation of counsel in ensuring that the parties recognize the need for full disclosure. If financial issues are being mediated, the mediator may ask the lawyers to assist their clients in preparing financial disclosure forms. In cases where custody of or access to children is an issue, counsel should be informed that clients will be asked to sign releases of information for schools, family doctors, mental health professionals, and other sources that may have information relevant to the needs of the children or the parenting skills of the parties.

If the mediator intends to have the clients sign a contract for mediation services, then the contract should be shown to the lawyers during this meeting. It is advisable for the mediator to obtain the signatures of the lawyers on the contract as well as those of the clients, in order to avoid any confusion in the future as to the terms of the retainer and whether the mediation is open or closed. Particularly in closed mediation cases, the mediator is advised to obtain the written agreement of the solicitors not to subpoena the mediator to court in the event that mediation fails and the matter proceeds to court. Having both the lawyers and the clients sign a written contract outlining their expectations of the mediator prevents future disputes about what the mediator is expected to do, what information the mediator will have available, and how the mediator will be paid.

The mediator should explain to counsel that he or she may contact the lawyers at various stages of the mediation process in order to give them feedback on progress and if necessary to seek assistance from the lawyers in resolving a conflict. It should be made clear that the mediator will not have a confidential relationship with one solicitor, but rather will have open communication with both solicitors, and if an issue of concern arises, both solicitors will be contacted and given full information.

Note that subsequent contacts can be by telephone, by letter, or by face-to-face meeting, if that is necessary. At times, it may be desirable to have a meeting of both counsel with the clients to resolve a particularly difficult issue. During such a meeting, the mediator may spend time with various combinations of persons, for example:

- with the parties alone;
- with the solicitors alone;
- with one solicitor and his or her client and then the other solicitor and his or her client; and/or,
- with all of the parties together.

That is, the mediator can use a form of shuttle diplomacy or hold caucuses with various subgroups in order to resolve a particularly difficult matter. It is advisable at the end of such a meeting to draw up a statement of those issues that have been resolved and the nature of the resolution reached. In addition, any issues not resolved should be noted and a statement made as to how those issues are to be dealt with in the future. Also, any agreement reached may be in the form of an interim agreement or may deal with only one of several issues that have been sent to mediation.

During the course of mediation, the parties may ask the mediator to discuss issues that were not part of the original mediation contract. For example, if the parties have been discussing custody of or access to children, the parties may also wish to discuss exclusive possession of the matrimonial home and possibly support. Usually this occurs in cases where the mediation has been successful in establishing a cooperative atmosphere and in building trust between the parties. The lawyers should be assured that the mediator will not deal with issues that have not been agreed upon without first contacting the lawyers and obtaining their approval. It would be advisable to confirm any changes to the original agreement in a letter sent to both counsel and both clients.

2. Meeting with Parties

(A) Objectives of Initial Meeting

The mediator tries to accomplish the following general objectives in the initial meeting with the parties:

- to establish that the mediator will act as an impartial person as between the parties;
- to observe the nature of the communication between the parties and to ensure that both appear to be able to articulate their views without threats or intimidation; and

- to reduce tension and help the parties develop more constructive ways of dealing with conflict (this is particularly important if children are involved).

In the event that custody of or access to children is an issue, the mediator attempts to fulfil these additional objectives:

- to help the parties appreciate that their parenting role will continue, even though their spousal role may end;
- to help the parents appreciate the importance to the children of cooperating in their parenting role;
- to provide the parties with information about the effects of separation and divorce on children;
- to obtain a relevant marital history, family history, and a description of the extent to which parenting tasks were shared during the marriage;
- to educate the parents with respect to options available under the law for resolving custody and access issues (that is, for sharing parental responsibilities such as sole custody arrangements and joint custody arrangements); and
- to determine other relevant sources of information with respect to the children's needs and the parenting capacity of each parent (for example, other primary caretakers such as nannies, new partners, members of the extended family, schoolteachers, and family doctors). Preference should be given to individuals with direct, frequent, and fairly long-term contact, especially if they have been involved in an impartial capacity with the family.

If financial matters are at issue, the mediator tries to meet the following objectives:

- to obtain full and complete financial disclosure;
- to obtain the names of relevant sources to contact with respect to financial matters (for example, the family accountant or an experienced real estate appraiser); and
- to educate the parties about the general guidelines provided under the law with respect to support obligations, division of assets, debts, pensions, and other financial matters. If the mediator is not a lawyer, the clients should be referred to their independent counsel for legal information prior to commencing mediation and certainly before signing any agreement. In any event, the mediator should be careful not to give any legal advice to either party regarding the position that he or she ought to take.

(B) PROCEDURE FOR MEETING WITH PARTIES

In order to achieve these objectives, the mediator will usually need to hold several meetings,during which the parties are seen together and individually. For the first meeting, some mediators prefer to meet with both parties together and others prefer to meet with both parties individually. There are advantages and disadvantages to each approach and, of course, the mediator should take into account the particular circumstances and feelings of the parties before adopting a particular approach.

An initial meeting with both parties together has the following advantages:

- It encourages the parents to see the mediator as an impartial person.
- It decreases the suspicion and mistrust directed at both the mediator and the other party.
- It highlights the importance of communication between the parties.
- It allows the parties to hear each other's views on why the marriage broke down and to deal with unresolved emotional feelings between the parties.
- It sets the stage for dispute resolution directly between the parties.
- It sets the focus on improved communication, particularly with respect to parenting, rather than on individual positions in the conflict.

The advantages of an individual meeting are as follows:

- The parties may be more comfortable meeting the mediator alone, prior to a confrontation with the other party.
- It permits each spouse to tell his or her version of the marriage breakdown without interruption by the other spouse.
- It allows each spouse to develop rapport individually with the mediator in a less stressful environment.
- It offers an opportunity for venting emotional feelings and for obtaining individual support from the mediator prior to beginning negotiations.
- It allows the mediator to evaluate each spouse individually and determine the relative bargaining power, the attitude to reconciliation, and any significant concerns or allegations about the other spouse with respect to the children.

In cases where domestic violence is suspected, or where there is insufficient background information, the first meeting should be an individual meeting. For inexperienced mediators, it is probably best to start with an individual meeting.

Whether the initial meeting is held jointly or with the parties individually, the mediator should ensure that the parties feel relaxed and comfortable. Each party should be reassured that he or she will have an opportunity to be heard without interruption and will have an opportunity to respond to any concerns or allegations raised by the other party. If the parties are particularly anxious, it may be easier to deal with basic demographic information at the outset, rather than highly charged emotional issues.

At this meeting, the mediator should review the mediation contract for the following purposes:

- to ensure that there is agreement on the issues to be resolved in mediation;
- to determine whether the mediation is open or closed;
- to determine whether the mediator is expected to make recommendations;
- to establish a basic procedure to be followed;
- to determine who needs to be seen; and
- to determine how the fees will be paid.

The mediator should then obtain a history of the marriage and a family and parenting history (this is particularly important if custody of and access to children are an issue). The mediator should also determine the present status of the parties with respect to each of the issues in dispute that are referred to mediation.

If the parties are meeting together, the mediator should ensure that each party has an opportunity to present his or her version of the marital and parenting history and his or her position on each issue, without being interrupted by the other party. It is advisable for the mediator to explain the communication process in advance, so that the parties do not feel personally attacked by the mediator if the mediator intervenes to discourage interruption. It is also advisable for the mediator to explain some basic ground rules, such as the following:

- Each party should make statements about how he or she personally feels, but not about how he or she believes the other person feels.
- Each party should not refute or criticize how the other person feels. That is, each person can only know how he or she feels and should not make disqualifying or denigrating statements about the other party.
- The parties should ask each other questions to determine how the other person felt or perceived an event, rather than presuming how the other person felt and then attacking that feeling or perception.
- If a party wishes to disagree with a factual statement or a perception of an event, the mediator should assure both parties that they will each have a turn to respond after the other party speaks. It is important for the mediator to encourage good listening skills from the initial meeting with the parties.

It is often important to clarify each person's position with respect to the marriage breakdown. Some individuals may still be hoping for a reconciliation, while others may be well along in the process of accepting a divorce. If there is a real imbalance between the parties in their attitude to the marriage breakdown, this could undermine the mediation process, whether the issues relate to children or to finances. If one partner is extremely angry, hurt, depressed, or unrealistically expecting a reconciliation, these feelings need to be discussed and clarified before the actual process of negotiation can begin.

The parties should then be asked their position on each of the issues to be mediated. It is helpful to put these on a flip chart to ensure clarity and to ensure that each party feels that his or her preferred outcome has been heard.

Beginning with the least contentious issue, the parties should be encouraged:

- to explain why they feel their positions are so important. That is, they should explain their interests so that each fully understands the needs and concerns of the other party.

Once the interests are understood, then the parties should be encouraged:

- to begin generating options or alternative solutions to each of the issues in dispute;
- to see that a successful settlement is usually one in which each party feels that he or she has made gains on some issues that are particularly important to that individual and has made concessions on other issues that may be more important to the other person; and
- to understand that negotiations are rarely successful if one party tries to be a total winner and to humiliate the other party by a total defeat.

The mediator should demonstrate good problem-solving techniques, such as helping the parties generate a range of alternatives and apply objective criteria to evaluate these alternatives.

In the first meeting it is important to obtain the parties' agreement to maintain the status quo with respect to the issues in dispute. It may be necessary to develop an interim plan for such matters as interim custody and access, interim support, or exclusive possession of the matrimonial home (if these issues are in dispute). To the extent possible, these interim plans should not unduly prejudice either party with respect to his or her legal position. However, both parties should recognize that interim arrangements may have long-term consequences if the parties do end up in court.

(c) PARENTING PLAN

The most important phase of the parenting meetings is the development of a Parenting Plan. This may take several meetings, depending on the level of cooperation between the parties and their ability to communicate with each other. The mediator tries to achieve the following objectives in these meetings:

- to clarify how each parent will contribute to carrying out the tasks or responsibilities of parenting (such as, who will transport the children to school, team sports, dance classes, swimming lessons, and doctor and dentist appointments; who will stay home with the child when he or she is ill or make daycare arrangements during school breaks or on professional development days if both parents are working);
- to determine how significant decisions concerning the children will be made (for example, will decisions about the children's health care, choice of school, religious upbringing, or extracurricular activities be made by one parent, by one parent after consultation with the other, or by both parents jointly?);
- to discuss and agree on the involvement of extended family members and new partners (for example, will new partners be introduced to the children? When? Will grandparents or new partners be welcome at extracurricular activities? What if the other parent plans to attend? How will the children feel about these decisions?);
- to clarify the times that the children will spend with each parent, during the school year (for example, will the children spend alternate weekends with each parent? If so, how is a weekend defined — that is, does it begin on Thursday or Friday after school or Saturday morning? Does it end Sunday night or Monday or Tuesday morning? Will the children have a midweek visit with the other parent? If so, will it be for dinner or for an overnight? As an alternative, will the children spend alternate weeks in each parent's home? Or will the parents alternate homes on a weekly basis? Will there be any opportunities for each parent to have some "one-on-one" time to plan for the separate interests of each child?);
- to clarify how the children will spend the school breaks, statutory holidays, professional development days, family birthdays, mother's day/ father's day, religious events, *etc.*;
- to establish the process for dealing with a material change in either parent's or the child's circumstances (for example, a parent's proposal to move to a different jurisdiction with the children of the marriage, the birth of children from a new relationship, or the inability to care for the children as a result of disability, death, or changed economic circumstances); and
- to determine a dispute resolution mechanism for handling disagreements about significant parenting issues (for example, discussion between the parents themselves, a return to mediation, negotiation between solicitors, or, if all previous steps fail, litigation).

It is important to clarify with the parents that as long as both have access to the child, they are equally entitled to information about the child's school progress, medical and dental care, and other information relevant to the child's wellbeing. For example, both parents can ask to attend parent-teacher meetings, request copies of report cards, or ask to speak to the child's health-care providers, as long as there is no order to the contrary. This is often reassuring to the parent who spends less time with the child.

The usual mediation process involves a number of joint as well as individual meetings and, depending on the nature of any issues to be resolved, may include meetings with children, new partners, grandparents, and other individuals who are relevant to the issues being mediated.

3. Meeting with Parents and Children

(A) OBJECTIVES

In the case of custody or access issues, it is generally recommended that the mediator meet with the children directly in order to determine their views, concerns, and preferences.

If the mediator is expected to prepare a report with recommendations, it is particularly important for him or her to see the children alone, and to see the children in conjunction with each parent, in order to form an impression about the parenting arrangements that may best meet the children's needs.

Depending on the issues in dispute, the parents' expectations of the mediator, and the mediator's preferred method of interviewing, the following types of meeting may be held.

A Meeting of the Entire Family

This is a meeting of all of the children, with both parents present. It is recommended in cases where the parties have not as yet separated and in cases where the parties have separated but there is a history of serious conflict involving polarization of the children's feelings about the parents. The primary aim of such a meeting would be for the parents to explain to the children together that the purpose of mediation is to arrive at a cooperative settlement.

A Meeting with Each Parent and All of the Children

This permits the mediator:

- to observe the parenting style of each parent separately with all of the children;
- to note the capacity of each parent to offer affectionate, supportive behaviour;
- to determine similarities and differences in each parent's ability to set reasonable limits and apply discipline techniques; and

- to assess the parents' respective awareness of the children's needs and their willingness to participate in various aspects of parenting.

This information could be the basis of an important discussion with the parents about their perception of the children's needs and differences in their approach to parenting.

A Meeting with Each Parent with the Children Individually

This is recommended where a child has a conflict with one parent. For example, the children are often caught up in a tug of loyalties between the parents and may express a great deal of anger toward one parent. An individual meeting may allow the child and parent to begin resolving their difficulties. Often, the source of the difficulties is that the child feels abandoned or rejected by the parent and is expressing his or her own feelings through anger.

A Meeting with All of the Children

This is particularly useful when the children are very supportive of each other or in cases where the children have been polarized as a result of a loyalty conflict, with each child supporting a different parent.

A Meeting with Each Child Individually

This meeting permits the mediator:

- to determine each child's individual concerns and preferences;
- to assess the emotional impact of the separation on each child; and
- to determine whether the child has experienced abuse or witnessed abuse.

A Meeting with Each Parent Individually

This gives the mediator an opportunity:

- to obtain relevant family history;
- to determine the specific concerns and wishes of each spouse, including concerns about abuse or intimidation;
- to give each parent feedback about the needs, interests, and wishes of each child; and
- to explore alternatives in a less threatening, more supportive atmosphere.

A Meeting with All of the Children and Both Parents to Achieve Closure

It may be desirable for the mediator to have the children present immediately after the parents reach an agreement, in order to explain the terms of the agreement as they affect the children. The children may be helpful in encouraging the parents to take a more cooperative approach in their future dealings with each other as parents. For example, the children can tell the parents how upsetting it is when they fight and ask the parents to behave in a friendlier, less hostile manner, particularly when the children are present. It should be agreed that the children will not be used as message carriers between the parents and that the children can object if either parent makes negative statements about the other.

(B) PROCEDURE FOR MEETING WITH PARENTS AND CHILDREN

Where some combination of meetings is being held between the parents and the children, the following procedures should be followed.

In cases where the mediator is expected to prepare a report with recommendations, it is preferable for the mediator to observe the children and their parents in a natural setting, such as their home, rather than in the more formal, unfamiliar atmosphere of the mediator's office. Children, particularly children under the age of ten, are far more comfortable in their home setting, and are likely to respond more openly and honestly in a familiar setting. However, this is a matter of individual preference for mediators, and may involve considerations such as the cost and convenience of a home visit.

The parents should give the children a clear statement that each child can speak freely and openly with the mediator and not fear any recriminations or pressure to divulge to the parents what they have said to the mediator. It is helpful if parents can explain to the children that they will not be hurt or upset by what the children say, but rather that the parents want the children to speak honestly because they want to create a parenting plan that will be in the children's best interests.

The mediator should ask each child what he or she does not want the mediator to share. The mediator should explain that he or she may not be able to keep confidential the information told to him or her by the children, particularly if the information suggests that the children are at risk of harm. However, the mediator should tell the children if information is likely to be shared with the parents or others. Depending on the circumstances, the children may be invited to be present when this feedback is given.

The mediator could give the children the mediator's office telephone number if there is a concern that they might experience parental pressure or repercussions for speaking openly. The parents should be aware that the mediator has taken this action.

The mediator should make it clear at the outset that the parents will be making the decisions about the children. That is, neither the children nor the mediator will be making the decisions; however, input from the children is important in arriving at decisions. The mediator should reassure the children that the mediator will not ask the children to state which parent they love most or who they want to live with.

The children need reassurance that each parent:

- will take care of the children's basic needs, despite the separation and divorce;
- will continue to love the children and that the children will be permitted to love both parents;
- will make an effort not to undermine the relationship between the children and the other parent (for example, by belittling, criticizing, or making negative comments about the other parent in the children's presence);
- will not pressure the children to reject the other parent or manipulate the children to choose him or her; and
- will support the children's right to respect and love both of their parents and their extended family and to maintain a close and loving relationship with all of these important individuals.

The mediator should ensure that the meeting held with the children individually is held in private and in a setting that is as comfortable as possible for the children, that is, preferably in their own home and in a room that the child chooses.

During the course of the meeting with each child, the mediator should determine the following types of information:

- feelings about the separation — depression, anger, feelings of rejection or abandonment, feelings of relief;
- reconciliation wishes — how realistic does the child feel these wishes are?
- the child's basic daily routine with each parent;
- the amount of time spent with each parent;
- how the child feels about the amount of time spent — too little or too much time with a particular parent?
- how the child feels about the pattern of visits — are they too frequent or too widely spaced, too short or too long, too few or too many overnight visits?
- the child's attitude to the matrimonial home and the neighbourhood — friends, school, community activities;
- the parenting responsibilities of each parent during the marriage and subsequent to the marriage (for example, feeding, bathing, shopping, doctor appointments, after-school activities, wake-up and bedtime routines);
- the attitude of both parents to visits and telephone contact by the other parent — does each parent encourage or obstruct contact by the other parent?
- whether the parents are prompt in picking up and delivering the children;

- whether the parents visit regularly;
- the attitude of the parents to each other at pickup and delivery or during visits;
- the child's feelings about access visits;
- the relationship of the child to each parent;
- the behaviour of the parents to each other, when the child is present;
- the relationship of the child with siblings;
- discipline techniques of each parent;
- loyalty conflicts — to what extent do these seem to be fostered by the parents?
- symptoms of stress or disabilities — school performance, difficulties with peers, nightmares, alcohol or drug abuse, emotional difficulties, physical symptoms;
- strengths and weaknesses of each parent in terms of parenting capacity and any disabilities, such as drug or alcohol abuse, life-threatening illness, emotional difficulties;
- the relationship between each parent and any new partner and between each child and that partner;
- the likelihood that the parents could act cooperatively in the best interests of the children in future parenting arrangements; and
- the child's wishes regarding changes in present arrangements or relationships.

4. Meeting with Significant Others and/or Collecting Information from External Sources

(A) OBJECTIVES

Depending on the type of issues being dealt with in mediation, and whether any individuals other than the parties are having a significant effect on the process (either facilitating or obstructing the mediation process), the mediator should consider the following meetings or data collection:

- Meeting individually with new partners and a joint meeting with both parties and any new partners. The purpose of this meeting would be to determine the new partner's role with respect to issues of custody of or access to children or with respect to financial matters such as contribution to household expenses and spousal support. It is recommended that an additional meeting be held with new partners and the two parties after an agreement has been reached by the parties, in order to ensure that the new partners will support the settlement and to reduce tension.
- Meeting with nannies or other significant caretakers to obtain information with respect to parenting arrangements, children's care,

special needs of children, and ability of each parent to meet these needs. This meeting would be more appropriate in open mediation if the mediator could be asked for recommendations.

- Telephone call or meeting with schoolteachers to obtain information with respect to each child's school performance, special academic needs, and involvement of parents in meeting these needs.
- Telephone call to family doctor to obtain health care information on each child and parent.
- Telephone call to other mental health professionals who have been offering counselling assistance, to obtain information about their emotional needs, family relationships, and other matters relevant to parenting arrangements.
- Telephone call or meeting with property appraisers, business valuators, or pension valuators to obtain appraisals of all interests in property.
- Telephone call or meeting with the accountant to obtain information on the financial needs and means of each party and on each party's net family property.

5. Contacts upon Completion of Mediation

At the point of termination of the mediation, either because an agreement has been reached or because the mediation process has been unsuccessful, both counsel should be contacted by the mediator.

If the parties have succeeded in resolving one or more of the issues in dispute, counsel should be informed that the mediator will be preparing a report or a draft memorandum of understanding that will be forwarded to both parties and their counsel for discussion, prior to signing any agreement.

If the mediation process has broken down, the mediator may suggest a meeting with both counsel to determine whether there is any possibility of breaking the impasse and resuming mediation or achieving a settlement on the outstanding issue(s) through negotiations between the lawyers.

Following the completion of the mediation process, the mediator should prepare a draft memorandum of understanding with respect to the issues that have been resolved. Copies should be sent to the parties and their solicitors, and the parties should be encouraged to obtain independent legal advice prior to signing any agreement.

If the mediator is not a lawyer, then one of the lawyers should redraft the agreement into a legal format with appropriate release clauses and other necessary legal formalities.

If the mediation was *closed mediation* and no issues were resolved:

- the mediator should send a letter to counsel indicating that no agreement was reached; and
- a copy of the letter should be forwarded to each party.

If the mediation was *closed mediation* and agreement was reached on some issues:

- the mediator should prepare a draft memorandum of understanding with respect to those issues that were resolved;
- the mediator should prepare a covering letter outlining which issues were not resolved;
- the mediator should not comment upon or make recommendations about the issues that were not resolved; and
- the mediator should send a copy of the memorandum of understanding and the covering letter to both counsel and both parties.

If the mediation was *open mediation* and one or more issues were not resolved:

- the mediator should prepare a draft memorandum of understanding with respect to those issues that were resolved;
- in a report or letter, the mediator should indicate those issues that were not resolved. If the mediator was asked to prepare recommendations, then the mediator should submit his or her recommendations for resolving the outstanding issues;
- the mediator should comment on the process followed and each party's position with respect to the unresolved issues; and
- the mediator should indicate that he or she would be willing to assist the parties should there be any difficulties in the implementation of the mediation settlement or should difficulties arise at a later date.

ANNOTATED BIBLIOGRAPHY

Adler, R. *Sharing the Children: How to Resolve Custody Problems and Get On With Your Life*. Bethesda, Maryland: Adler & Adler, Publishers, Inc., 1988. This book offers a step-by-step guide for parents going through the divorce process, including self-help checklists, suggestions for age-appropriate parenting schedules, and an outline of custody laws in the United States.

Bienenfeld, F. *My Mom and Dad Are Getting a Divorce*. EC. Corp., 1980. This is a book for children to read to help them deal with their feelings with respect to separation and divorce.

Blades, J. *Mediate Your Divorce: A Guide to Co-operative Custody, Property and Support Agreements*. New Jersey: Prentice Hall Inc., 1985. This book contains practical information with respect to mediation of custody, access, support, and property issues. It also contains a number of sample brochures and forms, as well as training materials, and is directed at both the mental health professional and the lawyer acting as mediator.

Blau, M. *Families Apart: Ten Keys to Successful Co-Parenting*. New York: Berkeley Publishing Group, 1995. Blau draws on her experience and research as a divorced parent. She identifies and discusses the factors that promote successful co-parenting.

Baruch Bush, R. and Folger, J. *The Promise of Mediation: Responding to Conflict through Empowerment and Recognition*. San Francisco: Jossey Bass Publishers, 1994. This is an important book dealing with the theoretical basis for or objectives of mediation. The authors describe four different theories or "stories" about the goals of mediation; namely, the "Satisfaction Story", the "Social Justice Story", the "Transformation Story", and the "Oppression Story", and recommend a transformative model in cases of ongoing relationships.

Coulter, L. *Two Homes: A Parent's Guide to Joint Custody in Canada*. Toronto: Harper Collins Publishers, 1990. Coulter, a divorced parent, writes this book as a guide for parents who are considering a shared parenting plan. She discusses different types of parenting plans, as well as the impact of divorce on children.

Erickson, S., and McKnight Erickson, M. *Family Mediation Casebook: Theory and Process*. New York: Brunner/Mazel, Inc., 1988. This book contains several case studies of families in mediation and is particularly helpful for new practitioners.

Fisher, R., and Ury, W. *Getting to Yes: Negotiating Agreement Without Giving In*. 2nd ed. Markham, Ont.: Penguin Books, 1991. This book sets out the model for principled negotiation or interest-based bargaining that underlies the mediation process. Both the principles and the model are useful for conflict resolution across a wide range of subject matters.

Fisher, R., and Brown, S. *Getting Together: Building Relationships as We Negotiate*. New York: Penguin Books, 1988. This book focuses on the relationship-building skills that are necessary for successful mediation.

Folberg, J., and Taylor, A. *Mediation: A Comprehensive Guide to Resolving Conflicts Without Litigation*. San Francisco: Jossey-Bass Publishers, 1984. See in particular Part Two, "Mediation Stages, Concepts and Skills", p. 38. This thorough text covers the theory and practice of mediation.

Gold, L. *Between Love and Hate: A Guide to Civilized Divorce*. New York: Plenum Press, 1992. This book looks at the impact of separation and divorce on parents and children. It has a number of practical tools for assisting parents in arriving at parenting arrangements post-separation. It is a very thorough and constructive guide that would be useful for mediators and parents to read.

Hansen, J.C., ed., and Grebe, S.C., vol. ed. *Divorce and Family Mediation: The Family Therapy Collections.* Aspen Systems Co., 1985. The authors describe several models of mediation for both family law and labour disputes. Mediators may be particularly interested in an article entitled "Including Children in Mediation: Considerations for the Mediator" by Karen K. Irvin, at p. 94. Her article outlines the arguments for and against including children in the mediation process.

Johnson, L., and Rosenfeld, G. *What You Need to Know to Help Kids Survive a Divorce: Divorced Kids, a Positive, Practical Guide to Help Children Cope With: the Loss of a Relationship, Feelings of Abandonment, Step-Families, Unspoken Fears, and Much More.* New York: a Fawcett-Crest Book, published by Ballantine Books, 1992.

Johnston, J., and Campbell, L. *Impasses of Divorce: The Dynamics and Resolution of Family Conflict.* New York: The Free Press, a division of MacMillan Inc., 1988. This book sets out a model and practical steps for dealing with high conflict couples.

Lemmon, J.A., ed. "Successful Techniques for Mediating Family Breakup" (1984), 2 *Mediation Quarterly.* This issue of the *Mediation Quarterly* contains a number of excellent articles with respect to the practice of mediation.

Ricci, I. *Mom's House, Dad's House: Making Shared Custody Work, How Parents Can Make Two Homes for their Children After Divorce.* New York: Collier Books, Macmillan Publishing Co., 1980. This is a practical and systematic guide for parents who are considering a shared parenting arrangement after divorce. Ricci describes how to shift from a spousal relationship, which is ending, to a parenting relationship, which is continuing. She has a number of practical tips, checklists, guidelines, sample agreements, *etc.,* which parents can use in their own situation.

Rofes, E. *The Kid's Book of Divorce: By, For, and About Kids.* New York: Vintage Books, a division of Randam House, 1982.

Saposnek, D. *Mediating Child Custody Disputes.* San Francisco: Jossey-Bass Publishers, 1983. See in particular Part II, "Structuring the Mediation Process," p. 44. This book would be useful to the mediation practitioner and contains a number of concrete suggestions and case examples of mediation in practice.

Saposnek, D. "Strategies in Child Custody Mediation: A Family Systems Approach". In "Successful Techniques for Mediating Family Break-ups" (1983), 2 *Mediation Quarterly* 29.

Tompkins, R. "Parenting Plans: A Concept Whose Time Has Come" (1995), 33 *Family and Conciliation Courts Review* 3, 286-297.

Ury, W. *Getting Past No: Negotiating With "Difficult People"*. New York: Bantam Books, 1991. This book contains suggestions for how to deal with "difficult people" It has helpful ideas for how to get others to try an interest-based approach, as well as suggestions for resolving impasses.

Visher, E., and Visher, J. *How to Win as a Step Family*. 2nd ed., New York: Brunner/Mazel, Publishers, 1991. This is a very helpful book to guide parents in creating a successful step-family.

Chapter Five

Mediation in Practice: Skills

A. BASIC INFORMATION

1. The Mediator as Educator: The Effects on Children of Separation and Divorce

Most parents are so caught up in their own pain, grief, and reduced self-esteem that it is difficult for them to focus on the needs of their children. In addition, most parents lack adequate information from which to predict their children's responses or to make decisions that would be in the best interests of their children. This information should be provided in an impartial, constructive manner that avoids laying blame on either parent for the children's responses to the separation.

In the initial meeting with the parents and in subsequent individual and joint meetings, it is important for the mediator to give the parents information about the likely impact of separation and divorce on the children and themselves.

As well, the mediator can assist the parents by discussing some helpful techniques for dealing with their children, so that the parents will feel more in control, less helpless in dealing with their children's reactions and will behave in a more constructive manner than if their energies were spent on self-blame or blaming the other spouse.

The mediator should emphasize that it is important for the parents to share information about the children's responses and to cooperate in their reaction, because this is in the children's best interests. If the parents undermine each other's approaches to discipline and caretaking, the children will quickly learn to play one parent off against the other and are likely to lose respect for both parents.

By emphasizing a cooperative parenting approach, the mediator is helping to divert the parties from their own battle and beginning to model the way in which they must pool their efforts to assist their children, even at a time of high emotional stress. The parents need to learn to focus on the needs of the children, rather than on the fault of the other spouse.

The following information may be helpful:

- Children are often unaware of conflict in a marriage or that the conflict is out of the ordinary until one parent is packing his or her bags to leave. Even though parents may see the marriage as intolerable and believe that this has been obvious for some period of time, children tend to accept their family as a "normal family" and do not anticipate a marriage breakdown. Parents need to understand that their children are likely to be shocked by a separation.

- Children are usually very attached to both parents and loyal to their family of origin. Most children are very upset and depressed at the loss of a parent and of their intact family unit.

- Children are sometimes ashamed and often fearful about the consequences of their parents' separation and/or divorce. They may see this as a failure, as contrary to moral or religious principles, and they may be afraid that this means the family is not "normal". They may be afraid to tell their friends or teachers, particularly if they do not know of other children from separated families. Also, they may worry about abandonment or about not being able to see both parents often enough or in a comfortable environment.

- The basic fears of most children at the time of separation relate to their own security. For example, children may have the following concerns:
  — Who will take care of me?
  — Will I be able to see both of my parents?
  — Where will I live?
  — Who will take care of the parent who is not living with me?

- Children may feel responsible for the marriage breakdown and may feel equally responsible for returning the family to an intact unit. That is, children often worry about such things as:
  — What did I do that was so terrible that my parent is leaving?
  — Was it my fault that the marriage broke down?
  — What can I do to save the marriage?
  — If I am really good, will the parent who left come back?

Children respond to separation and divorce in different ways at different developmental stages. The following material is based on the work of Dr. Judith Wallerstein and Dr. Joan Kelly. The "Children of Divorce Project" in California is summarized in their book, *Surviving the Breakup: How Children and Parents Cope with Divorce*.[1] Their information is based on follow-up studies of 60 divorcing families with 131 children who were living in California. These families were assessed at the time of separation, one year later, five years later, and then ten years later. The following is a brief summary of their findings with respect to the reactions of children at different stages of development.

---

[1] New York: Basic Books Inc., 1980.

Pre-school children — two to five years

- *Confusion, anxiety and fear*: Children are confused and unsure about the changes in their family life, because parents rarely explain the basis for the separation or divorce to children this age.
- *Regression*: Children may demonstrate their anxiety and insecurity by lapses in toilet training, increased clinging behaviour, increased fears, for example, of the dark, of changing routines, of being abandoned or hurt by another, or by expressing aggression.
- *Strong reconciliation fantasies.*
- *Feelings of guilt*: Children may experience feelings of self-blame for the marriage breakdown.
- *Increased aggression*: Children may display a greater irritability with siblings, parents, peers, or in school. This anger may stem from the child's feeling of loss or rejection. The child may have lost the psychological parent, that is, the one the child feels closest to. Also, both parents may be so preoccupied with their own feelings of hurt and depression that they are emotionally unavailable to the child.

School age — five to seven years

- *Pervasive sadness and grieving*: This is sometimes related to the intensity of turmoil in the home, but some children are intensely sad even when the parents are not demonstrating great distress.
- *Preoccupation with their own bitterness, humiliation, and plan for revenge.*
- *Yearning for the departed parent*: This is similar to grief for a dead parent.
- *Feelings of rejection, abandonment, and fear.*
- *Fantasy of responsibility for marriage breakdown.*
- *Reconciliation fantasies.*
- *Anger*: The child often directs anger at the custodial parent or whichever parent the child believes is responsible for the marriage breakdown. Anger is also directed at teachers, friends, and siblings in many cases.
- *Loyalty conflicts*: The child feels caught in a tug of war between both parents, that is, having to accept one parent and reject the other.
- *Changes in academic and social behaviour.*

School age — nine to twelve years

Children at this stage are more aware of parental conflict and the causes and consequences of divorce.

- *Profound feelings of loss, rejection, helplessness, and loneliness.*
- *Feelings of shame, moral indignation, and outrage at the parents' behaviour.*

- *Extreme anger, temper tantrums, and demanding behaviour.*
- *Fears, phobias, and use of denial.*
- *Fears with respect to the absent parent*: Children often worry about the well-being of the absent parent.
- *Increased somatic complaints*: Children may experience more head-aches, stomach aches, and sleep disorders at this age.
- *Loyalty conflicts*: The child identifies one parent as the good parent and one as the bad parent.
- *Low self-esteem*: The child may have increased problems in school and with peers and become involved in delinquent activities.

Adolescence — thirteen years and older

Adolescents often express anger at the parents because they experience the following feelings:

- *Overburdened*: They feel burdened by the increased responsibility for younger siblings and emotionally weak parents.
- *Anger and rejection*: They have to share visits with new partners and often hear the other parent criticized or discussed with disrespect.
- *Feelings of shame and insecurity*: They are ashamed of the parents' childish behaviour, particularly if the conflict continues over a considerable time period.
- *Confusion*: They feel torn between wanting to be with their friends and wanting to go on an access visit.
- *Anxiety*: They have fears about forming long-term relationships and they are anxious about their own future marriage.
- *Economic insecurity*: They worry about money, that is, whether the custodial parent will be able to provide for them.
- *Loyalty conflicts*: They are used to carry messages between parents in conflict.
- *Confusion re parental role*: They have a heightened awareness of their parents' sexual behaviour. As a result, adolescents often display increased promiscuous behaviour and tend to withdraw from parental contact and control.

Considerable research has been conducted on the impact of separation and divorce on children. Rhonda Freeman, Director of the Families in Transition Program in Toronto, has identified 11 key factors that affect children's adjustment to the divorce experience. While some children seem to cope quite well, particularly after a period of adjustment, others display long-term negative consequences. The differences can often be explained by the following factors, listed in order of their priority with respect to their impact on children:

1. *Level of Parental Conflict*: Research has consistently found that the level of conflict between the parents is the most significant factor in influencing children's post-divorce emotional, social, and academic adjustment.

2. *The Availability of Adequate Financial Resources*: Research has consistently documented the significant rise in child poverty in single parent families headed by women. Approximately 40% of these families fall below the poverty line following separation. This has an impact on children's nutrition, accommodation, access to post-secondary education, and recreational programs.

3. *Parenting Capacity*: The research of Wallerstein and Kelly[2] and others have documented the reduced ability of parents to carry out the tasks of parenting for up to several years following the divorce. Parents are preoccupied with meeting their own needs and are less available emotionally to deal with their children's needs, separate and apart from their own.

4. *The Establishment and Clarity of Parent/Child Boundaries and Roles*: Following a separation, parent/child boundaries are often blurred such that the child becomes the confidant and support person for the parent. Also, parents project their own needs and feelings on the children *vis-à-vis* their relationship with the other parent, rather than encouraging or even recognizing that the child may have very different needs or feelings.

5. *Encouragement of the Child's Relationship with Each Parent*: Children's adjustment is enhanced if both parents work out ways for the children to maintain a continuous (and relatively guilt-free) relationship with both of them.

6. *Ability to Minimize Disruption*: To the extent possible, children adjust more easily if changes can be implemented gradually. For example, if they can remain in the matrimonial home for a period of adjustment or at least in the same neighbourhood or school, this helps to ease the children into the myriad of changes in their lives.

7. *Child Care Arrangements*: To the extent possible, it is helpful to maintain similar child-care arrangements after separation, that is, familiar babysitters, day-care arrangements, *etc.*, to ease the child into the transition to separation.

---

[2]   *Ibid.*

8.   *Use of Language to Describe the Separation Experience*: It is helpful to avoid words such as "custody" or "custodial parent" and "access" or "access parent" in order to encourage a shift from a concept of children as the property of a parent to the concept of a parent-child relationship. For example, using terminology such as creating a "parenting partnership" or a "parenting plan" is more inclusive and respectful of the contribution of both parents to the ongoing development of the children.

9.   *Continuation of Predictable and Positive Routines*: The presence of familiar and predictable daily routines can reassure children, especially young children, that their relationship with both parents will continue. Children generally prefer a predictable schedule for spending time with each parent so they can look forward with some certainty to these times. This also gives the children and each parent an opportunity to make plans that do not conflict with the parenting schedule.

10.   *Alteration of the Divorce Environment*: It is important for parents to carefully explain, in advance, the changes that are necessary as a result of the separation. Children are better able to adjust if they have a rationale or can prepare for, for example, a move to a new location.

11.   *Child's Ability to Communicate*: The information given to children needs to be appropriate to their stage of development. For younger children, using stories or puppets may help the child to understand and express their feelings. Group programs for young children, such as Families in Transition or the Rainbows program, assist children to share their feelings with other children the same age who are facing similar experiences.

2. The Mediator as Fact Gatherer

Depending on the issues being mediated, the mediator must collect basic information from the parties and other relevant sources. In the case of open mediation or an assessment, the mediator should collect more background information than would be necessary for closed mediation. This is because the mediator may be asked for recommendations and should have a good factual basis for the recommendations. In the case of closed mediation, the mediator should use his or her discretion about what information might be desirable in order to understand the nature of the conflict and to facilitate a settlement.

For custody and access issues, the mediator should collect information with respect to the following:

- childhood history of each parent;
- courtship and marital history;
- involvement in child care during the marriage and following separation;
- employment history; and
- future plans (remarriage, residence, and employment).

If the mediation involves financial issues, then the mediator will need the following information:

- educational and employment history;
- past and present financial status; and
- future plans (education or retraining, employment, remarriage).

The following are examples of the type of information to be collected. Remember that detailed historical information may not be necessary for mediation, especially closed mediation. It is important to collect information that is relevant to the issues in dispute and that provides a context to understand the family members. What is relevant will vary with the circumstances of each case.

(A) CHILDHOOD HISTORY OF EACH PARENT

The childhood history of each parent gives valuable clues about the character development and personality of the parent. The type of care received by a parent significantly affects his or her approach to parenting.

Information could be collected with respect to such matters as:

- the relationship between the parent and each of his or her parents;
- the relationship of the parents to each other. Was there a marriage breakdown? If so, what were the circumstances and how did each family member react?
- the atmosphere in the home. Was it a happy home? Was there a great deal of conflict?
- the personality of each parent, particularly with respect to his or her parenting. Was each parent warm and able to show affection or cold and undemonstrative, patient or impatient, easygoing or demanding, interested and involved or preoccupied with matters outside the family?
- feelings of acceptance in the family. Did the child feel that he or she had met each of the parent's expectations? Or did the child feel inadequate in one or both parents' eyes?
- the nature of discipline used. What type of discipline was applied? How frequently was discipline used? Was the discipline seen as arbitrary or predictable? Was the punishment fair and reasonable or excessive?
- domestic violence. Were there incidents of domestic violence, either experienced directly or witnessed by the child?

- whether the parents were good providers/caretakers. Did they carry out their parenting responsibilities in a way that met the child's needs?
- the siblings, including the relationship with each sibling and the occupation and marital status of each sibling;
- the parents' attitude to religion and the role of religion or other moral values in the household;
- the history of significant problems with respect to alcohol, drugs, mental illness, or criminal activities in the family of origin;
- the work history, including time spent at home parenting; and
- other significant events or perceptions in relation to the childhood history.

It is important to determine whether the parent had a loving, secure, stable home environment or whether the parent grew up in an abusive, deprived, or neglectful environment. Of particular importance is the nature of discipline, the role that each parent played in the family, and the degree to which the child felt accepted and loved as opposed to unwanted and inadequate.

The type of family background and parenting experienced by the mother and father have a considerable influence on how each of them will parent and their expectations about how their partner should participate in parenting. The mediator should ask the parents how their own childhood history has affected their parenting and how they think the childhood history of their partner has affected their partner's parenting.

(B) COURTSHIP AND MARITAL HISTORY

It is important to determine the history of the relationship between the parents in order to find out:

- whether the relationship was satisfactory at any time;
- whether the parents loved and respected each other at any point during the relationship;
- at what point and for what reasons one or both parents changed their feelings about the relationship;
- whether the parties have similar feelings about the relationship at present or whether one party is hoping for a reconciliation and is unable to separate emotionally from the relationship; and
- whether the parents were able to cooperate with each other in the past and the present level of trust and cooperation, particularly with respect to the children.

At this point there may be some consideration of the possibility of reconciliation. That is, in appropriate cases, the mediator should clarify with both parties whether either or both feel that there is some possibility of saving the marriage. The fact that the parties would like to consider reconciliation does not mean that mediation would necessarily terminate. The parties might find it helpful to have an interim agreement worked out through mediation, so that they can then consider reconciliation free of anxiety about adversarial legal proceeding during this time period. In the event that the parties have separated or are considering a period of separation, such an agreement would help to preserve the parties' rights while they consider their future relationship.

If the parties have decided to separate permanently and if custody and access are issues, then the mediator should obtain a history of the courtship and marriage. This is particularly important for open mediation or for situations where the mediator has been asked to prepare an assessment report in the event that mediation does not resolve all of the issues in dispute. The following types of information should be gathered:

- a brief history of the relationship from the time of meeting until the time of the marriage, including what each parent found attractive and unattractive about the other, and whether the relationship was a stable relationship during the courtship period;
- who decided to marry and how the other partner felt about the marriage;
- the attitude of the extended family to the marriage;
- any major religious or cultural differences between the families and how these affected their relationship;
- when they decided to have children, who decided, and how the other partner reacted;
- the history of the pregnancy, including the involvement of both parties throughout the pregnancy and at the time of delivery; and
- how the marital relationship changed after the birth of each child.

If the parents had a strong marriage at one point and did love and respect each other, it is important for the mediator to help the parties recall the strengths of the marriage at a time when the parties may only be able to see the weaknesses and feel the disappointed expectations. If there was some evidence of parental cooperation during the lifetime of the children, the couple should reflect on how beneficial the cooperation was, not only for the parents, but particularly for the children. The mediator should emphasize that it is important for parents to continue to act cooperatively as parents, even though the spousal role may be at an end. By helping the couple to relive what is good in the relationship and bringing this to their attention, the mediator can sometimes begin to dissolve the present feelings of anger and hurt.

The review of the marital history is also useful for deterring the couple from blaming the marriage breakdown on one party or the other. The couple can be helped to reframe the reasons for the marriage breakdown so as to remove allegations of fault and feelings of guilt. For example, the couple may discover that the marriage broke down primarily because of differences in culture, values, personality, or interests, or because they had very different expectations about marriage and family life to begin with.

By reducing blame, the mediator can often begin the process of developing a more cooperative relationship. In addition, if the parties no longer feel they are personally to blame for the marriage failure, they will be less likely to feel the need to justify their behaviour to the children. This could help to reduce loyalty conflicts, where each parent blames and criticizes the other and encourages the children to take sides. Loyalty conflicts and a lack of cooperation create a tremendous emotional strain on children and are significantly related to poor adjustment to the separation and divorce.

An important reason for collecting the marital history, particularly with the couple present together, is to test the emotional climate between the parties and to help the mediator predict the likelihood that the parties will be able to cooperate in the future.

(C) PARENTAL INVOLVEMENT IN CHILD CARE

It is suggested that the mediator obtain information about each parent's involvement with the children and sharing of parental responsibilities within the context of the marital history. At this time, the mediator should deal with each parent's perception of his or her own attitudes and the other parent's with respect to the following:

- affection for the children and concern for their safety and welfare;
- method of discipline used by each parent and each parent's views on his or her own and the other parent's discipline techniques (do the parents approve of each other's methods? do they feel these methods are appropriate and effective for meeting the needs of the child?);
- sharing of parenting tasks and responsibilities from the birth of the child to the present time (did one parent take primary responsibility for the care of the child?) and attitude to each other's involvement and opinion of each other's competence to do parenting tasks, both in the past and in the future;
- competence in providing direct parenting, and interest and involvement in significant aspects of the child's life, for example, school, extracurricular activities, medical and health care needs.

It is preferable to obtain this information when the discussion is not centred on the question of custody, but rather more informally during a discussion of the marital history. It is also recommended that this discussion occur with the parties together, so that each party can respond to the other party's perception of his or her parenting role.

If information emerges that suggests abuse or neglect with respect to the children, the mediator should pursue these topics in more depth with each parent individually and, in addition, should check any external sources, such as doctors, hospital records, the Children's Aid Society, police records, and other relevant sources, to determine the extent of any harm done.

The mediator should avoid any prolonged discussion of these allegations with both parties present for the following reasons:

- The parent who is making the allegations is likely to make them in a more dramatic, forceful, and hostile manner when the other parent is present.
- The accused parent is likely to feel defensive and demoralized, and is therefore likely to minimize the incidents and their effects. In addition, the accused parent may feel the need to rebut any allegations, because of a desire not to lose face in front of the other parent, particularly with the mediator present.
- It may be easier for the mediator to get a more truthful, balanced account of any abusive incidents if the parties are seen individually.
- One parent may be afraid to make serious allegations in an open and honest manner in front of the other parent for fear of reprisal.
- A joint discussion of serious allegations is likely to make subsequent communication and cooperation between the parties more difficult.

For these reasons, the mediator should deal with serious allegations on an individual basis and in a constructive and supportive manner. Any recommendations made as a result of such discussions could then be reviewed with both parties present together, provided this would not jeopardize the safety of either parent.

If there are allegations of abuse or neglect, the mediator has a statutory obligation to report this information to the appropriate child welfare authorities. For example, in Ontario, the statutory duty is set out in s. 72 of the *Child and Family Services Act*.[3] The mediator should tell the parents that this is his or her legal duty, and should explain to each parent the essence of what he or she will say. The mediator should take steps to be sure the child is safe before disclosing his or her concerns to the parents. If the mediator prepares a written report, a copy should be given to the parents so that they are fully informed about any allegations.

If the mediator feels that one or both of the parents need some assistance in parenting skills or mental health counselling in relation to parenting ability, the mediator should make a referral to an appropriate professional or agency. The mediator should not become involved in an individual counselling relationship with one of the parents, as this would violate his or her impartial role.

---

[3]   R.S.O. 1990, c. C.11 [am. 1993, c. 27, Sch.].

(D) Employment History

This information is necessary for both financial mediation and for the mediation of custody and access disputes. The employment history gives some indication of the motivation of the parents, their stability, goals, lifestyle, and ability to relate to individuals outside the home. The work history also assists the mediator in understanding how the parents are likely to provide for the financial needs of the children in the future.

If one spouse has not been employed outside the home for several years, it is important to determine when that spouse can become self-supporting and at what financial level. It may be helpful to refer this spouse, usually the woman, to career counselling to assist with career selection and job skills. In addition, women who have been out of the workforce for some time often feel inadequate, insecure, and frightened at the prospect of re-entering the workforce. These concerns should be addressed, because they will have an impact on how quickly the individual will become self-supporting. If both parents will now be working outside the home, this usually necessitates a greater sharing of parenting responsibilities. This issue should be discussed with both parties to be sure the children's needs are met in a way that is fair and reasonable to both parents.

(E) Future Plans

The mediator should discuss the parents' work schedule, the likelihood that a parent will change jobs or move some distance away, any plans for remarriage, and other issues that may impact on the family's financial status or necessitate a change in the parenting arrangements. It would be important to take these factors into account in working out a plan for the present and in designing a procedure for changing the parenting arrangements, should the need arise in the future.

3. The Mediator as Communicator

One of the primary reasons given for marriage failure is difficulty in communication between the parties. Spouses will often state that one or both of them are unable to understand:

- each other's feelings — often spouses give ambivalent messages to each other about their satisfaction with the marriage;
- each other's motives for leaving the marriage or for wanting it to continue;
- why one or both were unhappy during the marriage; and/or
- what was expected of them by the other spouse to save the marriage.

The spouses often report that they never clarified or discussed feelings of anger, disappointment, or resentment, and as a result, important issues in the marriage were unresolved. Such couples generally have a long history of distrust and suspicion about the other partner's motives and behaviour.

Mediation is a technique that depends on effective communication in order to reach an agreement. The task is made difficult because the mediator is faced with two people who by this time usually dislike each other, are very poor communicators, are highly distrustful, and are fearful of being hurt again. It is essential that the mediator help the parties to develop more effective communication techniques from the very beginning or the mediation will likely fail.

Because the mediation sessions, particularly the initial sessions, are likely to be highly emotionally charged, it is important for the mediator to explain certain basic communication skills or rules of procedure prior to beginning the content of the discussion. There are several reasons for establishing basic communication skills in the initial meeting, namely:

- The parties can begin to communicate more effectively right from the beginning of mediation.
- The parties are more likely to absorb information about communication techniques when they are not in the midst of discussing emotionally charged information.
- The parties are likely to present their information more effectively and more constructively, that is, with less conflict and assignment of blame, if they have discussed appropriate methods of communication.
- By developing more effective communication skills from the beginning, the mediator is improving the chances of the parties listening to each other, reducing their tension, and beginning the process of talking constructively about the issues in dispute.

The following examples of listening and communication techniques should be taught to the parties:

- *Speaking in the first person.* That is, if a party has a concern, the party should state that concern as his or her own concern, not as a general concern or as a concern of some other person. For example, "I am concerned about the fact that you make hostile comments about me in front of the children", rather than, "It is not a good idea for children to hear parents badmouthing each other."
- *Making eye contact with each other* when they are speaking.
- *Directing comments about the other spouse to that spouse* rather than to the mediator.
- *Speaking one at a time* and not interrupting the other.
- *Making direct statements about how they feel* rather than trying to elicit the mediator's disapproval of the other spouse (and approval of themselves). For example, "I think that you should pick up the children for an access visit at the time that you agreed. It is very disap-

pointing to the children when you are late", rather than a question addressed to the mediator, "Don't you think that it is psychologically damaging to children when parents are late for access visits?"

- *Stating specifically the behaviour that is upsetting* rather than attacking the other spouse in more general terms. In addition, each spouse should state the behaviour that he or she would prefer, so that the discussion can become focused on what behaviour is upsetting and what changes are needed, rather than defending against personal attacks. For example, "It is upsetting to me when you change access arrangements at the last minute. I would appreciate it if you would notify me of changes at least two days in advance" (statement of the problem); "I would be much more willing to cooperate if you would ask me if it was convenient to change the access arrangements rather than just telling me that you are changing them, without any concern for alternative plans that I may have made" (specifying the preferred behaviour).
- *Paraphrasing what he or she heard the other spouse saying.* This ensures that both spouses are listening to each other, and it also helps to clarify any confusion or misinterpretation.
- *Asking for clarification* rather than attacking the other spouse. That is, they should be sure that they have correctly understood any communication, before they become upset. Too often, couples who are already upset and distrustful of each other misinterpret both the intent and the actual content of the communication. A great deal of hostility can be eliminated if they learn to ask for clarification. For example, "I am not sure that I understood what you just said, could you explain that again please", or, "Could you give me some more information about that?" rather than, "You are a liar and you have always tried to undermine me and there you are doing it again — I knew I could not trust you!"
- *Using direct versus indirect statements.* For example, "I was upset when you telephoned last night and did not tell me about the parent-teacher interviews to be held next week", rather than, "You never communicate with me about how the children are doing in school."
- *Identifying feelings,* that is, the person's own feelings and his or her perception of the feelings expressed by the other person. For example, "It made me feel hurt when you said that I was not a good mother", or, "I guess it must have made you feel angry when I refused to share the transportation of the children for access visits."
- *Talking about feelings* rather than acting them out through aggressive retaliatory behaviour. For example, one spouse might say, "It makes me feel that you do not really care about your children when you refuse to pay child support", rather than cutting off access to the non-paying spouse. An even better approach would be for the spouse to *ask for clarification*. For example, "Is there some reason why

you are not paying child support?" This permits the other spouse to give some explanation for his or her behaviour, such as, "I am now unemployed", or "I feel that you are interfering with my relationship with the children so that I did not feel like paying child support". By asking for clarification, important issues that need to be dealt with in mediation can be identified. These issues would not be resolved if the parties resorted to acting-out behaviour.

- *Accepting the fact that each person is entitled to his or her own perception of a situation.* That is, rather than putting the mediator in the position of judging who is right or wrong, or who is lying or truthful, both parties need to accept that they may perceive situations differently and therefore may feel and act differently.

Once the mediator has taught the parties basic communication techniques, the next step is to help the parties orient toward their future relationship rather than dwelling on events and feelings of the past. The mediator should emphasize the following:

- What has happened in the past cannot be changed. While these events will certainly colour the parties' perceptions, nevertheless it is important for them to make a commitment to be different today. The focus of mediation should be on determining what type of relationship the parties would like to have in the future.
- The parties should not expect that the relationship will change overnight or that there will be no setbacks. The important thing is to recognize and encourage each other when positive steps are made and not to become overly upset or discouraged when difficulties arise. The parties should use the communication techniques explained above in order to avoid undue hostility.
- Each spouse should tell the other spouse when he or she has done something right. For example, "I really appreciated it when you called to ask whether it would be convenient for me to change the access arrangements this weekend. I felt that you were giving me a choice and that you were concerned about disrupting my plans. It felt good to cooperate." So often in cases of marriage breakdown, the parties get no positive reinforcement, but only hear about the things that they did wrong. This is particularly true of cases that go to litigation. In order to use more cooperative behaviour in the future, the parties must learn to give each other positive reinforcement for improved behaviour in the present.

In addition to improving the parties' ability to communicate, the mediator needs to focus the discussion on the particular issues in dispute. If the mediator has been successful in establishing some level of trust, a willingness to cooperate, and an improvement in communication skills, then the next step is to help the parties identify some objective criteria or governing principles for resolving those issues that are in dispute. For example, if one issue is custody of or access to children, then the mediator might determine whether the parents agree that the best interests of the children ought to be the primary criterion for evaluating a solution, as opposed to whether one parent wins or loses. The mediator could spend some time with the parents identifying what is meant by "best interests of the children". For example, the parties might agree on the following:

- It is desirable for children to have a close, loving relationship with both parents.
- Children should feel comfortable expressing feelings of love and respect for one parent in the other parent's presence.
- Parents (and their new partners and extended family members) should not criticize or demean the other parent in the children's presence.
- Children should spend considerable time with both parents, in keeping with the children's needs, stage of development, and wishes, and with the ability and willingness of the parents to spend time with the children.

It is important for the mediator to establish these general principles or criteria before dealing with the specific questions of where the children will live and at what specific times the children will see each parent. The aim is to help the parents deal with these issues in terms of the children's needs rather than their own bargaining position.

As a further example, if the mediation is with respect to spousal or child support, the parties could be asked to come to some agreement on the basic principles to apply in resolving this dispute. Of course, the parties should first be advised by their solicitors of any criteria set out in the family law legislation or child support guidelines established by the government. Until guidelines are in place, the criteria might be, for example, that the level of child support should be fair and reasonable given each spouse's ability to earn income and each spouse's financial needs. The parties could then be asked to identify specific criteria or factors to be taken into consideration in determining spousal support:

- what amount of support should be paid; and
- for how long, or until what conditions occur, should support be paid.

The parties might agree that the following criteria would be important, for example:

- the present level of income of both spouses;
- the educational history;
- work experience;
- the length of time out of the workforce;

- the need for retraining;
- the financial responsibilities of both spouses;
- the age and health of the spouses;
- the age and health of the children;
- the standard of living enjoyed by the spouses prior to separation;
- the level of income required for both spouses to be self-sufficient; and
- a realistic time frame for achieving financial independence. For some spouses it may be unrealistic ever to achieve full financial independence, but perhaps some partial goal could be reached.

It is important to focus the parties on realistic, objective criteria, rather than each party's position, which may be based on emotional factors, such as a desire for revenge for a matrimonial fault.

The previous discussion centred on improving communication techniques and changing behaviour patterns, which should in turn increase the chances of reaching a settlement. While many couples will successfully resolve all of the issues in dispute, some couples will not settle some or all of the issues because:

- One or both do not wish to end the spousal relationship.
- One spouse wants to punish the other spouse for feelings of hurt or humiliation suffered in the marriage breakdown.
- Delaying a settlement is to the spouse's advantage in the courts.
- There is not sufficient trust by one or both spouses to reach a full settlement.
- One spouse has strong feelings of guilt about settling. That is, a spouse may not be able to settle the issue of custody because of a concern that the children will later blame him or her for abandoning them. This type of parent often needs a court order or at least a professional's recommendation before he or she can agree to the other spouse having the primary residence or sole custody of the children.

These are important factors for the mediator to recognize when they arise in the mediation process. The mediator needs to be prepared with some special techniques for dealing with each of these potential obstacles to mediation.

In addition, there are circumstances in which the parties reach agreement that should cause the mediator some concern. For example, situations where one party is too eager to settle, particularly where the settlement may not be in the best interests of the children or may be an unfair or unreasonable financial settlement. This often occurs when:

- one spouse feels completely dominated by the other spouse, or is under physical or emotional duress to reach a settlement (whether the duress is real or perceived). In this situation a spouse may submit to the other spouse's demands to avoid conflict or prevent some feared retaliation;

- the spouses are of such unequal bargaining power, for example, in verbal skills, self-confidence, or control of important resources, that one spouse gives up immediately in defeat;
- one spouse may be prepared to accept an unreasonable settlement on one issue in order to win on the issue that is most important to him or her. For example, in a custody battle, a spouse may forgo reasonable support or a reasonable division of property in order to gain custody.
- one spouse feels totally responsible for the marriage breakdown and wants to atone for his or her guilt by giving up everything to the other spouse; or
- one spouse is so anxious to end the marriage and not have to deal face to face with the other spouse that he or she is prepared to concede everything in the mediation. A variation of this type of individual is a spouse who is so angry at the other spouse that he or she cannot accept anything from that spouse, even if it would be reasonable for the spouse or the children to do so.

Both the failure to settle and an unreasonable settlement should be of concern to the mediator, particularly when it affects the welfare of children. Three examples will be given of situations described above in order to give the mediator a better appreciation of the problem and of the techniques for resolving or dealing with these situations.

(A) THE STONEWALLING PARENT

The mediator should be alert to the fact that it may be in one party's interest to delay a settlement. This can arise in cases involving custody and access, and in financial disputes. For example, in custody cases, the party who has *de facto* custody of the children is at a considerable advantage in that a court usually awards custody to the parent who has had the primary care and control of the children from the date of the separation. The reason for this is that the court considers the stability of the children to be a very significant factor in determining custody. As a result, the parent who has the care and control of the children at the time of mediation will have less motivation to settle than the party who does not have *de facto* custody. If the mediation is delayed or prolonged and no resolution is reached, the party with *de facto* custody will have gained a considerable advantage over the other party by the time the matter reaches trial.

A stonewalling or delaying tactic can also be used in financial mediation to the advantage of one party over the other. For example, in determining the level of spousal or child support to award, the court will take into consideration the level of support and the length of time an interim arrangement has been in effect. If one party has managed to survive financially for some period of time on a low level of support, the court will take this level of support into account. It is therefore to the advantage of the payor spouse to delay matters in mediation and to agree to a low level of support in any interim agreement.

The reasons for stonewalling set out above are related to improving a spouse's position in court. In some cases a spouse may stonewall for very different reasons, such as:

- not wanting to end the spousal relationship;
- not wanting to lose face by making concessions to the other spouse; or
- not wanting to lose face in the eyes of a third party (for example, a new partner or the spouse's lawyer).

When a mediator suspects that one party is not negotiating in good faith, the mediator should take the following steps:

- *discuss with the parties the mediator's concerns about possible stonewalling.* Perhaps a better of way of dealing with this issue is to discuss the significance of a time delay in the first meeting, that is, before either party has shown any evidence of stonewalling. By raising the issue the mediator may prevent this problem from arising;
- *encourage the parties to come to an interim agreement* that would be the least prejudicial to both parties during the course of mediation;
- *help the parties to agree on an early termination date,* or at least a date by which progress will be reviewed, at the outset of the mediation in order to prevent one side from prolonging matters unnecessarily.

These are preventive steps that it is hoped will avoid or minimize the effects of stonewalling. If the problem continues, then the mediator could use some of the following techniques to resolve the impasse:

- *Breaking the issues in dispute into sub-parts,* so that the parties can deal with each issue in smaller pieces, rather than an all-or-nothing approach. For example, if access is in dispute, rather than dealing with each spouse's entire access plan, the discussions could focus on whether access should be supervised or unsupervised; whether access should be daytime only or should include over-night visits; whether access should include midweek visits; and whether telephone access should be specified or left open to the parents' discretion. Once agreement has been reached on these types of parameters, then the discussion can focus on such things as how many weekends and for what length of time on a weekend, or on what special days during the year, such as Mother's Day, Father's Day, Christmas Day, or the child's birthday. In the event that the parties reach agreement on some of the sub-issues, they should be praised and encouraged by the mediator for making progress toward a settlement. It is often easier to reach agreement on smaller issues and gradually build toward resolving the entire issue.

- *Meeting individually with each spouse.* This is often called an individual caucus. The individual caucus can be held on a separate day or can be part of a joint session. That is, the mediator can ask one spouse to leave the room so that the mediator can spend some time with each spouse individually before returning to a joint session. During the individual sessions, the mediator can determine what the road blocks are to agreement and can encourage each of the parties to generate some realistic alternatives that may lead to a settlement. It may be easier for the mediator to arrive at more reasonable proposals in an individual session rather than in a joint meeting, because the parties may be concerned about losing face in each other's presence.

- *Helping the parties refocus their attention on the principles they have agreed upon as the basis for a settlement.* For example, the best interests of the children or a fair and reasonable financial settlement could be discussed in the context of a time delay. The parties could be asked whether it is in the best interests of the children to have a long period of uncertainty with respect to a parenting plan, or whether it is fair and reasonable for the children to suffer unnecessary hardship as a result of a delay in determining child support.

If the parties fail to respond to these techniques and if the delay is significantly prejudicing one spouse, then the mediator should state his or her concerns to the parties and their counsel and should terminate or suspend the mediation. This would allow the disadvantaged spouse to make an immediate application to court for resolution of the dispute.

(B) THE REJECTED PARENT

A parent who is rejected will respond in one of several ways, namely:

- *intense anger* at the other partner, often in proportion to the feelings of lowered self-esteem, humiliation, or rejection;
- *depression* — the parent may be immobilized from taking any constructive action because of strong feelings of inadequacy resulting from the rejection; or
- *cautious hope* — the parent may believe that the rejection is temporary, or that if he or she makes a change in behaviour a reconciliation will be possible.

It is extremely important to deal with each of these feelings at an early stage. The spouses will not be able to deal with the practical issues in dispute until their feelings have been addressed. Therefore, dealing with feelings actually facilitates mediation and removes a primary obstacle to settlement, namely, the client's self-esteem and feelings about the other partner. It is also important for the parties to stop blaming each other so that they can be mobilized to take more constructive action. This is in their own interests as well as in the interests of their children.

The Angry Parent

There are a number of techniques that the mediator can use to deal with an intensely angry parent:

- *Arrange individual sessions* in the early stages of mediation. The client needs an opportunity to ventilate in a supportive atmosphere; however, it could be extremely destructive to the mediation process if the client were permitted to ventilate in the other partner's presence.
- *Help the spouse to identify the source of the anger.* For example, "I am angry because my partner humiliated me by leaving me for someone else." Encourage the spouse to talk through what it is that he or she is specifically concerned about and to share the fears and frustrations that are behind the anger.
- *Determine whether the reasons for the anger are grounded in the past or are continuing in the present.* Ask the spouse to determine in what way the anger will affect the spouses' future relationship.
- *Ask the spouse to consider ways in which the anger could be reduced.* For example, is it important that the partner recognize the cause of the anger and apologize for the humiliation? Does the spouse need to rebuild his or her self-confidence independent of the previous relationship (for example, through a new more satisfying relationship or through psychotherapy)?
- *Help the spouse to develop techniques* for controlling the anger or expressing it more constructively.
- *Help the spouse to appreciate the effects* on the other partner, and in particular on the children, of hanging on to the anger, rather than learning more constructive techniques for dissipating or controlling the anger.

Parents are often motivated to change their behaviour when they recognize the destructive impact on them and in particular on their children. These spouses often need some concrete suggestions for changing their behaviour and some positive feedback to rebuild their self-confidence.

The Depressed Parent

If the mediator believes that a parent is very depressed and overcome by feelings of inadequacy as a result of the marriage breakdown, the mediator should recommend that the individual obtain appropriate professional assistance such as:

- individual psychotherapy or counselling;
- group therapy, that is, a support group of individuals with similar problems;
- vocational counselling; or
- assistance with budgeting or financial management.

The mediator should discuss the client's emotional state with him or her in an individual session before making a recommendation for additional assistance. In the event that the client is too depressed to reasonably negotiate the issues in dispute, the mediator should consider:

- *delaying the mediation for some period of time* until the individual has the appropriate counselling. This should not be done without discussions with both clients and their counsel. It would be important to discuss the implications of a time delay as opposed to the implications of attempting to mediate when one party is not emotionally able to negotiate on equal terms;
- *continuing the mediation once the supportive assistance has been initiated.* In cases where the individual is still functioning at a fairly reasonable level, this might be a desirable alternative; or
- *terminating the mediation.* Mediation is not an appropriate technique when the client is extremely depressed.

The Hopeful Parent

It is important to clarify whether the parties intend to separate or reconcile at an early stage of the mediation. If one party is hoping for a reconciliation and the other is determined to separate, then this information must be clarified so that the parties are not bargaining under a false impression.

It is often the case that one party is unrealistic in his or her hopes for reconciliation. This party may offer to give up virtually everything in order to please the other party, in the hope that the party will return to the marriage. Once the party is disillusioned, he or she is often angry at the mediator as well as himself or herself for permitting an unfair bargain. While the parties are in a joint session, the mediator should ask each party to clarify his or her position on reconciliation versus separation.

It is recommended that the mediator discuss this issue further in an individual session to determine whether the hopeful parent is acting out of love for the other partner or out of an anxiety about being left alone. If the spouse is concerned about how he or she will cope with loneliness or new responsibilities, these specific issues should be dealt with. The mediator may feel that, as with the depressed person, the individual needs some counselling, and should make an early referral for appropriate assistance. For example, if the spouse is anxious about managing financially on his or her own, he or she should be referred for career counselling and budgeting assistance. Such specific information may increase self-confidence and help the spouse to accept being single again.

If the mediator believes that one party is making an unreasonable settlement because of unrealistic hopes, the mediator should encourage the parties to reach an interim, time-limited agreement that can be reviewed at some point in the future when the party may be more realistic.

(c) THE GUILTY PARENT

In this case, the parent who feels responsible for the marriage breakdown may make concessions to the other parent out of guilt, rather than out of a firm belief that a particular plan is fair, reasonable, or in the children's best interests. For example, a parent who has committed adultery may agree to give up all of his or her assets, pay an unreasonably high level of support, or give custody of the children to the other parent in order to atone for his or her behaviour. For this reason the mediator should:

- *be sensitive to non-verbal as well as verbal cues* to indicate that a parent is feeling extremely guilty (for example, excessive crying or little eye contact);
- *determine whether one parent is behaving out of guilt and the other parent is behaving out of a need for revenge.* Once the mediator has identified the problem, he or she should encourage the parties to talk about this issue both together and separately;
- *help both of the spouses refocus* away from the assignment of blame and onto the particular issues in dispute. That is, even though a party may have caused the marriage breakdown, that does not necessarily mean that that person is not needed by the children and does not have good parenting skills. Both spouses should be made aware of the fact that in many provinces the legislation specifically states that marital misconduct is not a factor in determining custody of or access to children unless that conduct is relevant to parenting. The federal *Divorce Act*,[4] which applies to all provinces and territories, also takes this position. If the spouses understand that the court will not use matrimonial fault as a factor in determining custody, this should help to refocus the mediation onto the best interests of the children;
- *explain to spouses who are mediating financial issues* that most provinces specifically exclude marital misconduct as a factor to be considered in determining eligibility for support or the quantum of support. This is the same type of approach as with custody, and should be discussed because spouses often believe that they will be entitled to a higher level of support if they are the innocent party in the marriage breakdown. It is particularly important to clarify this matter, because previous legislation in most provinces did award support

---

[4] R.S.C. 1985, c. 3 (2nd Supp.), s. 16(9).

on the basis of matrimonial fault. Matrimonial fault is specifically eliminated as a criterion in the *Divorce Act*,[5] which applies across all provinces and territories.

If the mediator is unable to resolve successfully the issue of guilt, and if this guilt is interfering with the ability to mediate a reasonable solution, then the mediator should discuss this matter with the spouse individually and should suggest delaying the mediation until that spouse receives individual counselling. If the spouse agrees to a delay, this should be discussed with both spouses and both counsel. Following the discussion with the mediator, if the parent who is feeling guilty wishes to continue the mediation, the mediator should encourage the spouses to reach an interim settlement that is time limited, so that the spouse can review his or her decision at a later date.

If the guilty spouse wishes to proceed to a final settlement, the mediator should document the advice given to the client and should give the client a copy of the memorandum outlining the mediator's concerns. The client should be strongly encouraged to get independent legal advice before finalizing any agreement. If despite these efforts the client wants to proceed, as long as the settlement reached does not jeopardize the health or safety of the children, the mediator should exercise his or her discretion as to whether or not to terminate the mediation. For example, if the mediator feels that the bargain reached in a financial mediation is unreasonable because of the party's feeling of guilt, the mediator may decide not to interfere with the agreement, provided that there has been full financial disclosure and the mediator has indicated his or her concerns both to the client and to counsel for the client.

B. DEALING WITH IMPASSES

The mediator may find that the parties get stuck or reach an impasse at several points during the mediation. Often the reason for the impasse has to do with how the parties are feeling about each other rather than with the substance of the issues in dispute. In order to resolve impasses successfully, the mediator has to avoid being caught up in the conflict between the spouses, and has to skillfully redirect the spouses to the practical task of arriving at a mediated settlement. There are a number of techniques for dealing with impasses, some of which were mentioned previously under the discussion of communication techniques.[6] Examples of approaches that could be used by the mediator are:

- *Reframing the issue.* For example, "I wonder whether the issue is that the children must be returned home by 5:00 p.m. on Sunday, or

---

[5]   *Ibid.*
[6]   See *supra*, "A.(3) The Mediator as Communicator".

whether the issue is really that you feel it is important for the children to have time to unwind and readjust before going to bed following an access visit. If it is the latter, let's discuss how long it takes your children to readjust before their bedtime."

- *Identifying the underlying feelings or problem.* For example, "I get the feeling that you are very angry about having to do all the transporting of the children for access visits. Is that a factor in your refusal to agree to more frequent visits?"
- *Recognizing the impasse.* For example, "We seem to be stuck on this point."
- *Identifying the criteria that can be used to evaluate different alternatives.* For example, if the issue is the choice of a doctor for the children, the parents might suggest such criteria as location of the office, hours of business, specialization (pediatrician versus general practitioner), and access to a particular hospital. Or, if the issue is division of particular assets, the criteria might include the appraised value of the property or a particular mechanism for selection, such as one spouse drawing up two lists of items and the other spouse selecting the list he or she wants.
- *Having each of the clients take responsibility for the impasse.* That is, "We seem to be stuck, what can you do about this?"
- *Providing information to the clients to break the impasse.* For example, information about the effects of parental conflict upon the children.
- *Suggesting several substantive or procedural alternatives,* particularly face-saving options. For example, if one party wants to spend every weekend with the children and the other party wants to offer every other weekend, the mediator might consider alternatives for a compromise. One possibility is that, in those months where there are five weekends, one party could have three of the weekends and the other party two weekends. Another option would be to offer a greater number of long weekends that occur on statutory holidays or professional development days.
- *Holding an individual caucus with each spouse* and then bringing them together after considering the options separately.
- *Letting the parties think about the session and come back with a proposal the next time.* The mediator could give the spouses homework to complete, such as listing the advantages and disadvantages of each of the options that have been considered.
- *Asking the spouses to write out the advantages and disadvantages of the proposals from the other spouse's point of view.* This technique attempts to get each spouse to stand in the other spouse's shoes; that is, it encourages both spouses to consider the others' point of view.
- *Having the spouses submit a written final offer to the mediator.* The mediator picks the best proposal and uses it as the basis for discussion. This technique is moving somewhat closer to arbitration, although

the mediator does not make the final decision. The final decision is still left to the parties.

C. POWER IMBALANCES

The mediation process presumes that the parties are able to negotiate with each other on relatively equal terms. If there is a significant imbalance in power between the two spouses, this may undermine the mediation process.

The following are some reasons for an imbalance of power between the parties:

- domestic violence, including physical, verbal, and psychological abuse;
- lack of information;
- difference in education;
- difference in intellectual ability;
- difference in verbal ability;
- difference in culture or language;
- difference in age;
- difference in socio-economic status;
- difference in personality (for example, dominant versus submissive);
- difference in the availability of a support system for each spouse (for example, extended family, close friends, or organizations such as the church); or
- difference in attitude to the marriage breakdown; that is, one spouse may feel responsible for the marriage breakdown and very guilty about its effects on the family.

The following are methods that the mediator might use for dealing with the various types of power imbalance:

- Referring both the victims of abuse and abusers to appropriate resources, such as shelters, women's advocates, anger management groups, and counselling. In these cases, mediation would usually be terminated.
- Ensuring that the spouses make full disclosure to each other of all relevant information.
- Ensuring that the spouses obtain independent legal advice before signing any agreement.
- Referring the spouses for appropriate outside assistance, such as to an accountant, mental health professional, or vocational counsellor.
- Ensuring that only one individual speaks at a time.
- Preventing the spouses from interrupting each other.
- Preventing one spouse from attacking the other personally;

- Restating the position of the weaker spouse. That is, if the weaker spouse is not as articulate as the stronger spouse, the mediator can help to state the spouse's position more clearly.
- Helping the clients to make more direct statements about their wishes. The mediator can assist the weaker spouse to voice his or her demands, rather than continuing to carry all the responsibility and resenting the more dominant spouse. For example, "I want you to assist with the transportation of children to and from access visits".
- Pointing out certain process aspects of the communication that the spouses may not be conscious of. For example, one spouse may always look at the mediator when he or she wants assistance rather than make demands directly to the other spouse, or one spouse may always precede a request for cooperation with a criticism. The mediator should draw attention to the process and to the response of the other spouse to this behaviour.
- Requesting an individual session with one spouse or recommending an individual caucus during a joint session in order to assist a weaker spouse.
- Giving positive reinforcement and support during the session whenever the weaker spouse demonstrates more assertive behaviour.
- Giving positive reinforcement to the more dominant spouse whenever he or she demonstrates cooperative behaviour.

If the imbalance of power is so great that one or both spouses is unable to assert his or her own position without fear or duress or if the possibility of a fair outcome is in doubt, then the mediator should discuss this directly with both clients and also with their counsel and should terminate the mediation.

D. REFERRAL TO OUTSIDE PROFESSIONALS

There are some problems that arise during mediation that require the expertise of another professional. In some situations, mediation can continue concurrently with the involvement of the other professional. In other instances, mediation may have to be suspended or even terminated. This would depend on the reason for referral. The mediator should discuss both the reason for referral and its effect on the mediation process with both clients before the referral is made.

The following list includes examples of professionals who may have special skills to offer:

- *accountants* — for information about tax implications, help in understanding corporate financial statements, business valuations, *etc.*;

- *property appraisers* — for appraisals of commercial, residential, and personal property;
- *investment analysts and pension experts* — to determine the present value of pensions, RRSPs, and annuities, and to obtain information regarding returns on investments;
- *mental health professionals* (for example, psychologists, psychiatrists, and social workers) — for emotional support and counselling;
- *vocational counsellors* — for information on career alternatives and retraining; and
- *budget counsellors* — for assistance in money management, particularly with respect to managing household expenses.

E. SUMMARY

This chapter has discussed the role of the mediator:

- as *educator*, informing the spouses about the effects on them and their children of separation and divorce;
- as *fact gatherer*, collecting relevant information with respect to the parties' history, present behaviour and future plans; and
- as *communicator*, helping the parties to communicate more effectively.

If the mediator successfully fulfils these three roles, the clients are likely to reach and maintain a settlement and to relate to each other more constructively in the future.

ANNOTATED BIBLIOGRAPHY

Ahrons, C. *The Good Divorce: Keeping Your Family Together when Your Marriage Comes Apart*. New York: Harper-Collins Publishers, 1994. Ahrons defines the "good divorce" and challenges the myth that divorce inevitably turns adults into bitter enemies. Ahrons provides a number of specific suggestions to help families continue to meet the needs of their children.

Ahrons, C., and Rogers, R. *Divorced Families: Meeting the Challenge of Divorce and Remarriage*. New York: W.W. Norton & Co., 1987. The primary focus of this book is how different families cope with the normal but complicated relationship changes that result from divorce and remarriage.

Bach, G., and Wyden, P. *The Intimate Enemy: How to Fight Fair in Love and Marriage*. New York: Avon Books, 1968. This is a very readable book dealing with communication problems in marriage. It is a useful guide to clients for effective conflict resolution and uses examples with which all of us can identify.

Barsky, M. "Emotional Needs and Functional Communication as Blocks to Mediation". In "Successful Techniques for Mediating Family Break-ups" (1983), 2 *Mediation Quarterly* 55. This article explores techniques for improving communication during the mediation process.

Behrman, R., ed. *The Future of Children: Children and Divorce*. Volume 4, number 1. Los Altos, California: The David and Lucile Packard Foundation, Spring 1994. This issue contains a number of articles by leading lawyers and mental health professionals on a wide range of topics about the impact of divorce on children.

Brown, E. *Patterns of Infidelity and Treatment*. New York: Brunner/Mazel, Inc., 1991. This book explores why spouses are unfaithful and what the consequences are for the marriage.

Folberg, J., and Taylor, A. *Mediation: A Comprehensive Guide to Resolving Conflicts Without Litigation*. San Francisco: Jossey-Bass Publishers, 1984. See Chapter 3, "Stages in the Mediation Process", p. 38; Chapter 4, "Counselling Concepts for Developing Mediation Skills", p. 73; and Chapter 5, "Methods of Enhancing Communications", p. 100.

Francke, L.B. *Growing Up Divorced: How to Help Your Child Cope with Every Stage —From Infancy Through the Teens*. New York: Fawcett Crest Books, 1983. This book was written by a parent who experienced divorce. She has combined her own perceptions with a review of major research in the field.

Freeman, R. *Successful Family Transitions: An Evaluation of Intervention Strategies*. Toronto: Family Service Association of Metropolitan Toronto, 1995.

Gardner, R. *The Boys and Girls Book About Divorce*. New York: Bantam Books, 1970.

and

Gardner, R. *The Parent's Book About Divorce*. New York: Bantam Books, 1979. These two books are written by an experienced clinician who offers many insights about the impact of divorce and separation on children and their parents. The children's book can be read with children or by an adolescent and can be used as the basis for their discussions during a counselling process.

Gold, L. *Between Love and Hate: A Guide to Civilized Divorce*. New York: Plenum Press, 1992. See, *supra*, Chapter 4, Annotated Bibliography.

Goldhar-Lerner, H. *The Dance of Anger: A Woman's Guide to Changing the Patterns of Intimate Relationships*. New York: Harper & Row, Publishers, 1985. This book is an excellent resource for couples who want to understand (and change) their repetitive patterns of conflict.

Gray, J. *Men are from Mars, Women are from Venus: A Practical Guide for Improving Communication and Getting What You Want in Your Relationships*. New York: Harper-Collins, 1990.

and

Gray, J. *Men, Women, and Relationships: Making Peace with the Opposite Sex*. Hillsboro, Oregon: Beyond Words Publishing, Inc., 1993.

and

Gray, J. *Mars and Venus Together Forever: Relationship Skills for Lasting Love (A New, Revised Edition of "What Your Mother Couldn't Tell You and Your Father Didn't Know")*. New York: Harper Perennial (a division of Harper-Collins Publishers), 1994. John Gray has written a valuable set of books about male-female communication, including techniques for improving relationships between men and women.

Haynes, J. M. *Divorce Mediation: A Practical Guide for Therapists and Counsellors*. New York: Springer Publishing Co., 1981. See Part I, "Professional Intervention in Divorce Situations"; in particular, Chapter 2, "The Emotional Aspects of Divorce", and Chapter 3, "The Special Problems of Children", p. 15. These two chapters help the mediator focus on the unique problems faced by families who are separating and divorcing and on the role of children in the mediation process.

Haynes, J. *The Fundamentals of Family Mediation*. Suny Press:, 1994.

Hess, R.D., and Camara, K.A. "Post-Divorce Family Relationships as Mediating Factors in the Consequences of Divorce for Children" (1979), 35 *Journal of Social Issues* 39.

Hetherington, E.M., Cox, M., and Cox, R. "The Aftermath of Divorce". In I.J.P. Stevens, Jr., and M. Mathews, eds., *Mother-Child, Father-Child Relations*. Washington, D.C.: National Association for the Education of Young Children, 1979.

Hetherington, E.M., Cox, M., and Cox, R. "Play and Social Interaction in Children Following Divorce" (1979), 35 *Journal of Social Issues* 26. This article presents the results of a longitudinal study on the effects of divorce on play and social interaction in 48 middle-class white preschool children from divorced families. These children were compared to 48 children from non-divorced families and were studied at intervals of two months, one year, and two years after divorce. This study found that the adjustment to divorce appeared to be more difficult for boys than girls.

Hickey, E., and Dalton, E. *Healing Hearts: Helping Children and Adults Recover From Divorce.* Carson City, Nevada: Gold Leaf Press, 1994. This is an excellent book to help parents to heal emotionally so that they can in turn help their children deal constructively with the challenges and changes brought by divorce.

Hodges, W. *Interventions for Children of Divorce: Custody, Access, and Psychotherapy.* 2nd ed. New York: John Wiley and Sons, Inc., 1991. This book reviews the literature on different parenting arrangements and their impact on children at different ages. The author also discusses mediation and custody assessments as two interventions that may assist parents going through separation.

Ives, S.B., Fassler, B., and Lash, M. *The Divorce Workbook: A Guide for Kids and Families.* Vermont: Waterfront Books, 1985. This is a practical workbook for use by therapists to help children express their feelings about separation and divorce through art .

Johnston, J., and Campbell, L. *Impasses of Divorce: The Dynamics and Resolution of Family Conflict.* New York: The Free Press, 1988. This book makes an important contribution toward understanding the dynamics of high conflict couples and offers innovative approaches to mediation.

Johnston, J., and Campbell, L. "A Clinical Typology of Interparental Violence in Disputed —Custody Divorces". (1993), 63 *American Journal of Orthopsychiatry* 1. Based on two studies of high-conflict divorcing families, four characteristic profiles of interparental violence were identified: ongoing or episodic battering by males, female-initiated violence, interactive violence controlled by males, and violence engendered by separation or post-divorce trauma. A fifth profile consisted of psychotic and paranoid reactions. These different profiles generate different issues to consider in mediation.

Kalter, N. *Growing Up With Divorce.* New York: The Free Press, 1990. Kalter, a psychologist, describes how children experience divorce and makes recommendations for ways in which parents and professionals can reduce children's stress and enhance their adjustment. This is a valuable book for both parents and professionals.

Kelly, J. "Power Imbalance in Divorce and Interpersonal Mediation: Assessment and Intervention" (1995), 13 *Mediation Quarterly* 2, 85-98.

This article presents a framework for understanding the conditions that create unequal power in mediation. A variety of mediator interventions are discussed which may empower disputants when differences in power threaten the integrity of the mediation process and its outcome.

Kruk, E. *Divorce and Disengagement: Patterns of Fatherhood Within and Beyond Marriage*. Halifax: Fernwood Publishing, 1993.

Lansky, V. *Divorce Book for Parents: Helping Your Children Cope with Divorce and its Aftermath*. New York: Signet (a division of Penguin Books U.S.A., Inc.), 1989. Lansky is a divorced parent with many practical tips for preparing both adults and children for the experience of separation.

Lund, M. "A Therapist's View of Parental Alienation Syndrome" (1995), 33 *Family and Conciliation Courts Review* 3, 308-323. This article explores many possible reasons for Parent Alienation Syndrome and suggests possible interventions.

McKnight-Erickson, M., and Erickson, S. *The Children's Book...For the Sake of the Children: A Communication Workbook for Separate Parenting After Divorce*. West Concorde, Minn.: CPI Publishing 1992.

Myers, S., and Filner, B. *Mediation Across Cultures: A Handbook about Conflict and Culture*. San Diego: 1993.

Santrock, J.W., and Warshak, R.A. "Father Custody and Social Development in Boys and Girls" (1979), 35 *Journal of Social Issues* 112. This study examined 33 boys and 27 girls from 60 white middle-class families ranging in age from 6 to 11 years. One-third of the children came from families in which the father was awarded custody, one-third from families in which the mother was awarded custody, and one-third from parentally intact families. Videotaped observations were used to evaluate the children's social development in the three research groups.

Saposnek, D. *Mediating Child Custody Disputes*. San Francisco: Jossey-Bass Publishers, 1983. See particularly Part III, "Strategies Used by Children, Parents and Mediators", and Chapter 6, "How Children Contribute to Custody Disputes"; Part II, "Structuring the Mediation Process", particularly Chapter 4, "Phases of Mediation: From Gathering Information to Reaching Agreements", p. 71. Also, see Part III, "Strategies Used by Children, Parents and Mediators", Chapter 8, "Strategies for Eliciting Cooperation Between Parents", and Chapter 9, "Skills and Techniques for Managing Conflict". This book contains many useful clinical techniques for resolving disputes during mediation.

Trafford, A. *Crazy Time: Surviving Divorce*. New York: Bantam Books, 1982. Trafford, a journalist who experienced divorce, interviewed several hundred separated people in order to better understand the experience of separation. This is a helpful book for parents who are recently separated.

Wallerstein, J.S. "Children of Divorce: The Psychological Tasks of the Child" (1983), 53 *American Journal of Orthopsychiatry* 230. This article attempts to conceptualize the major coping tasks faced by children who are experiencing separation and divorce.

Wallerstein, J.S. "The Long Over-burdened Child: Some Long-term Consequences of Divorce" (1985), *Social Work* 116. This article looks at the needs of children under circumstances where their parents' capacity to parent has been diminished by the effects of separation and divorce.

Wallerstein, J.S., and Blakeslee, S. *Second Chances: Men, Women, and Children a Decade After Divorce*. New York: Ticknor & Fields, 1988. This book follows the same families as *Surviving the Breakup* (see below), ten years after divorce. Wallerstein's conclusion is that divorce is not a short-term crisis, but a profoundly life-changing event for all concerned. The focus in this book is on adolescents and young adults a decade after divorce.

Wallerstein, J.S., and Kelly, J.B. *Surviving the Breakup: How Children and Parents Cope with Divorce*. New York: Basic Books Inc., 1980. This is the best-known report of research on the effects of separation and divorce on children and parents. It is a longitudinal project, and at the time the book was published, children and parents were studied at various intervals up to five years following separation or divorce. This is an extremely readable, enlightening book that can be used to assist parents in understanding the consequences, and to help parents plan a strategy for dealing with the aftermath, of separation and divorce.

Ware, C. *Sharing Parenthood After Divorce: An Enlightened Custody Guide for Mothers, Fathers and Children*. Toronto: Bantam Books, 1984. This is a book written by a parent who attempted mediation as a method of resolving a contested custody dispute. She reports on her own experience and the experience of many other couples with respect to sharing parenthood after divorce. She is a strong advocate for both the mediation process and for a shared approach to parenting.

Weiss, R.S. "Growing Up a Little Faster: The Experience of Growing Up in a Single-Parent Household" (1979), 35 *Journal of Social Issues* 97. The author concludes that there may be some positive benefits for children in single-parent households in terms of increased self-esteem, independence, and a sense of competence as a result of being given increased responsibility.

Chapter Six

Major Issues: Custody and Access

A. CUSTODY AND ACCESS

Often the most significant issue in dispute between parents is who will have custody of the children. On a psychological level, this is often a competition for control, affection, continuity of lifestyle, and acceptance as a parent. Feelings of anger, a desire for revenge, fear of loneliness, and guilt compete with feelings of genuine concern about the welfare of the children and the knowledge that children need both parents and usually show better psychological adjustment if the conflict between the parents is kept to a minimum.

Often the party who is successful in winning custody succeeds in other aspects of the dispute, such as obtaining exclusive possession of the matrimonial home, support, and familiar family possessions. The party who loses custody of the children faces the most radical change in lifestyle, and even if that parent chooses to leave the marriage, he or she often experiences strong feelings of loneliness, depression, a sense of failure, guilt, or rejection.

The more adversarial the process for determining custody and the more the law establishes one parent as a winner and the other as a loser in custody matters, the more devastating the psychological effect on both parents and children. Within this psychological context, the following is a discussion of the law of custody, at both provincial and federal levels, including alternative orders that can be made by the court.

1. What is Custody?

In the context of parental disputes over children, custody refers to the totality of rights and duties in relation to the child. That is, it encompasses both control of the physical person of the child and the right to make decisions about the child's upbringing.

Custody essentially includes the following rights:

- the right to control the child;
- the right to make decisions regarding the child's education, religion, and lifestyle; and
- the right to grant or withhold consent to the marriage of an underage child.

Custody also includes such responsibilities as:

- providing for the child's physical, mental, and moral care and development; and
- providing for the child's basic needs, such as food, clothing, and housing.

Custody is often used interchangeably with guardianship; however, guardianship is really a broader term that applies in situations other than "legal custody" in the sense described above.

2. What is Access?

Access is defined as the right of the non-custodial parent to visit with the child. An order for access does not include the legal right to make decisions with respect to the child's upbringing nor does it include the legal responsibility for the child's care and control. The purpose of access is to encourage the continuation of a parent-child relationship following a marriage breakdown. A non-custodial parent who has access rights no longer has a legal right to participate as a parent in many significant areas of the child's life, such as determining the child's residence, education, or religion.

The non-custodial parent has the same responsibilities for the care of the child as any adult acting in a caretaking capacity. That is, the non-custodial parent is responsible for emergency health care, informing the custodial parent of any delay in returning the child at the agreed-upon time, and requesting in advance any changes in the visitation schedule.

In some provinces, such as Ontario, and under the federal *Divorce Act*,[1] anyone who has access to the child has a legal right to make inquiries and receive information about the health, education, and welfare of the child.

3. Custody Disputes: The Historical Context

Under the English common law, children were considered to be the property of their fathers, and custody awards were routinely made to fathers.

During the 19th century, the industrial revolution resulted in many fathers working away from the home and mothers remaining in the home as the primary caretakers of children. In addition, society began to place a higher value on children as more children survived the high risk of infant mortality. Legally, the courts shifted from a preference for fathers as custodians to mothers as custodians. This was particularly true of young children. During the early 1900's, the "tender years" doctrine was applied as the principal rule for determining custody disputes. That is, custody was routinely awarded to mothers, particularly for children under the age of seven, unless the mother was found to be unfit.

---

[1]   R.S.C. 1985, c. 3 (2nd Supp.).

In the mid-1970's a further cultural change took place that had an effect on the criteria for awarding custody. The child's needs and interests became a more important factor, and custody was awarded on the basis of "the best interests of the child". Custody awards were not supposed to be contingent on the sex of the parent, but rather were to reflect the best interests of the child. In fact, the courts still demonstrated a considerable preference for maternal custody, unless the mother was demonstrated to be unfit.

In the 1980's, a number of social factors had an impact on custody awards; for example, such changes as:

- more women were in the workforce and out of the home;
- more men were participating in child rearing and household tasks; and
- there was a greater concern about discrimination on the basis of sex, both as it applied to women and to men.

In keeping with the movement toward greater sharing of parental rights and responsibilities during the marriage, the early 1990's saw an increased trend toward continued sharing of the parental role even after marriage breakdown. This trend was responsible for the movement away from a determination of sole custody to one parent (that is, exclusive parental rights to one parent) toward a concept of continued parental cooperation and sharing after the marriage has ended. This trend has led to a number of variations in the traditional award of custody to one parent and access to the other.

4. Custody Arrangements

(A) SOLE CUSTODY

Sole custody refers to an order whereby one custodial parent is awarded the totality of rights and duties in relation to the child. Custody can be determined by the courts, or it can be determined by the parties through their own agreement.

(B) SPLIT CUSTODY

Split custody means that one parent has full custody of one or more children and the other parent has full custody of one or more of the other children. Usually each parent would have the right of access to the other child or children.

(C) ALTERNATING CUSTODY

Alternating custody means that one parent has full custody, including care and control of the child, for a specified time period, and then the other parent has full custody, including care and control, for a specified time period (not to be confused with alternating or rotating residence, which is described below in (d) "Joint Custody").

While the child is residing with one parent, that parent is entirely responsible for all decisions with respect to the child's upbringing, although the non-custodial parent usually has the right to access. This custody arrangement divides, rather than shares, the custodial responsibilities between the parents. This is to be distinguished from joint custody, which will be discussed next.

(D) JOINT CUSTODY

In contrast to alternating custody, joint custody preserves, at all times, both parents' joint legal responsibility for the upbringing of the child. That is, even following separation, both parents maintain their legal rights and responsibilities for significant decisions affecting the child.

Joint legal custody does not necessarily mean that the child spends an equal amount of time physically living with each parent. There is no requirement that the child spend any particular amount of time with each parent, although both parents retain their legal status as parents.

In California and some other jurisdictions in the United States, courts distinguish between joint legal custody and joint physical custody:

- *Joint legal custody* means that both parents retain the right to make decisions with respect to the child.
- *Joint physical custody* means that the child spends a substantial amount of time living with each parent. In California, children who live at least 30 per cent of the time with each parent are considered to be in a joint physical custody arrangement.
- *Sole legal custody* means that one parent has the legal right to make all decisions with respect to the child's upbringing.
- *Sole physical custody* means that the child primarily resides with one parent and has access visits with the other parent.

In California, any combination of the above-mentioned aspects of custody is possible. That is, a family can have joint legal and joint physical custody, or joint legal but sole physical custody, or sole legal and sole physical custody, or sole legal but joint physical custody.

In Canada, couples who have joint custody of their children generally share decisions with respect to upbringing, but have an arrangement whereby the child has a primary residence with one parent. However, there are a growing number of cases in which parents share both decision making and physical care and control on an approximately equal-time basis.

Under both provincial and federal legislation, it is possible for a court to order joint custody, particularly in cases where the parties consent to such an order. However, the Northwest Territories is the only jurisdiction in Canada to specifically include the term "joint custody" as an option available to the judge under its custody provisions. The legislation does not contain either a presumption or a preference for joint custody, but rather permits the judge, in appropriate cases, to make such an order.

In practice, Canadian courts usually do not make joint custody orders in cases where the parties do not request it, particularly if there is evidence that the parties cannot cooperate with each other in the interests of their children. There are some recent exceptions to this general rule, particularly at the stage of an interim custody order. At this point, the court may make a joint custody or alternating custody award to preserve the status quo as between the parties until the date of trial.

A number of couples who mediate rather than litigate the issues of custody and access decide on a shared parenting arrangement, that is, in effect, some form of joint custody. According to the research data collected by Howard Irving in the early 1980's on a sample of 201 Ontario couples, joint custody appears to have many benefits for both parents and children. Particularly where these arrangements were arrived at voluntarily, the parents reported a higher level of satisfaction; it was found that co-parental relationships were likely to be less litigious than sole custody arrangements: the children tended to be happier when they maintained frequent, reliable, and ongoing contact with both their parents, and this arrangement encouraged joint fiscal responsibility, with a far higher percentage of joint custodial fathers paying support.

Some studies have not found this relationship between joint custody and payment of support. For example, in jurisdictions such as California, where support obligations are reduced if a father agrees to spend a substantial amount of time with the children, research[2] shows that despite these agreements, children usually spend the majority of their time living with their mother. In Canada, the proposed federal support guidelines could have the same effect; that is, support obligations are likely to be reduced if couples agree on joint physical custody (if both parents have *equal overnight* time), although most children will likely continue to spend the majority of their time living with their mother. This issue is discussed in greater detail in Chapter 7.

Other studies[3] have found that the level of conflict between the parents is an important factor in parental satisfaction, as is the fact that they reached a joint custody agreement voluntarily. Another factor is the proximity of the parents' residences to each other and to the children's schools.

5. The Criteria for Awarding Custody as Determined by Provincial and Federal Statutes

Custody decisions are made under both provincial legislation and federal legislation. Usually, custody decisions reached prior to divorce are made

---

[2]   See E. Maccoby and R. Mnookin, *Dividing the Child: Social and Legal Dilemmas of Custody* (Cambridge, Mass.: Harvard University Press, 1992).

[3]   See H.H. Irving and M. Benjamin, "Shared Parenting in Canada; Questions, Answers and Implications" (1986), 1 *Canadian Family Law Quarterly* 79; J. Kelly, "Current Research on Children's Post-Divorce Adjustment: No Simple Answers" (1993), 31 *Family and Conciliation Courts Review* 1; and E. Maccoby and R. Mnookin, *supra*, note 2.

pursuant to a provincial statute, although interim orders can be made under the federal *Divorce Act*.

At the time of divorce, custody and access decisions are considered a part of corollary relief, that is, relief that the courts can grant in conjunction with their power to grant a divorce under the federal *Divorce Act*. It is also possible to apply for a custody order under a provincial statute at the time of divorce.

When an action for divorce is commenced under the *Divorce Act*, any application for custody under a provincial statute that has not as yet been determined by the court is stayed, except by leave of the court. This is because the decision under the federal Act would be constitutionally paramount to a decision under a provincial Act. Therefore, there would be no reason for competing claims under the two Acts to proceed at the same time.

Provincial statutes and the federal *Divorce Act* vary in the way in which they describe custody and in the criteria that are used in determining custody. Some statutes refer only to the best interests of children, whereas other statutes set out specific criteria for the judges to consider in making a custody award.

For example, the Ontario *Children's Law Reform Act*[4] sets out very specifically the criteria to be applied by a judge in making an order of custody. These criteria reflect the common law position on custody awards. As a result, even in those provinces that do not set out elaborate criteria for determining custody, most jurisdictions would apply the same or similar criteria on the basis of common law.

The Ontario *Children's Law Reform Act* deals with custody as follows:

24(1) The merits of an application under this Part in respect of custody of or access to a child shall be determined on the basis of the best interests of the child.

(2) In determining the best interests of the child for the purposes of an application under this Part in respect of custody of or access to a child, a court shall consider all the needs and circumstances of the child including,
- (a) the love, affection and emotional ties between the child and,

  (i)   each person entitled to or claiming custody of or access to the child,
  (ii) other members of the child's family who reside with the child, and
  (iii) persons involved in the care and upbringing of the child;
- (b) the views and preferences of the child, where such views and preferences can reasonably be ascertained;
- (c) the length of time the child has lived in a stable home environment;

---

[4]   R.S.O. 1990, c. C.12.

(d)   the ability and willingness of each person applying for custody of the child to provide the child with guidance and education, the necessaries of life and any special needs of the child;

(e)   any plans proposed for the care and upbringing of the child;

(f)   the permanence and stability of the family unit with which it is proposed that the child will live; and

(g)   the relationship by blood or through an adoption order between the child and each person who is a party to the application.

(3) The past conduct of a person is not relevant to a determination of an application under this Part in respect of custody of or access to a child unless the conduct is relevant to the ability of the person to act as a parent of a child.

It is important to note that this statute apparently does not establish a preference for biological parents over psychological parents, and in addition it specifically excludes matrimonial fault or other aspects of past conduct if they are not relevant to parenting ability. It is often necessary for the mediator in discussions of custody, as well as in discussions of support, to point out to the parties that the court does not make awards of custody or support on the basis of matrimonial fault.

By way of contrast, the federal *Divorce Act* does not set out the criteria for evaluating the child's best interests, although it does adopt "best interests" as the sole test for determining custody awards. One unique feature of the federal Act is that it places a heavy emphasis on ensuring that the child has an opportunity to spend considerable time with both parents. In fact, to preserve the child's relationship with both parents, the Act directs the court to give consideration, when determining custody awards, to the parent who is most likely to encourage the involvement of the non-custodial parent. This Act is similar to the Ontario Act in that matrimonial fault is expressly excluded as a factor in awarding custody or access, unless the conduct is relevant to parenting. The custody provisions of the *Divorce Act* are set out below:

16(8) In making an order under this section, the court shall take into consideration only the best interests of the child of the marriage as determined by reference to the condition, means, needs and other circumstances of the child.

(9) In making an order under this section, the court shall not take into consideration the past conduct of any person unless the conduct is relevant to the ability of that person to act as a parent of a child.

(10) In making an order under this section, the court shall give effect to the principle that a child of the marriage should have as much contact with each spouse as is consistent with the best interests of the child and, for that purpose, shall take into consideration the willingness of the person for whom custody is sought to facilitate such contact.

The federal and provincial statutes also differ in their descriptions of entitlement to custody, and the rights and privileges of the custodial and the non-custodial parents. For example, the Ontario *Children's Law Reform Act* deals with these issues in the following way:

> 20(1) Except as otherwise provided in this Part, the father and the mother of a child are equally entitled to custody of the child.
>
> (2) A person entitled to custody of a child has the rights and responsibilities of a parent in respect of the person of the child and must exercise those rights and responsibilities in the best interests of the child.
>
> (3) Where more than one person is entitled to custody of a child, any one of them may exercise the rights and accept the responsibilities of a parent on behalf of them in respect of the child.
>
> (4) Where the parents of a child live separate and apart and the child lives with one of them with the consent, implied consent or acquiescence of the other of them, the right of the other to exercise the entitlement to custody and the incidents of custody, but not the entitlement to access, is suspended until a separation agreement or order otherwise provides.
>
> (5) The entitlement to access to a child includes the right to visit with and be visited by the child and the same right as a parent to make inquiries and to be given information as to the health, education and welfare of the child.

It is clear that this Act sets up an equal statutory entitlement on the part of fathers and mothers to custody of their children. In addition, while the Act does not prevent an order of joint custody, it is written from the perspective of a sole custody award. It does not at any time specifically mention joint custody or split or alternating custody.

This Act does give some of the rights of a parent to the non-custodial parent. That is, it does give the non-custodial parent a right to make inquiries and be given information with respect to the child's health, education, and welfare. However, it should be noted that this is a right to information and not a right to participate in decision making.

Under the federal *Divorce Act* the entitlement to custody and the allocation of rights and privileges between the custodial and non-custodial parent are as follows:

> 16(1) A court of competent jurisdiction may, on application by either or both spouses or by any other person, make an order respecting the custody of or the access to, or the custody of and access to, any or all children of the marriage.
>
> (2) Where an application is made under subsection (1), the court may, on application by either or both spouses or by any other person, make an interim order respecting the custody of or the access to, or the custody of and access to, any or all children of the marriage pending determination of the application under subsection (1).
>
> (3) A person, other than a spouse, may not make an application under subsection (1) or (2) without leave of the court.
>
> (4) The court may make an order under this section granting custody of, or access to, any or all children of the marriage to any one or more persons.

(5) Unless the court orders otherwise, a spouse who is granted access to a child of the marriage has the right to make inquiries, and to be given information, as to the health, education and welfare of the child.

(6) The court may make an order under this section for a definite or indefinite period or until the happening of a specified event and may impose such other terms, conditions or restrictions in connection therewith as it thinks fit and just.

(7) Without limiting the generality of subsection (6), the court may include in an order under this section a term requiring any person who has custody of a child of the marriage and who intends to change the place of residence of that child to notify, at least thirty days before the change or within such other period before the change as the court may specify, any person who is granted access to that child of the change, the time at which the change will be made and the new place of residence of the child.

This statute does not presume that the parents have an equal entitlement to custody. There is no reference to joint custody in the legislation (only in a marginal note, which has no statutory significance); however, the *Divorce Act* does establish a right to information by the non-custodial parent, including the right upon application to be notified of a change of address if the custodial parent decides to move to a new location.

6. CURRENT ISSUES

(A) CUSTODIAL DESIGNATION

This chapter has used the traditional legal language of "custody" of and "access" to the child. However, over the past decade, in North America, Australia, and England, there has been an increasing interest in the impact on parents of the language used to describe their ongoing role with their children. In the first place, "custody" is an ownership concept. We use it to describe who owns or has possession of an object, such as, "I have custody of the dining room chairs". In criminal law, it has connotations of detaining people against their will, such as, "We took the prisoner into custody". Neither of these concepts is an attractive way to describe a parent-child relationship, nor does it address the fears, concerns, or needs of many parents. Also, the concept of custody is, "If I have it, you don't". It is a win/lose term which suggests that if a parent loses custody, he or she will lose the opportunity to have an important role or relationship with the child. It is this fear that propels most custody battles.

Fighting over the custodial label usually does not address the important responsibilities of parenting. In England, the *Children Act*[5] clearly illustrates the shift in language from "custody" of children to that of "parental responsibility", which is defined as "all the rights, duties, pow-

---

[5]   1989 (U.K.), c. 41, s. 3(1).

ers, responsibilities and authority which by law a parent has in relation to the child and his property".

Most parents who fight over "custody" are not fighting over who will carry out the tasks or responsibilities of being a parent; they are usually fighting over their own rights as parents. This is not in the child's best interests because, especially after a separation, it is difficult for either parent to meet all of the needs of the child on his or her own. A better approach would be for both parents to arrive at a parenting plan that shares the responsibilities, regardless of the choice of custodial designation.

The trend, particularly by mediators, is to try to shift the focus to how the parents are going to carry out their responsibilities as parents, and as a last step, to decide on a custodial label where necessary. By helping parents to focus on how they will each contribute to a parenting plan (rather than on what to call it), there are usually several benefits, namely:

- Neither parent carries the entire burden of responsibilities, which is particularly important if both parents are in the workforce after separation.
- Children's needs are met more adequately and cooperatively. Single parents are often unable to offer their children the same opportunities as they could prior to separation.
- Both parents continue to see themselves as having a significant parenting role.
- Both parents have some time to meet their own personal needs, which will likely enhance their ability to parent.

The same concerns apply to the term "access". Access is a possessory term and has little to do with maintaining a relationship between a parent and child. Parents (usually fathers) often feel disenfranchised by the terminology of being reduced to an "access" parent, which often feels like being relegated to the stature of a visitor or distant relative. Access parents may feel no commitment to carrying out responsibilities, particularly if their efforts are not recognized as contributing to parenting. Ironically, the access parent is often resented by the custodial parent as being the "Santa Claus" parent, while the custodial parent feels overburdened by the weight of trying to meet all of the practical, economic, and recreational needs of the children.

When parents fight over a custodial label, what they usually want is to have an important role or to maintain a significant relationship with the child. Even if the main issue is to have the child primarily reside with that parent, most parents would really appreciate the other parent's assistance in carrying out parenting tasks and would expect to consult the other parent on significant issues. Both parents are usually satisfied with this type of parenting plan, but the label is often the focus of a divisive battle that undermines any cooperation.

Today the trend is to avoid battles over custodial labels and, instead, to encourage mediation clients to work out a parenting plan that will define their roles and responsibilities in relation to the children. The emphasis is on the *responsibilities* of parenting rather than on the *parent's rights*.

The plan should clarify which parent will carry out specific parenting tasks and how each parent will participate in decision making. Also, it should deal with what time the child will spend with each parent on a regular basis and during school breaks, statutory holidays, and other special days. It should also clarify the process to be followed if a material change in circumstances occurs, such as a move to another city, a remarriage, or a parent's illness, and how the parents will resolve significant conflicts in the future. To the extent that the parenting plan offers a clear road map, the number of future conflicts will reduced. Mediation is a very effective process for designing parenting plans that are tailored to the special needs and circumstances of the entire family.

(B) MOBILITY

For many years the courts have struggled with the issue of whether, or under what circumstances, a custodial parent can remove a child from the jurisdiction where he or she lived at the time of separation. Initially, the courts took the position that, unless the decision was unreasonable (for example, the move was only to prevent the non-custodial parent from exercising access) or there were special circumstances, the custodial parent had the right to move with the child. As in *Wright v. Wright*,[6] the focus was on the rights of the custodial parent, unless that was contrary to the terms of a separation agreement. Following passage of the *Divorce Act, 1985*[7] and the *Ontario Children's Law Reform Act, 1977*[8] (or similar statutes in other provinces), the courts adopted the "best interest of the child" test, as in *Carter v. Brooks*[9] and *Young v. Young*.[10]

In the *Carter v. Brooks* decision, Morden A.C.J.O. rejected the idea of developing a fixed list of criteria or a presumption in favour of the custodial parent in mobility cases. Instead he stated:[11]

> I think the preferable approach in the application of the standard [*i.e.*, the best interests test] is for the court to weigh and balance the factors which are relevant in the particular circumstances in the case at hand, without any rigid preconceived notion as to what weight each factor should have. . . . At the end of the process the court should arrive at a determinate conclusion on the result which better accords with the best interest of the child.

[6]   (1973), 1 O.R. (2d) 337, 40 D.L.R. (3d) 321, 12 R.F.L. 200 (C.A.).
[7]   S.C. 1986, c. 4 [see now R.S.C. 1985, c. 3 (2nd Supp.)].
[8]   S.O. 1977, c. 41 [now R.S.O. 1990, c. C.12].
[9]   (1990), 2 O.R. (3d) 321, 30 R.F.L. (3d) 53 (C.A.).
[10] [1993] 4 S.C.R. 3, 108 D.L.R. (4th) 193, 49 R.F.L. (3d) 117.
[11] *Carter v. Brooks, supra*, note 9, at p. 328 O.R.

However, in the case of *MacGyver v. Richards*,[12] Abella J.A. took a different approach. She started from the observation that the custodial parent "must be understood as bearing a disproportionate amount of responsibility"[13] and therefore:[14]

> In deciding what restrictions, if any, should be placed on a parent with custody, courts should be wary about interfering with that parent's capacity to decide, daily, what is best for the child. . . . Those judgments may include whether to change neighbourhoods, or provinces, or partners, or jobs, or friends, or schools, or religions.

She concluded that[15]

> When, therefore, a court has been asked to decide what is in a child's best interests, and a choice must be made between the responsible wishes and needs of the parent with custody and the parent with access, it seems to be manifestly unfair to treat these wishes and needs as being on an equal footing.

This issue of mobility was decided by the Supreme Court of Canada in the case of *Gordon v. Goertz*.[16] The majority decision written by McLachlin J. held that the sole test was "the best interests of the child, having regard to all the relevant circumstances relating to the child's needs and the ability of the respective parents to satisfy them."[17] The focus of the inquiry is not the interests and rights of the parents. Each case turns on its own unique circumstances and the only issue is the best interests of the child in the particular circumstances of the case. "The inquiry does not begin with a legal presumption in favour of the custodial parent, although the custodial parent's views are entitled to great respect."[18] In assessing the best interests of the child, the judge should more particularly consider, *inter alia*:[19]

> (a) the existing custody arrangement and relationship between the child and the custodial parent; (b) the existing access arrangement and the relationship between the child and the access parent; (c) the desirability of maximizing contact between the child and both parents; (d) the views of the child; (e) the custodial parent's reason for moving, *only* in the exceptional case where it is relevant to that parent's ability to meet the needs of the child; (f) disruption to the child of a change in custody; (g) disruption to the child consequent on removal from family, schools, and the community he or she has come to know.

In the end, the importance of the child's remaining with the parent to whose custody it has become accustomed in the new location must be

---

[12] (1995), 22 O.R. (3d) 481, 11 R.F.L. (4th) 432 (C.A).
[13] *Ibid.*, at p. 490 O.R.
[14] *Ibid.*, at p. 491 O.R.
[15] *Ibid.*, at p. 492 O.R.
[16] (1996), 134 D.L.R. (4th) 321, 19 R.F.L. (4th) 177.
[17] *Ibid.*, at 342 D.L.R.
[18] *Ibid.*
[19] *Ibid.*

weighed against the continuance of full contact with the child's access parent, its extended family and its community. The ultimate question in every case is this: what is in the best interests of the child in all the circumstances, old as well as new?

This decision will have a significant effect on the position taken by the parties in mediation.

Since the child's best interest in each case is the appropriate test, the mediator will need to help the parties consider the criteria set out by McLachlin J. in addition to such factors as:

- whether the move would improve the quality of life for the child and custodial parent;
- whether there is a new partner, and the child's relationship with that person;
- if there is a new partner, the stability of this family unit;
- the child's ties to extended family, friends, school, and the community in the current versus the proposed location;
- the distance proposed, and the willingness of the custodial parent to facilitate a meaningful access plan;
- the financial resources of both parents for carrying out a meaningful access plan; and
- the age of the child and any special needs or abilities.

In mediation, the question of mobility is often the most difficult issue on which to reach agreement, even if there is no move contemplated at the time of separation. It is important for the mediator to be familiar with the current statutes and case law on this subject because they will have an important impact on the negotiations. Also, it is a reality that today's families are more mobile than in the past, and therefore the issue of mobility should be discussed in every mediation involving custody and access. Any agreement reached will need to be described with great care to ensure that the parties' wishes are clearly and accurately reflected. Most often parties do not know what the future will hold, and it is often reasonable to set out some general principles about mobility and a method for resolving disputes should they arise. For example, parties might agree to

- first inform the other parent at least 30 days (or preferably more) in advance as to the location and reason for the proposed move;
- discuss the implications of a proposed move directly with the other parent in the hope of reaching a mutually acceptable plan; but if an impasse is reached, then
- return to mediation; and if this does not result in an agreement within a specified time, then
- request that the lawyers be involved in trying to negotiate a resolution; and if this is unsuccessful in a specified time period, then

- proceed to arbitration or litigation with respect to any unresolved issues.

It may be appropriate for the parties to agree that during the time they are trying to resolve the conflict, the custodial parent may move, but the child remains in the jurisdiction. This provision would encourage parents to give as much notice as possible of a pending move and would also encourage them to set a reasonable time frame for reaching a resolution.

7. Summary

This chapter has examined different types of custodial arrangements. It is important to understand the various options for custody, because the parties may be unaware of the alternatives, and this information could facilitate a settlement. In addition, a number of current issues in the field were explored in terms of their significance for mediation. Mediators need to continually update their knowledge about such issues as they will have an impact on the positions taken by the parents and will help to identify the underlying concerns that need to be addressed.

ANNOTATED BIBLIOGRAPHY

Adler, R. *Sharing the Children: How to Resolve Custody Problems and Get On With Your Life*. Bethesda, Maryland: Adler & Adler, Publishers, Inc., 1988. See *supra*, Chapter 4, Annotated Bibliography.

Bowman, M.E. and Ahrons, C.R. "Impact of Legal Custody Status of Fathers' Parenting Post-Divorce" (1985), *Journal of Marriage and the Family* 481. This study examines 28 joint-custodial fathers and 54 non-custodial fathers with respect to (a) contact and activities with the children and (b) shared responsibility and decision making. The results demonstrated that joint-custodial fathers were more involved with their children than non-custodial fathers one year after divorce.

Coulter, L. *Two Homes: A Parent's Guide to Joint Custody in Canada*. Toronto: Harper Collins Publishers, 1990. See *supra*, Chapter 4, Annotated Bibliography.

Dillon, P., and Emery, R. "Divorce Mediation and Resolution of Child Custody Disputes: Long-Term Effects" (1996), 66 *American Journal of Orthopsychiatry* 1.

Irving, H.H., and Benjamin, M. "Shared Parenting in Canada; Questions, Answers and Implications" (1986), 1 *Canadian Family Law Quarterly* 79. This article reports on the results of the Shared Parenting Project, a research study comparing the experience of 201 shared parents with that of 194 (maternal) sole custody parents. This is a very informative article that explodes some of the myths about joint custody.

Irving, H.H., and Benjamin, M. "Mobility Rights and Children's Interests: Empirically-Based First Principles as a Guide to Effective Parenting Plans" (1996), 13 *Canadian Family Law Quarterly* 3, 249-60.

Joyal-Poupart, R. "Joint Custody". In E. Sloss, ed., *Family Law in Canada: New Directions*. Ottawa: Canadian Advisory Council on the Status of Women, 1985, p. 107. This author examines custody legislation and jurisprudence in a number of jurisdictions. Arguing from the feminist point of view, he takes the position that joint custody should be granted in cases where parents expressly request it.

Kelly, J. "Current Research on Children's Post-Divorce Adjustment: No Simple Answers" (1993), 31 *Family and Conciliation Courts Review* 1. This is a sophisticated research summary on the current knowledge about factors affecting children's post-divorce adjustment.

Maccoby, E., and Mnookin, R. *Dividing the Child: Social and Legal Dilemmas of Custody*. Cambridge, Mass.: Harvard University Press, 1992. This is the report of an extensive longitudinal study of California families post-separation. It looks at the parenting arrangements as well as the economic consequences of divorce.

McWhinney, R. "The 'Winner-Loser Syndrome': Changing Fashions in the Determination of Child 'Custody'" (1995), 33 *Family and Conciliation Courts Review* 3, 298-307.

Mills, B.C. (Judge), and Belzer, S. "Joint Custody As a Parenting Alternative" (1982), 9 *Pepperdine Law Review* 53. The authors present the legislative history of the California Joint Custody Statute and summarize a variety of viewpoints with respect to joint custody. This article contains a discussion of the legislative intent behind the statute and the issue of whether the current law is the most effective means of protecting the best interests of children and of assuring children a frequent and continuing contact with both parents following a marriage breakdown.

Ricci, I. *Mom's House, Dad's House: Making Shared Custody Work, How Parents Can Make Two Homes for their Children After Divorce*. New York: Collier Books, Macmillan, 1981.

Roman, M., and Haddad, W. *The Disposable Parent*. New York: Holt Rinehart & Winston, 1978. This book explores the impact on fathers, in particular, and on children of sole custody awards. The book makes a case for a shared parenting approach.

Ryan, J. "Joint Custody in Canada: Time for a Second Look" (1986), 49 R.F.L. (2d) 119, and published in B. Landau, ed. *Children's Rights in the Practice of Family Law*. Toronto: Carswell Publishing Co., 1986. This article reviews the literature on joint custody and reflects the optimism of the 1980's that joint custody would be a preferred approach to parenting following divorce.

Thompson, R. "Beam Us Up Scotty: Parents and Children on the Trek" (1996), 13 *Canadian Family Law Quarterly* 3, 205-47.

Tompkins, R. "Parenting Plans: A Concept Whose Time Has Come" (1995), 33 *Family and Conciliation Courts Review* 3, 286-97. This article encourages parents and those assisting them to develop detailed parenting plans to increase clarity and reduce conflict after separation.

Wilson, J. *Wilson on Children and the Law*. Toronto: Butterworths, 1994.

Chapter Seven

Major Issues: Support and Property

A. SUPPORT FOR SPOUSE

Financial provision for a spouse or former spouse is often called alimony, maintenance, or support, often interchangeably. For the purposes here, we will use the term "support" to include financial provision for either a spouse or former spouse. Support is designed to provide financial assistance to a dependent spouse. Support can be provided to a spouse during separation but prior to divorce, or after a divorce. Provincial statutes have the jurisdiction to deal with spousal support prior to divorce. After a divorce, and during divorce proceedings themselves, the federal government has exclusive jurisdiction to deal with support under the *Divorce Act*.[1] The definition of who qualifies for spousal support under the provincial and federal statutes is very different in some instances. However, the criteria for awarding support are generally very similar, regardless of whether the provincial or federal legislation is being applied.

1. The *Divorce Act*

(A) WHO QUALIFIES?

Under the *Divorce Act*, only spouses who were married to each other can obtain support upon dissolution of the marriage. The jurisdiction to award support under the *Divorce Act* depends on a judgment for divorce being granted.

(B) CRITERIA

The *Divorce Act* sets out in s. 15(2) that a court may make whatever order it deems "reasonable" for the support of a spouse. The major criteria, or factors, that a court·is to consider are set out in s. 15(5), which reads as follows:

> 15(5) In making an order under this section, the court shall take into consideration the condition, means, needs and other circumstances of each spouse and of any child of

---

[1]   R.S.C. 1990, c. 3 (2nd Supp.).

the marriage for whom support is sought, including

(*a*)   the length of time the spouses cohabited;
(*b*)   the functions performed by the spouse during cohabitation; and
(*c*)   any order, agreement or arrangement relating to support of the spouse or child.

In addition to these factors, the Act sets out specific objectives of an order for support in s. 15(7), which reads as follows:

15(7) An order made under this section that provides for the support of a spouse should

(*a*)   recognize any economic advantages or disadvantages to the spouses arising from the marriage or its breakdown;
(*b*)   apportion between the spouses any financial consequences arising from the care of any child of the marriage over and above the obligation apportioned between the spouses pursuant to subsection (8);
(*c*)   relieve any economic hardship of the spouses arising from the breakdown of the marriage;
(*d*)   in so far as practicable, promote the economic self-sufficiency of each spouse within a reasonable period of time.

The main considerations of the court in awarding support are the means, needs, and other circumstances of the parties. Means and needs emerge as the major factors. What means does each party have? Are they sufficient to meet his or her needs? And if they are not, to what extent does the other spouse have means to contribute?

The previous legislation[2] included a reference to the conduct of the parties as a factor to be considered by the court in making an order for support. Now, by virtue of s. 15(6), any misconduct of a spouse is not to be taken into account in making an order for spousal support.

In addition to the general criteria of "means and needs", the court is directed to consider the length of cohabitation, the functions each spouse performed during cohabitation, and any other order or agreement relating to support. These factors suggest (although certainly not clearly) that a divorce court may award less support in the case of a marriage of short duration or more support if the marriage has been a lengthy one. Similarly, where one spouse has performed all household functions and has been out of the workforce, this may warrant a greater or lengthier support order.

The objectives of an order for support of a spouse are interesting. For the first time, federal legislation squarely addresses the issue of a dependent spouse becoming self-sufficient. The Act provides as an enumerated objective that an order is to promote economic self-sufficiency within a reasonable period of time. Since the passage of the legislation, the issue

---

2   *Divorce Act*, R.S.C. 1970, c. D-8.

of spousal support has gone through considerable growing pains. We have seen the emergence and decline of the notion of "causal connection" and issues of "compensatory support". Most recently (in 1995) judgments of the Supreme Court of Canada have held that spousal support is always open for review and must specifically address the principles and objectives stated in s. 15(7) of the Act. These are

- to recognize economic advantages and disadvantages arising out of the marriage or its breakdown;
- to apportion financial consequences arising out of taking responsibility for the care of children;
- to relieve economic hardship arising out of marriage breakdown; and
- to promote economic self-sufficiency within a reasonable period of time.

All the criteria are equally important, and must be looked at in conjunction with one another. The primary goal of spousal support can be seen as "promoting the equitable distribution of the economic consequences of the marriage and its breakdown".[3]

These areas bear further comment. The notion of "*causal connection*" required that a dependant spouse's dependency be "causally connected" to the marriage. For example, if a spouse had stayed out of the workforce to raise the children, and was thus economically disadvantaged as a result, his or her dependency was "causally connected" to the marriage, and support would be ordered. If, however, the lack of economic independence was caused by illness or wilful action, it was not "causally connected", and support might be denied. At the same time as the causal connection theory was popular, the goal of promoting economic independence as the primary goal of support was given primacy over all others. We saw numerous support orders limited to a short period of time. These cases arose primarily in the economic boom times of the mid-1980's. As with so many things, this analysis fell out of favour, and is rarely used any more.

The next notion which gained popularity was the idea of "*compensatory support*". In this support model, the needs of the dependant spouse are only part of the analysis. In addition, support is regarded as having an element of compensation — that is, to compensate the spouse for lost income and opportunities "suffered" as a result of roles taken on in the marriage. On this analysis, the spouse who has curtailed career opportunities to take on the necessary roles and responsibilities in the marriage looks to the other spouse as an insurer for that loss. While the notion of compensation is part of the overall analysis of spousal support, it should be approached with caution. Lump sums are often sought as compensa-

---

[3] *Ibid.*, s. 15(7)(*d*).

tion; they are rarely ordered. Rather, compensation becomes simply one other factor to consider when working out a reasonable level of support. It cannot be looked at in isolation, however. The losses that are sought to be compensated for must be analyzed in the context of overall gains within the marriage, particularly on the side of equalization or division of property.

In the 1990's we have seen a further swing of the pendulum, away from time-limited and compensatory models, to the notion that support may be for life in many instances. The quantum of support orders has been steadily rising. Economic self-sufficiency is seen as only one of the criteria to be considered. The notion of compensation is looked at more in the context of the duration of the award. If the support order has a compensatory element, that portion of it will not necessarily terminate on the spouse's remarriage or cohabitation, since neither of those two events negate the need for compensation. The whole spousal support area is in a state of flux. The only thing which can be stated with certainty is that nothing is predictable or certain.

Practically speaking, notwithstanding the enumerated criteria in the *Divorce Act*, it is suggested that the primary analysis of the support obligation will be a practical rather than a philosophical one. While it may be an enumerated goal of a support order to promote economic self-sufficiency, in most situations there is simply not enough money to support two households, and the promoting of economic self-sufficiency is a practical imperative, rather than a philosophical or legal one. Accordingly, the prime considerations will always be the degree of dependency, the extent to which the dependency can be decreased by the dependent spouse's own efforts to become self-sufficient, and the extent to which the other spouse has the means to contribute to the dependant's needs and still meet his or her own needs.

2. Provincial Statutes

(A) WHO QUALIFIES?

In many provinces, the legislation relating to spousal support applies not only to spouses who have married one another, but in some circumstances extends the right to be supported to common law partners as well. The qualifications may vary from province to province, but generally speaking, the legislation is designed to recognize situations of economic dependency and to provide for support when these types of economic units break down, notwithstanding that there may be no marital relationship between the parties. An example of this type of extension of support rights is found in the Ontario *Family Law Act*.[4] Part III of the Act deals

---

[4]   R.S.O. 1990, c. F.3.

with support obligations, and extends the definition of "spouse" to include not only spouses who are married to one another, but also:

> 29 . . . . either of a man and woman who are not married to each other and have cohabited,
>
> (a)   continuously for a period of not less than three years, or
> (b)   in a relationship of some permanence, if they are the natural or adoptive parents of a child.

These two categories of "common law" spouses have the same rights and obligations relating to support as do married spouses.

(B) Criteria

In Ontario, the general rule is that each spouse has an obligation to provide support for himself or herself, and also to support his or her spouse in accordance with need, to the extent that he or she is capable of doing so. Accordingly, the primary obligation is to be self-supporting and to provide support in accordance with means and in accordance with the needs of the other spouse. The twin factors of "means" and "needs" are therefore the paramount criteria for support under provincial legislation, as they are under the federal *Divorce Act*. In each case "needs" will reflect the lifestyle of the parties while they were together, so reasonable needs will vary from couple to couple.

Like the federal legislation, the Ontario legislation, for example, sets out the purposes of an order for support of a spouse. This is done in s. 33(8), which reads as follows:

> 33(8) An order for the support of a spouse should,
>
> (a)   recognize the spouse's contribution to the relationship and the economic consequences of the relationship for the spouse;
> (b)   share the economic burden of child support equitably;
> (c)   make fair provision to assist the spouse to become able to contribute to his or her own support; and
> (d)   relieve financial hardship, if this has not been done by orders under Parts I (Family Property) and II (Matrimonial Home).

The court is to consider all the circumstances of the parties in determining the amount of support, including the following criteria, which are set out in s. 33(9):

> 33(9) In determining the amount and duration, if any, of support in relation to need, the court shall consider all the circumstances of the parties, including:
>
> (a)   the dependant's and respondent's current assets and means;
> (b)   the assets and means that the dependant and respondent are likely to have in the future;
> (c)   the dependant's capacity to contribute to his or her own support;
> (d)   the respondent's capacity to provide support;

(e)   the dependant's and respondent's age and physical and mental health;

(f)   the dependant's needs, in determining which the court shall have regard to the accustomed standard of living while the parties resided together;

(g)   the measures available for the dependant to become able to provide for his or her own support and the length of time and cost involved to enable the dependant to take those measures;

(h)   any legal obligation of the respondent or dependant to provide support for another person;

(i)   the desirability of the dependant or respondent remaining at home to care for a child;

(j)   a contribution by the dependant to the realization of the respondent's career potential;

(k)   if the dependent is a child,

  (i)   the child's aptitude for and reasonable prospects of obtaining an education, and,
  (ii)   the child's need for a stable environment;

(l)   if the dependant is a spouse,

  (i)   the length of time the dependant and respondent cohabited,
  (ii)   the effect on the spouse's earning capacity of the responsibilities assumed during cohabitation,
  (iii) whether the spouse has undertaken the care of a child who is of the age of eighteen years or over and unable by reason of illness, disability or other cause to withdraw from the charge of his or her parents,
  (iv)   whether the spouse has undertaken to assist in the continuation of a program of education for a child eighteen years of age or over who is unable for that reason to withdraw from the charge of his or her child,
  (v)   any housekeeping, child care or other domestic service performed by the spouse for the family, as if the spouse were devoting the time spent in performing that service in remunerative employment and were contributing the earnings to the family's support,
  (vi)   the effect on the spouse's earnings and career development of the responsibility of caring for a child; and,

(m)   any other legal right of the dependant to support, other than out of public money.

As under the *Divorce Act*, conduct does not affect the obligation to provide support. The focus of the Ontario legislation is very similar to that of the *Divorce Act*. The criteria can be viewed as essentially the same, the only difference between the two pieces of legislation, in general terms, being who qualifies for an order for support.

The issue of "spousal" rights and obligations for couples of the same sex is one which has been grappled with to a degree by many courts.

While there is some recognition that these relationships are "marriage-like", with many of the same economic dependencies arising from them, the courts have not extended the legal rights and obligations of the legislation to these relationships. Although (for example, in Ontario) there have been some law reform bodies recommending changes to legislation which would extend these statutory rights and obligations to same-sex couples, to date it has not occurred. These couples must therefore set up their own contractual sets of rights and obligations on the breakdown of their relationships. The case of *M. v. H.*[5] (at June 1996 under appeal to the Ontario Court of Appeal) dealt specifically with the rights of same-sex couples. On an interim basis, support was ordered forthe "dependant" partner in the relationship, Epstein J. holding that the limitation of the definition of "spouse" in s. 29 of the *Family Law Act* to partners of the same sex was unconstitutional. The case is under appeal, and the operation of the interim order has been stayed pending appeal. Any suggestion that same-sex couples have the same rights as heterosexual couples should therefore be approached with extreme caution.

B. SUPPORT FOR CHILDREN

1. The *Divorce Act*

(A) WHO QUALIFIES?

To be supported pursuant to the provisions of the *Divorce Act*, a child must fall within the definition of the term "child of the marriage" in the legislation. This means a child who is either under the age of 16 years, or 16 years of age or over and under the charge of the parents but unable, by reason of illness, disability, or other cause to withdraw from their charge or to obtain the necessaries of life. This definition includes children who are completing their education (including post-secondary education) and who are unable by this reason to support themselves. Generally speaking, when considering the issue of child support under divorce legislation, children are considered to be entitled to support until they complete their first post-secondary diploma or degree, as long as they remain in full-time attendance at school. At the time of writing (June 1996), significant amendments to the *Divorce Act* have received first reading in Parliament.[6] The proposed amendments, if passed in their present form, will substitute the following for the definition of "child of

---

[5] (1996), 27 O.R. (3d) 593, 17 R.F.L. (4th) 365 (Gen. Div.); supplementary reasons Ont. Gen. Div. (Doc. 93-FC-804), June 28, 1996.

[6] See Bill C-41, 2d Sess., 35th Parl., 1996. At the same time, the Department of Justice published a working draft of the Federal Child Support Guidelines, which enumerates the proposed regulations that will set out the Guidelines themselves and how they will operate.

the marriage".[7] It will be defined as a child who:

(a)   is under the age of majority and who has not withdrawn from their charge, or

(b)   is the age of majority or over and under their charge but unable, by reason of illness, disability, pursuit of reasonable education or other cause, to withdraw from their charge or to obtain the necessaries of life;

(B) CRITERIA

Again, under the *Divorce Act*, when dealing with an order for support of a child, the court may make such order as it thinks reasonable. The same factors as are relevant in determining an order for support of a spouse are also to be taken into account in determining an order for support for a child, namely, the conditions, means, needs, and other circumstances of each spouse and any child of the marriage for whom support is sought, including the length of time the spouses cohabited, the functions performed by the spouse during cohabitation, and any order, agreement, or arrangement relating to support of the spouse or child.

As was the case with spousal support, objectives of an order for support of the child are also set out in the Act, in s. 15(8), which reads as follows:

15(8) An order made under this section that provides for the support of a child of the marriage should

(a)   recognize that the spouses have a joint financial obligation to maintain the child; and

(b)   apportion that obligation between the spouses according to their relative abilities to contribute to the performance of the obligation.

This section is really a codification of the law as it has developed since 1968, namely, that child support is the joint obligation of the parents, and that the obligation should be apportioned between the parties in accordance with their ability to pay.

More and more, child support is being examined more closely, and parties are being asked to direct their minds very carefully to the issue of the items necessary to support their children. These include not only the obvious, such as clothing and babysitting, but also all of or a portion of the following types of expenses, depending on the needs, interests, and ages of the children:

- day-care expenses;
- housing expenses, including mortgage, taxes, utilities;
- transportation expenses, including family car, public transit, and the like;

---

[7]   *Ibid.*, s. 1(2), amending the *Divorce Act, supra*, note 1, s. 2(1).

- entertainment, including such items as birthday parties;
- recreation, including such things as club memberships, Cubs, Beavers, Brownies, Girl Guides, music lessons, skating lessons, art, drama, *etc.*;
- allowances;
- special education or tutoring;
- costs incidental to religious education, confirmation, *etc.*;
- university tuition;
- diapers, formula, related sundries;
- medical expenses, including drugs, eye glasses;
- dental expenses, including orthodonture;
- summer vacation, including holidays, trips, summer camp.

This list is designed as an initial guide to isolating the children's expenses. Once this is done, it becomes easier to apportion the load between the parents in accordance with their ability to pay, taking into account income tax consequences that will flow from certain types of payments. These consequences are dealt with more thoroughly below in "E. Income Tax Implications: Support".

The March 1996 federal budget brought in two significant and lasting changes to child support. The first is the institution of "child support guidelines", to determine child support in all cases decided under the *Divorce Act*. The guidelines are to come into effect on May 1, 1997. At the time of publication, the child support guidelines were still under revision and not available in their final format. It is critical that any mediator consult the appropriate guidelines for his or her province before mediating the issue of child support. After the federal guidelines come into effect, all child support under the *Divorce Act* must be determined in accordance with the guidelines. The guidelines are presumptive, meaning that a court cannot depart from them except in cases of "add-ons" or "undue hardship", which must be enumerated by the judge. The guidelines do not consider the income of the custodial parent, only that of the paying parent. The guidelines are designed to cover the average expenses of children. It will be possible to increase the guideline amounts for "add-ons" such as net child-care expenses; medical and health related expenses over $200 per year that are not covered by provincial or territorial health insurance plans; educational expenses for primary, secondary, or post-secondary education; and extraordinary expenses for extracurricular activities that allow a child to pursue a special interest or talent, or attend a specialized program. The expenditures of the family prior to separation will be considered in determining whether these "add-ons" are appropriate. It is currently (as of June 1996) unclear as to how the paying spouse's contribution to these add-ons will be determined. In addition, the guideline amounts can be departed from (either higher or lower) in cases of "undue hardship". Factors can include things like an unusually high level of debt incurred to support the family or earn a living, significant access expense, like travel and accommodation, and obligations for the support of other children, or spousal support obligations.

The guidelines will also provide a method for adjusting the support amount, in cases of split custody, where each parent has custody of one or more children, and in cases of shared custody, where the parents share custody in a substantially equal fashion.

The second change to child support includes a complete revision of the rules concerning the taxation of child support. This will be dealt with in detail below in "E. Income Tax Implications: Support".

2. Provincial Statutes

(A) WHO QUALIFIES?

Under provincial statutes, support for a child is generally required as long as that child is a minor. Definitions of minority will vary from province to province. In Ontario, the obligation of a parent to support a child extends to any unmarried child who is a minor, or is enrolled in a full-time program of education. The obligation to support a child does not extend to a child who is 16 years or over and has withdrawn from parental control. As is the case under the *Divorce Act*, generally, under provincial legislation, support obligations apply to children who are still at school.

(B) CRITERIA

The *Family Law Act* of Ontario sets out specifically the purposes of an order for support of a child. These are found in s. 33(7), which reads as follows:

> 33(7) An order for the support of a child should,
>
> (a) recognize that each parent has an obligation to provide support for the child;
> (b) recognize that the obligation of a natural or adoptive parent outweighs the obligation of a parent who is not a natural or adoptive parent; and
> (c) apportion the obligation according to the capacities of the parents to provide support.

This is very similar to the provision under the *Divorce Act*.

Section 33(7)(b) is interesting in that, for the first time, it focuses attention on the fact that a child may have several "parents". Under the *Family Law Act*, a parent includes a person who has demonstrated a settled intention to treat a child as a child of his or her family. Accordingly, in a combined family situation, a stepparent may well be recognized as a "parent" for the purposes of the legislation. What this provision makes clear is that a stepparent's obligation to support a stepchild is not as great as the obligation of that stepchild's natural or adoptive parent to support him or her.

In determining the amount of support, the same criteria are relevant, including the child's aptitude for and reasonable prospects of obtaining an education and the child's need for a stable environment.

Notwithstanding all of these enumerated criteria, the basic issue will still be what the child realistically needs by way of support, having regard to the lifestyle the parties enjoyed while they were living together, and the extent to which this level of lifestyle can be maintained by the parents now that they are living apart. As part of the move to guidelines for child support, the federal government is hoping that provinces will enact similar or identical guidelines to those which will govern child support under the federal divorce statute. It remains to be seen whether this will, in fact, occur. As a practical matter, courts are likely to apply the guidelines to all issues of child support, whether under the *Divorce Act* or under provincial legislation.

C. FINANCIAL DISCLOSURE

1. Legal Obligation to Disclose

Financial disclosure is a necessary precondition for working out resolutions of property and support issues. There are both practical and legal reasons for this.

Practically speaking, it is impossible for the parties to agree on a reasonable level of support without having a clear idea of the income and needs of each of them. Similarly, the parties cannot approach the question of property division without knowing what property there is to be divided and what the value of the property is. Often the property will not be divided in kind, but property that each party has will be set off against property that the other one has, and equalization payments will be made to ensure that each spouse ends up with an equal value of whatever property or assets provincial legislation decrees should be shared.

Legally speaking, financial disclosure is crucial. Agreements can be set aside if the parties failed to disclose to each other their significant assets, income, and liabilities existing at the time an agreement was made. For example, in Ontario the relevant section of the *Family Law Act* is s. 56(4)(*a*), which reads as follows:

> 56(4) A court may, on application, set aside a domestic contract or a provision in it,
>
> (*a*) if a party failed to disclose to the other significant assets, or significant debts or other liabilities, existing when the domestic contract was made.

The reason this is so is clear. For example, if a husband fails to disclose to his wife an asset worth $100,000 that yields annual income of $10,000, and the wife accepts a level of support that she believes is all the husband can afford, she has been misled and has relied on misleading information to reach her decision about settlement. Similarly, if the asset hidden by the husband is one that provincial legislation says should be shared, she has been cheated out of $50,000 of her settlement. All decisions should be informed ones; if the wife in either case had known the true state of affairs, she would not have accepted either the level of support she did or the property settlement she did. Because she did not have a complete picture, she would be able to attack the agreement in the future. Since the goal of mediation is to reach not only an agreement, but one that will be legally binding and that the parties can live with comfortably in the future, there is no point in mediating financial issues without complete financial disclosure; to do so is to invite an attack on whatever agreement is reached, and makes the mediation process a waste of time, money, and energy.

(A) WHAT CONSTITUTES FULL DISCLOSURE?

To make full disclosure, all income, assets, and liabilities must be disclosed. Even though a party might object, he or she must still disclose the following assets:

- property acquired after separation;
- property the other knows nothing about;
- income the other party knows nothing about;
- property owned prior to the marriage;
- property acquired by inheritance or gift;
- property that provincial law exempts from sharing; and
- property that will be shared pursuant to provincial legislation.

(B) VALUATION OF ASSETS, DEBTS, ETC.

Disclosure of assets has two elements:

- identifying the asset; and
- valuing the asset.

Identifying the asset is usually quite simple. Valuing the asset may be extremely complicated. Valuators can differ wildly in their estimates of the value of any particular asset, and valuation in itself has been the subject of numerous and lengthy articles. Generally speaking, the value of any particular asset will be its fair market value — the price a willing buyer will pay a willing seller on the open market. It is not book value, replacement value, or cost. In complex situations, it will often be necessary to obtain professional opinions on the valuation of various assets such as real estate, employment pensions, shares in private companies, family businesses, professional practices, and things of that nature.

Debts and liabilities must be disclosed also. These may include contingent liabilities, such as notional costs of disposition that would be attracted on the sale of the asset. For example, when valuing the matrimonial home, it is customary to take the estimated sale price of the matrimonial home and deduct from it any

- outstanding mortgages, liens, or encumbrances;
- real estate commission that would be paid, (perhaps discounted); and
- legal fees and other costs of sale.

The value then remaining is the net value that would be subject to division. The issue of notional disposition costs or tax costs should be approached with care. Of course, if an asset is being sold as part of the overall settlement, these costs will be incurred, and should be deducted as reasonable liabilities. If the asset is not being sold, the issue arises as to whether there should be any deduction for what are truly "notional" costs, or whether there should be no deduction at all. The party who owns the asset will argue that he or she will incur the costs at some point in the future, at the very least on his or her death, when the *Income Tax Act*[8] will deem a disposition. The other party, who may be looking to the value of the asset as part of his or her equalization entitlement, will want to have the highest value. Generally, therefore, the issue of notional disposition costs and possible discounting of their value must be addressed as part of the overall valuation issue. Pensions and their valuation pose particularly difficult valuation issues, and are extremely difficult, conceptually, to understand. An actuarial report of value, prepared by an actuary skilled in this area according to the specific guidelines mandated by the Canadian Institute of Actuaries, will be required in virtually every case. Even these reports must be scrutinized with care, and analyzed in accordance with the prevailing valuation principles of the case law.

Most provinces have regimes of property or asset sharing that provide for calculating the net value of assets in order to determine what should be shared.

2. Supporting Documentation

Most jurisdictions have specific court forms that are used to make financial disclosure. There is usually a section to list income from all sources, a budget section to list monthly expenses, assets sections (often broken down by categories such as land, bank accounts, stocks and bonds, and the like), and a section for debts and liabilities. The financial statement that is used in the Ontario Court (General Division) pursuant to the *Family Law Act*, and in Ontario divorce actions, is an example of this type of financial form. It is reproduced below in "F. Example of Financial Disclosure Form".

---

[8] R.S.C. 1985, c. 1 (5th Supp.).

Although the form is designed for court use, it is not limited that way. The form is usually used as the method of complying with the initial requirements of financial disclosure in negotiation situations, and should be used the same way in mediation. It is customary for the parties to exchange sworn financial statements and then to produce whatever additional documentation is required in order to substantiate the figures set out in the form.

The statements in the financial form should be verified by the clients or their solicitors to the extent possible by requesting additional supporting documentation to corroborate the figures set out in the statement. Examples might include some or all of the following:

- income tax returns to substantiate income;
- financial statements to substantiate corporate value;
- bank statements to substantiate values in bank accounts;
- RRSP statements to substantiate total value of RRSPs;
- real estate appraisals to substantiate the value of land, buildings, and homes, *etc.*;
- pension statements and actuarial valuations of pensions to substantiate pension values;
- benefits package statements to disclose the total benefits available to an employee and their value, particularly things like stock options and employee share loans, *etc.*, for senior employees;
- corporate valuations to substantiate the value of an interest in a closely held corporation;
- partnership agreements to show any particular rights the partners have against one another, and to give some indication of the value of a partnership interest;
- shareholder's agreements to show the potential value of a shareholder's interest;
- insurance policies to confirm the choice of beneficiary, the extent of insurance, and benefits payable;
- copies of leases, telephone bills, VISA and department store accounts, utility bills, and tax bills, *etc.*, to corroborate estimated expenses.

This list is not meant to be exhaustive, but to indicate some areas where supporting documentation and professional valuations could, and often should, be obtained.

D. INCOME TAX IMPLICATIONS: PROPERTY

All the provinces have slightly different regimes for property sharing, ranging from deferred community for certain assets only, to more complete deferred property sharing. A "deferred" regime is one in which the actual sharing of the property or its value is postponed until a triggering event happens, usually something like separation, divorce, or death. Until one of the triggering events happens, the parties remain "separate as to property", which means that each can deal with his or her own property as he or she sees fit.

Most provinces treat the family home in a special way, both in terms of eventual sharing and its treatment during cohabitation. For example, in Ontario the general rule is that the value of the matrimonial home will be shared equally regardless of any special circumstances relating to its acquisition; during cohabitation of the parties neither spouse may sell or mortgage the family home without the other spouse's consent.

Whatever the scheme, the mediator must know and understand it fully before attempting to mediate these issues, and must be aware of tax consequences to certain property transfers. Property is an extraordinarily complex and difficult area of family law. It is usually important to have the help of outside experts, such as chartered accountants, valuators, or others, to help with the resolution of property issues.

It should be noted that since 1993, the special tax rules for spouses concerning attribution, joint elections, principal residence exemptions, and RRSP transfers apply to common law spouses as well. The *Income Tax Act* defines common law spouses as "Persons of the opposite sex, cohabiting in a conjugal relationship who cohabited throughout the preceding twelve months or who are the parents of the same child".

1. Property Transfers Between Spouses

The federal *Income Tax Act* is quite old-fashioned in terms of its treatment of married couples when dealing with transfers of property between spouses, essentially treating husband and wife as one person. The Act taxes the income or capital gains of the party who is the original owner of the asset, even if the other spouse receives the benefit. This taxation rule, known as "attribution", may be acceptable when couples are together, but is most unfair when applied to separating couples who are making a property settlement.

2. The Attribution Rules

(A) THE GENERAL RULE

An attribution rule is one that disallows the split of income between spouses, and attributes it all to the donor spouse who had the asset in the first place. Attribution applies in two separate situations:

- income; and
- capital gains.

Income attribution applies where the property transferred is income producing. For example, if the wife has an income-producing asset, like shares paying high dividends, and wishes to transfer some or all of the shares to her husband in order to split the income on the shares between them and save some income tax, the *Income Tax Act* will not permit this to happen. Even if the wife transfers the shares to her husband, the *Income Tax Act* will treat all the income on all the shares as being the wife's, and will tax it all in her hands. She must pay all the tax, but the husband will get to keep the dividend income. If, however, in that example, the husband sold the shares for more than the wife had bought them, this would trigger a capital gain — an increase in value of capital property from the date it is acquired to the date it is sold. Again, the general rule is that the capital gain would be attributed back to the wife, who would have to pay tax on the taxable portion. This is how attribution generally works between spouses. As mentioned before, this is quite unfair when applied to separating spouses who are attempting to resolve financial issues between them.

(B) SPECIAL RULES FOR SEPARATED SPOUSES

Because the general attribution rules caused a great deal of hardship to separated spouses, and property transfers often would have to be delayed until after a divorce (when the parties are no longer husband and wife), special rules were enacted to avoid the hardship. There are two kinds of special rules relating to attribution:

- automatic; and
- by election.

Automatic: If a couple has separated pursuant to a written separation agreement or court order, and there are transfers of income property between them, there is no longer any attribution of income between them. This occurs automatically.

By election: If the separated couple (living apart pursuant to a written separation agreement or court order) does not wish to have attribution of capital gains between them, they must jointly choose this option. To make this choice, they must sign a joint written election not to have the capital gains attribution provisions of the *Income Tax Act* apply to them.

3. Principal Residence Exemption

The family home is given special treatment, not only by provincial family law legislation in terms of how it is to be shared and how each spouse's right to live in it is to be protected, but also by the federal *Income Tax Act* in terms of its tax treatment. The *Income Tax Act* gives a taxpayer's "principal residence" special tax treatment, and if certain conditions are met, when the principal residence is sold any capital gain realized on the sale of the property will be tax free. Each family unit may have only one principal residence, which may be designated as such if, and only if:

- the property is solely or jointly owned;
- the taxpayer, his or her spouse or former spouse, or dependent child ordinarily inhabits the property after 1981;
- no other property is designated in this way by the taxpayer or his or her spouse (except for a spouse who has been living separate and apart from his or her spouse throughout the year); and
- the taxpayer is a resident of Canada.

If the spouses separate, and one of them owns the home and the other spouse lives in it, it will still remain the principal residence of the spouse who owns it. The spouses will continue to be viewed by the *Income Tax Act* as a single family unit until the end of the year in which they separate, and during that time they can only have one principal residence. If they remain living separate and apart, in the following years each can have his or her own principal residence with the special tax treatment.

The principal residence provisions of the *Income Tax Act* are very complex. This is a very general overview of what they are and cannot be relied on as a statement of the law. This description is designed to alert the mediator to the issues and potential problems of the family home, and to suggest that expert advice be obtained to deal with this issue.

4. Registered Retirement Savings Plans

Registered Retirement Savings Plans (RRSPs) provide a popular way to amass savings and create a tax deferral at the same time. A yearly contribution to an RRSP to the statutory maximum is fully tax deductible, creating an immediate tax saving, and all interest earned on all contributions to the RRSP (whether these have been fully deductible or not) are completely tax sheltered as long as the money remains in the plan.

As soon as funds are withdrawn from the plan, they are fully taxable in the hands of the recipient. This is why the plans create only a deferral of tax. Payment of income tax is postponed until the funds are withdrawn. It is generally expected that the funds will be accumulated until the taxpayer's retirement years, when he or she has no other income, and that the funds will therefore be able to be withdrawn gradually when the taxpayer has a low taxable income and will be taxed at a lower rate than they would have been when they went into the plan.

If, as part of a property settlement, it is necessary to use the funds in a RRSP and withdraw them in the recipient's prime earning years, a huge tax liability would result if the general rules were applied.

Again, there are special rules for separated spouses that allow for a less onerous result. All or part of one spouse's RRSP can be transferred completely tax free to the other spouse's RRSP if the following conditions are met:

- the transfer is made on or after marriage breakdown;
- the transfer is made pursuant to a written separation agreement or court order;
- the order or agreement requires the transfer in settlement of issues that arise out of the marriage; and
- the funds must go directly from one plan into another.

Revenue Canada must receive a copy of the order or agreement and a special form within 30 days of the transfer.

While it will be advantageous from a tax point of view for the original owner of the RRSP to make use of these special rules, it may not be to the advantage of the recipient spouse to receive the funds this way. As has been mentioned, the funds must go directly into an RRSP of the recipient spouse. If he or she needs the funds immediately to purchase a home or meet living expenses, the collapse of his or her plan or the withdrawal of any funds from it will trigger an immediate income tax liability in the hands of the recipient. What this means is that if a lump sum payment is funded by an RRSP transfer, the recipient spouse will end up with less cash in hand than he or she would receive if a simple lump sum cash payment were made.

As is the case with all matters relating to income tax, issues are complicated and expert advice should always be obtained.

E. INCOME TAX IMPLICATIONS: SUPPORT

There are income tax implications not only for property transfers, but also for support payments.

1. Lump Sum Versus Periodic Payments

A support payment can be a single, once-and-for-all payment designed to sever all ties between the spouses (a lump sum) or may be a series of payments over either a fixed period of time, or continuing until the happening of certain events (periodic payments). Each type of payment has certain advantages and disadvantages.

Lump sums have the advantage of being once and for all, and of severing ongoing ties between the parties. Once paid, the recipient spouse need not worry about default in the future and difficulties in collection. Their disadvantages are that they are not tax deductible to the payer, may carry the risk of being varied in the future to provide for more money if the other spouse has used up the lump sum, and cannot be gotten back if the other spouse immediately gets married or lives in a common law relationship, two situations that might terminate or vary an ongoing support obligation.

Periodic payments have the advantage of being tax deductible to the payer, of being terminable if certain conditions are met (such as remarriage or cohabitation), and of usually being variable if either spouse suffers or enjoys a change in circumstances. Their disadvantages are that they continue an ongoing and often lengthy financial relationship between the spouses, carry the risk of default and the related cost and aggravation of attempts to collect, and provide a fertile ground for continued conflict and resentment between the spouses. Periodic payments are far more common than lump sums, because generally ongoing funds are required by a dependent spouse to meet day-to-day expenses, and there is usually not enough capital to fund an adequate lump sum payment.

2. Deductibility of Support Payments

As we have already seen, the general income tax rules disallow attempts to split income between spouses. However, where spouses separate, special rules come into play that allow this kind of division. The separated family unit usually still has only the same amount of family income, which must now support two households rather than only one. The deductibility of support payments operates as a method of splitting income between the two households and generally reducing the overall amount of tax paid by the family as a whole, thus creating slightly more family income.

The *Income Tax Act* has very stringent requirements that must be met in order to make support payments deductible. The requirements are as follows:

- the parties are living separate and apart, and remain living separate and apart during the remainder of the taxation year;
- the payments are made pursuant to a written separation agreement signed by the parties or pursuant to a court order;
- the payments are for the maintenance of the recipient;
- the payments must be a predetermined amount of money payable on a periodic basis, that is, at fixed, recurring intervals; and
- once paid, the funds must be at the sole discretion of the recipient.

Formerly, to be deductible, the payments had to occur after the signing of an agreement or a granting of a court order, which meant that if the payer had made any voluntary payments before, or had paid in anticipation of an agreement being signed or an order being granted, the payments would not be deductible. These stringent rules have been somewhat relaxed, and payments made prior to the signing of an agreement may still be deductible if:

- the payment is made in the year of or the year immediately preceding the signing of the agreement;
- the agreement refers to the prior payments specifically and states that they are to be deductible to the payer and includable in the income of the recipient; and

• all other criteria regarding deductibility have been met.

If a payer has been making voluntary payments and wishes to claim a deduction for them, a negotiated agreement that allows this deduction will often provide for the payer to pay the tax attracted by these earlier payments. The reason for this is that the recipient will likely not have planned for the eventual tax deductibility of these payments, not knowing that this would be the case, and often the money will have already been spent. Making prior payments deductible confers a very great benefit on the payer, and even if he or she pays the tax attracted by the payments in the hands of the other spouse, there is usually still a significant benefit to be gained.

Where the payment is deductible in the hands of the payer, the receipt of the support will be included in the income of the recipient.

3. Changes to Tax Treatment of Child Support

The government of Canada in the 1996 budget announced significant changes to the tax treatment of child support, to come into effect at the same time as the child support guidelines. From May 1, 1997, child support agreements or orders made on or after that date will no longer be tax deductible to the payer, nor income to the payee. The payments will be tax neutral. Orders and agreements existing up to May 1, 1997 will be unaffected, and the old tax rules will apply to them. However, if variations are made to existing agreements or court orders after May 1, 1997, the new tax rules will apply. Once the new tax rules apply, there is no "going back" to the old tax treatment. Third party payments must also be approached with particular caution. Unless a third party payment is specifically designated as being for the benefit of the spouse, and it is further agreed that the payment will be deductible or taxable, the payment will be deemed to be for the benefit of the child and therefore tax neutral. Similarly, payments on account of arrears will first be credited against child support, and will not be deductible or taxable. Only when all child support arrears are paid in full will payments on account of arrears begin to be credited against spousal support arrears, with its different tax treatment.

Where an order or agreement has a single payment of support for a spouse and children, combined, the support will be deemed to be for the child and children only, and thus tax neutral. It is therefore critical to address not only the allocation of support between a spouse and children, but how best to maximize the tax benefits available to the family by way of that allocation.

4. Other Relevant Tax Provisions for Marriage Breakdown

When dealing with the issue of support in the context of separation, it is not enough for the mediator to consider only the questions of the deductibility or includability of the proposed support payments. Two additional areas that should be reviewed are the tax deductions available to each spouse, and the potential use and tax effect of third party payments.

(A) Personal Income Tax Credits

There are various credits that can be claimed by taxpayers to reduce the amount of tax they pay. Everyone is entitled to a personal credit and, in some cases, a married or equivalent to married credit is available. For separated spouses, the spouse who has custody of the children can claim the equivalent to married credit for one child, and the dependant credit for other children, in order to reduce the tax payable. Certain child-care expenses are also deductible, and can be used to reduce the tax payable. There are various computer programs available which will calculate the respective tax positions of the parties, given various scenarios concerning support. It is strongly suggested that any mediator whose practice includes financial mediation of any kind should invest in this type of computer assistance, and learn how to use it. Tax rates and rules change frequently. It is critical to keep up to date. The *Income Tax Act* should of course be consulted and, as is the case with all tax matters, expert advice should be obtained to explore fully the most advantageous tax position for the parties.

(B) Third Party Payments

Often, for many different kinds of reasons, a payer spouse may wish to make certain payments for the benefit of the other spouse and children directly to a third party. These types of payments may include:

- medical and dental insurance;
- medical and dental costs;
- school fees;
- university tuition;
- camp fees; and
- mortgage and utilities.

Because the requirements to make a support payment tax deductible are so very stringent, it has been very difficult to make this type of payment fall within the defined criteria, and complex wording has been necessary in agreements or court orders to accomplish this. However, changes in the law since 1983 have made the task much easier. Third party payments will be tax deductible if the following criteria are met:

- The parties are living separate and apart both when the expense is incurred and when it is paid.
- There is a written separation agreement or court order that specifically describes the obligation to pay (for example, "the husband will pay all camp fees").
- Both parties must agree specifically that the payments are to be tax deductible to the payer.
- The agreement or court order must refer specifically to the application of ss. 60.1(2)[9] and 56.1(2)[10] of the *Income Tax Act*.
- The payments must be for the maintenance of a spouse or former spouse.

With the proposed changes to the taxation of child support effective May 1, 1997, it should be noted that only those third party payments that are clearly referable to the support of a spouse, rather than a child, will be eligible for the tax deduction following the changes to taxation of child support effective May 1, 1997.

Payments relating to the family home, that is, mortgage payments, utilities, and the like, will *not* be deductible if the payer owns the home or has any interest in it.

F. EXAMPLE OF FINANCIAL DISCLOSURE FORM

The following is a mediator's financial and property worksheet modelled on the financial disclosure form that is used in the Province of Ontario in the Ontario Court (General Division) for the purposes of both the *Family Law Act* and the *Divorce Act*.

This worksheet is reproduced with the permission of DIVORCEmate Software Inc.

---

[9] Am. S.C. 1994, c. 7, Sched. VIII, s. 22(1).
[10] Am. S.C. 1994, c. 7, Sched. VIII, s. 18(1).

Financial and Property Mediation Worksheet
Wife and Husband

FINANCIAL STATEMENT – Part 1
Incomes and Current Budgets

    1. Particulars of our financial situations and of all our property are accurately set out below, to the best of our knowledge, information and belief.

ALL INCOME & MONEY RECEIVED – MONTHLY
(Include all income & other money received from all sources, whether taxable or not. Show gross amount here and show deductions on pages 3, 4, 5, & 6. Give current actual amount where known or ascertainable. Where amount cannot be ascertained, give your best estimate. Use weekly, monthly, & yearly column as appropriate.)

CATEGORY	WIFE	HUSBAND	COMMENTS
1. Salary or Wages			
2. Bonuses			
3. Fees			
4. Commissions			
5. Child Tax Benefit			
6. Unemployment Insurance			
7. Workers' Compensation			
8. Public Assistance			
9. Pension			
10. Dividends			.
11. Interest			
12. Rental Income			
13. Allowances & Support from others			
14. Other (Specify)			
MONTHLY TOTALS			

or ANNUAL TOTALS		
or WEEKLY TOTALS		

OTHER BENEFITS

(Show all non–monetary benefits from all sources, such as use of a vehicle or room and board, and include such items as insurance or dental plans or other expenses paid on your behalf. Give your best estimate where you cannot ascertain the actual value.)

ITEM AND PARTICULARS	WIFE	HUSBAND
TOTAL		

GROSS MONTHLY INCOME & BENEFITS _____

CURRENT BUDGETS

CATEGORY	WIFE'S BUDGET for twelve (12) month period From To Show current expenses, or your best estimate where you cannot ascertain the actual amount.			HUSBAND'S BUDGET for twelve (12) month period From To Show current expenses, or your best estimate where you cannot ascertain the actual amount.		
	WEEKLY	MONTHLY	YEARLY	WEEKLY	MONTHLY	YEARLY
HOUSING						
1. Rent						
2. Real property taxes						
3. Mortgage						
4. Common expenses						
5. Water						
6. Electricity						
7. Natural gas						
8. Fuel oil						
9. Telephone						
10. Cable T.V.						
11. Home Insurance						
12. Repairs and maintenance						
13. Gardening and snow removal						
14. Other – specify						
FOOD, TOILETRIES & SUNDRIES						
15. Groceries						
16. Meals outside home						
17. Toiletries & sundries						
18. Grooming						
19. General household supplies						
20. Laundry, dry cleaning						
21. Other – specify						

CATEGORY	WIFE'S BUDGET			HUSBAND'S BUDGET		
	WEEKLY	MONTHLY	YEARLY	WEEKLY	MONTHLY	YEARLY
CLOTHING						
22. Children						
23. Self						
TRANSPORTATION						
24. Public transit						
25. Taxis, car pool						
26. Car insurance						
27. Licence						
28. Car maintenance						
29. Gasoline, oil						
30. Parking						
31. Other – specify						
HEALTH & MEDICAL						
32. Doctors, chiropractors						
33. Dentist (regular care)						
34. Orthodontist, or special dental care						
35. Insurance premiums						
36. Drugs						
37. Other – specify						
DEDUCTIONS FROM INCOME						
38. Income tax						
39. Canada Pension Plan						
40. Unemployment insurance						
41. Employer pension						
42. Union or other dues						
43. Group insurance						
44. Credit union loan						
45. Credit union savings						
46. Other – specify						

CATEGORY	WIFE'S BUDGET			HUSBAND'S BUDGET		
	WEEKLY	MONTHLY	YEARLY	WEEKLY	MONTHLY	YEARLY
MISCELLANEOUS						
47. Life insurance premiums						
48. Tuition fees, books, etc.						
49. Entertainment						
50. Recreation						
51. Vacation						
52. Gifts						
53. Babysitting, day care						
54. Children's allowances						
55. Children's activities						
56. Support payments						
57. Newspapers, periodicals						
58. Alcohol, tobacco						
59. Charities						
60. Income tax (not deducted at source)						
61. Other — specify						
LOAN PAYMENTS						
62. Banks						
63. Finance companies						
64. Credit unions						
65. Department stores						
66. Other — specify						

CATEGORY	WIFE'S BUDGET			HUSBAND'S BUDGET		
	WEEKLY	MONTHLY	YEARLY	WEEKLY	MONTHLY	YEARLY
SAVINGS						
67. RRSP / RSP						
68. Other – Specify						
TOTALS						

TOTALS OF WIFE			TOTALS OF HUSBAND	
Monthly Total	=		Monthly Total	=
Weekly Total x 4.33	=		Weekly Total x 4.33	=
Yearly Total / 12	=		Yearly Total / 12	=
MONTHLY WIFE'S BUDGET			MONTHLY HUSBAND'S BUDGET	

SUMMARY OF INCOME & EXPENSES WIFE		SUMMARY OF INCOME & EXPENSES HUSBAND	
Gross monthly income		Gross monthly income	
Subtract wife's monthly budget	–	Subtract husband's monthly budget	
WIFE'S MONTHLY SURPLUS / (DEFICIT)		HUSBAND'S MONTHLY SURPLUS / (DEFICIT)	

Property Statement – Part 2
LAND

(Include any interest in land owned on the valuation date, including leasehold interests and mortgages, whether or not you are registered as owner. Include claims to an interest in land, but do not include claims that you are making against your spouse in this or a related proceeding. Show estimated market value of your interest without deducting encumbrances or costs of disposition, and show encumbrances and costs of disposition under Debts and Other Liabilities on page 12.)

NATURE & TYPE OF OWNERSHIP *(State percentage interest where relevant.)*	NATURE & ADDRESS OF PROPERTY	ESTIMATED MARKET VALUE OF YOUR INTEREST AS OF VALUATION DATE: *(See instructions above)*		
		WIFE	**HUSBAND**	**COMMENTS**
		Valuation Date:		
	Matrimonial Home			
	TOTALS			

GENERAL HOUSEHOLD ITEMS & VEHICLES

(Show estimated market value, not cost of replacement for these items owned on the valuation date. Do not deduct encumbrances here but show encumbrances under Debts and Other Liabilities on page 12.)

ITEM	PARTICULARS	ESTIMATED MARKET VALUE OF YOUR INTEREST AS OF VALUATION DATE: *(See instructions above)*		
		WIFE	HUSBAND	COMMENTS
General household contents including special items a) matrimonial home(s)				
b) elsewhere				
Jewellery				
Works of art				
Vehicles & boats				
Other special items				
	TOTALS			

SAVINGS & SAVINGS PLANS

(Show items owned on the valuation date by category. Include cash, accounts in financial institutions, registered retirement or other savings plans, deposit receipts, pensions and any other savings.)

CATEGORY	INSTITUTION	ACCOUNT NUMBER	AMOUNT AS OF VALUATION DATE:		
			WIFE	HUSBAND	COMMENTS
		TOTALS			

SECURITIES

(Show items owned on the valuation date by category. Include shares, bonds, warrants, options, debentures, notes and any other securities. Give your best estimate of market value if the items were to be sold on the open market.)

CATEGORY	DESCRIPTION	NUMBER	ESTIMATED MARKET VALUE AS OF VALUATION DATE:		
			WIFE	HUSBAND	COMMENTS
		TOTALS			

LIFE & DISABILITY INSURANCE

(List all policies owned on the valuation date.)

COMPANY & POLICY NO.	KIND OF POLICY	OWNER	BENEFICIARY	$ FACE VALUE	CASH SURRENDER VALUE AS OF VALUATION DATE:		
					WIFE	HUSBAND	COMMENTS
				TOTALS			

ACCOUNTS RECEIVABLE

(Give particulars of all debts owing to you on the valuation date, whether arising from business or from personal dealings.)

PARTICULARS	AMOUNT AS OF VALUATION DATE:		
	WIFE	HUSBAND	COMMENTS
TOTALS			

BUSINESS INTERESTS

(Show any interest in an unincorporated business owned on the valuation date. A controlling interest in an incorporated business may be shown here or under Securities on page 9. Give your best estimate of market value if the business were to be sold on an open market.)

NAME OF FIRM OR COMPANY	INTEREST	ESTIMATED MARKET VALUE AS OF VALUATION DATE:		
		WIFE	HUSBAND	COMMENTS
TOTALS				

OTHER PROPERTY

(Show other property owned on valuation date by categories. Include property of any kind not shown above. Give your best estimate of market value.)

CATEGORY	PARTICULARS	ESTIMATED MARKET VALUE AS OF VALUATION DATE:		
		WIFE	HUSBAND	COMMENTS
TOTALS				

DEBTS & OTHER LIABILITIES

(Show your debts and liabilities on the valuation date, whether arising from personal or business dealings, by category such as mortgages, charges, liens, credit cards, notes and accounts payable. Include contingent liabilities such as guarantees and indicate that they are contingent.)

CATEGORY	PARTICULARS	VALUE AS OF VALUATION DATE		
		WIFE	HUSBAND	COMMENTS
		TOTALS		

PROPERTY, DEBTS & OTHER LIABILITIES ON DATE OF MARRIAGE

(Show by category the value of your property and your debts and other liabilities calculated as of the date of your marriage. Do not include the value of a matrimonial home that you owned at the date of marriage.)

CATEGORY PARTICULARS	VALUE AS OF MARRIAGE DATE:	
	WIFE'S	HUSBAND'S
Land, excludes Matrimonial Home owned on Date of Marriage		
General Household Items and Vehicles		
Savings and Savings Plans		
Securities		
Life and Disability Insurance		
Accounts Receivable		
Business Interests		
Other Property		
Debts and Other Liabilities *(input as negative number)*		
TOTALS		

EXCLUDED PROPERTY

(Show the value by category of property owned on the valuation date that is excluded from the definition of "net family property".)

CATEGORY	PARTICULARS	WIFE	HUSBAND
TOTALS			

DISPOSAL OF PROPERTY

(Show the value by category of all property that you disposed of during the two years immediately preceding the making of this statement, or during the marriage, whichever period is shorter.)

CATEGORY & PARTICULARS	WIFE	HUSBAND
TOTALS		

CALCULATION OF NET FAMILY PROPERTY

	WIFE	HUSBAND
Value of all property owned on valuation date		
Subtract value of all deductions −		
Subtract value of all excluded property −		
NET FAMILY PROPERTY	$ 0.00	$ 0.00

	WIFE PAYS TO HUSBAND	HUSBAND PAYS TO WIFE
EQUALIZATION PAYMENT		

Notes and Comments:

Children's Expenses Budget – Part 3
Wife – Monthly

CATEGORY FROM WIFE'S BUDGET (NOTE: The following categories do NOT include "Other – specify" subheadings except as noted below.)	WIFE'S BUDGETED MONTHLY	%AGE ALLOCATED TO CHILD(REN)	$ TOTAL ALLOCATED TO CHILD(REN)
1. Housing (mortgage/rent, utilities, etc.)			
2. Groceries			
3. Meals outside home			
4. Toiletries & sundries			
5. Grooming			
6. General household supplies			
7. Laundry & dry cleaning			
8. Children's clothing		100%	
9. Transportation, personal car expenses			
10. Transportation (public, busing, taxi, etc.)			
11. Doctors, chiropractors			
12. Dentists (regular care)			
13. Orthodontist, special dental care			
14. Health & medical insurance premiums			
15. Prescription Drugs			
16. Life insurance premiums			
17. Tuition fees, books			
18. Entertainment			
19. Recreation			
20. Vacation			
21. Gifts			
22. Babysitting, day care		100%	
23. Children's allowances		100%	
24. Children's activities		100%	
25. Newspapers, publications, magazines			
26. Other – specify			
27.			
28.			
29.			
30.			
31.			

CHILDREN'S MONTHLY EXPENSES TOTAL _____

PARAS FORMULA GUIDELINE:

(Enter appropriate spousal income)	Spousal Income	%age of Total Income	Paras $ Share
WIFE		0.00%	
HUSBAND		0.00%	

COMMENTS & NOTES:

ANNOTATED BIBLIOGRAPHY

Abel, S., and Sussman, E. "Child Support Guidelines: A Comparison of New York, New Jersey, and Connecticut — A Synopsis" (1995), 33 *Family and Conciliation Courts Review* 4, 426-45.

Achten, S. "Living Life By Formula" (1996), 13 *Canadian Family Law Quarterly* 3, 205-17.

Cochrane, M. *The Everyday Guide to Canadian Family Law.* Toronto: Prentice-Hall Canada Inc., 1991. See *supra*, Chapter 2, Annotated Bibliography.

Davies, C. "The Emergence of Judicial Child Support Guidelines" (1995), 13 *Canadian Family Law Quarterly* 2, 89-110.

Finnie, R. "Child Support Guidelines: An Analysis of Current Government Proposals" (1995), 13 *Canadian Family Law Quarterly* 2, 145-62.

Hewlett, S. *When the Bough Breaks: The Cost of Neglecting Our Children.* New York: Basic Books, a division of Harper-Collins Publishers, 1991.

Mamo, A. "Apportionment of Child-Care Costs: The Emergence of Judicial Guidelines" (1995), 13 *Canadian Family Law Quarterly* 2, 111-43.

Weitzman, L. *The Divorce Revolution: The Unexpected Social and Economic Consequences for Women and Children in America.* New York: The Free Press, 1985. This is an important book documenting the serious hardship faced by women and children after divorce.

Wolfson, L. "Reflections on R. v. Thibaudeau" (1995), 13 *Canadian Family Law Quarterly* 2, 163-71.

Wolfson, L. *The New Family Law.* Toronto: Random House, 1987. This is an easy-to-read description of the *Family Law Act* of Ontario. It would be a helpful reference for Ontario parents.

Chapter Eight

Mediation in Practice: Professional Conduct

A. STANDARDS OF PRACTICE

Mediation is a relatively new field in professional practice, particularly the area of divorce mediation. While there have been court-connected mediation services for over 35 years in some jurisdictions in the United States, such as California, and in some parts of Canada for almost 25 years, namely, Alberta and Ontario, nevertheless the real impetus for developing mediation as a profession dates back to approximately 1980. Today, increasing numbers of mental health professionals, lawyers, and judges are endorsing mediation as a preferred approach for resolving family law disputes, and as a result, mediation is gaining recognition as a distinct mode of professional practice.

As the use of mediation becomes more widespread, there is considerable agreement among mediators themselves, as well as among legislators, lawyers, judges, and potential clients, that the following issues require clarification, namely:

- What is mediation?
- What are the standards of practice that define responsible, competent professional practice as a mediator?
- Is there a mechanism for supervision and discipline of mediators? That is, does a member of the public or another profession have a mechanism for complaining about conduct by a mediator that is inept, unprofessional, or unethical?
- If there is a governing body, what are its powers and procedures for decision making?
- What are the qualifications, that is, the training and experience, necessary to be a mediator?
- Are there guidelines for appropriate procedures to follow, a fee structure and other rules of practice that distinguish a good mediator from a poor one?
- Are there or should there be special rules of practice for lawyers acting as mediators?
- Are there potential conflicts between the lawyer's role as counsel and the lawyer's role as mediator?
- Similarly, are there possible conflicts between the role of the mental health professional as clinician and his or her role as mediator?

These basic questions deal with the issues of standards of practice, ethical conduct for professional mediators, and the qualifications necessary to become a mediator. It is important to address these issues for the following reasons:

- Mediation is a practice that crosses professional boundary lines; that is, at present there is no single profession that governs mediation and monitors the standards of practice within the profession.
- Mediators come from a variety of disciplines, namely, law, psychology, social work, psychiatry, counselling, and other disciplines whose standards of professional conduct may be in conflict with the standards that are considered desirable for mediators.
- In cases of lawsuits against mediators, the liability insurance that is usually held by professionals may or may not cover the practice of mediation.
- The interests of the public need to be protected. One of the distinct advantages of mediation is the fact that parties can arrange their own settlement of issues in dispute in an atmosphere of confidentiality. The key elements of mediation are private ordering of dispute resolution and confidentiality. However, these elements also create a great risk if the parties are unequal in bargaining power, if the mediator is incompetent or unethical, or if the parties fail to disclose adequate information for reaching an appropriate solution. Because litigation tends to be conducted in public, while mediation tends to be conducted in a private setting, protection of the public can only be achieved by the enforcement of standards of practice, codes of professional conduct, and, eventually, procedures for certification and licensing.

1. Definition of Mediation

Most definitions of mediation incorporate the following elements: Family mediation is a *non-adversarial* process, in which a qualified and *impartial third party* (the mediator) helps the family resolve their disputes *voluntarily* by agreement, which is based on *sufficient information*, and includes *independent legal advice* for each participant.[1]

Most definitions of mediation emphasize the fact that the mediator must act in an impartial role.

The mediator must:

- ensure that the parties reach a consensual agreement, that is, without duress;

---

[1] This definition is taken from the Code of Professional Conduct, in the Code of Ethics of the Ontario Association for Family Mediation, set out below in Appendix 10B, and the Code of Professional Conduct of Family Mediation Canada, set out below in Appendix 10D.

- ensure that the parties are properly informed, that is, that all relevant information has been exchanged;
- ensure that the agreement reached is fair and reasonable, particularly where children are involved;
- ensure that the parties are not under a disability (such as emotional disturbance, intellectual impairment, or fear of physical abuse) during the negotiations;
- clarify with the clients his or her professional role, that is, that the mediator is acting as a mediator and not as a lawyer, psychologist, or other professional. For example, the mediator (if a lawyer) should clarify with the clients that he or she cannot be the solicitor for either client if he or she has been their mediator. Similarly, the mediator should explain that he or she cannot be the individual clinician for either party after he or she has acted in the impartial role of mediator.

2. Codes of Professional Conduct

Codes of professional conduct contain both standards of practice and a code of ethical conduct. These terms can be described as follows:

- *Standards of practice* refer to the minimally acceptable, commonly understood practices of a profession. These standards are designed to protect the public and ensure a reasonable level of competence among practitioners. If followed, the standards of practice should protect a mediator from liability, because the standards establish the reasonable level of care to be exercised by a person practising mediation.
- A *code of ethical conduct* is usually thought of as the moral and social obligations of the professional that are imposed by the governing body on members of the profession. Adherence to an ethical code is usually required as a prerequisite to certification or licensing. Ethical codes have been described as the "do nots" of each profession. There are a number of conflicts still to be resolved between the ethical code of mediators and the ethical codes of some other disciplines, such as law or certain mental health professions. In addition, guidelines for the qualifications for mediators, their licensing and certification are still in the early stages.
- *Codes of professional conduct* are intended to govern the behaviour of professionals when they are acting in their capacity as mediators. These codes are not intended to replace or in any way compete with the codes of conduct of the mediator's basic profession, that is, law, psychology, social work, or other. The major elements that are present in most codes of professional conduct for mediators are set out below.

(A) COMPETENCE

It is recognized that mediators may be trained in different professional disciplines; however, the following levels of competence are essential:

- The individual should have specific training in the skills, knowledge, and techniques necessary to be an effective mediator.
- The mediator should agree to mediate only those issues for which he or she has adequate training and experience. That is, lawyers should not mediate custody and access issues unless they have specific training and knowledge with respect to such matters as child development, family dynamics, the effects on children and adults of separation and divorce, appropriate parenting techniques, and stages of physical, emotional, and social development of children. Similarly, a mental health professional should not agree to mediate such issues as property division, support, or complex financial arrangements unless he or she has adequate training in family law, income tax, and in some cases, accounting.
- Mediators should cooperate with other professionals who are assisting the clients, such as lawyers, accountants, or business evaluators and, in fact, should suggest that relevant professionals be retained to assist with specific issues in the mediation. For example, if the mediation is dealing with the issue of division of property, specialists such as business evaluators, accountants, or real estate appraisers may be needed to provide the necessary background information for mediating the issues in dispute.
- The mediator should attend continuing education programs and read recent literature with respect to mediation to ensure that his or her mediation skills are up to date.

(B) DUTY TO DESCRIBE MEDIATION PROCESS AND ITS COST AT OUTSET

The mediator should discuss the following information with the clients by telephone prior to the first session and/or during the first session:

- the process to be followed during mediation, including whether the meetings will be conjoint, individual, or a combination of conjoint and individual; also, who will be included in these meetings and the location of the meetings;
- a definition of mediation, and the difference between mediation and other forms of conflict resolution that would be available to the parties (such as litigation, arbitration, or marital counselling);
- the issues to be discussed in mediation;
- whether the mediation is to be open or closed, that is, the issues of privilege and confidentiality;
- the requirement to make full disclosure of all relevant information with respect to the issues being mediated;

- the advisability of both parties having independent legal advice throughout the mediation process and certainly prior to signing any mediated agreement;
- the process for terminating the mediation by either the clients, the mediators, the lawyers, or the court; and
- the mediator's fees and billing practices, including the hourly rate, the activities for which the clients will be charged, the method of billing, whether a retainer is required, cancellation policy, and expert witness fees if required in court.

During the process of explaining the mediation process to the clients, the mediator should also be assessing the suitability of the clients for mediation — that is, whether the clients show significant signs of emotional disturbance, or whether it appears that one party is under duress by the other party to the point where mediation would not be possible.

If for some other reason related to the client's personality or the ability of the mediator to relate to the clients, the mediator believes that the mediation is unlikely to be successful, then the mediator should share this information with the clients and either terminate the mediation or refer the clients to some other mediator who might be more successful.

If the mediator does not have the special knowledge or expertise to deal with the particular issues in dispute in the case, then he or she should terminate the mediation and assist the clients in finding a mediator with the requisite background.

(C) IMPARTIALITY

One of the primary features of mediation is the private ordering of dispute resolution. The role of the mediator in this process is to facilitate communication, offer educational input, and ensure that the parties are fully informed. All of these roles must be fulfilled in an impartial manner. That is, the mediator must disclose to the clients any biases the mediator might hold that are relevant to the issues in dispute. For example, if the mediator has strong beliefs that the custodial spouse should not be employed outside the home, or that young children should be in the primary care of a mother, or that it is important for children to have a strong religious upbringing, or that it is important for children to be raised in a home setting with mother and father figures, then these biases or beliefs should be communicated to the parties if custody of and access to children is being discussed. The mediator should discuss these beliefs or biases during the orientation session, that is, before the mediation process is under way. If relevant biases or beliefs do not become apparent until later, then they should be raised at the first opportunity.

The mediator should not mediate those cases where he or she has had a significant prior involvement, that is, if the mediator or a partner or an associate of the mediator has conducted individual therapy or counselling with either of the parties previously, or if the mediator has acted as legal counsel for either of the parties. In some cases the mediator may have offered marital counselling to the couple, and this may create some problems with respect to ethical standards. This is less of a problem if the clients initially contracted with the mediator to provide marital counselling but, if the counselling should fail or the couple decide to separate, to mediate some or all of the terms of a separation agreement. That is, the contract contemplated from the beginning that mediation would be tried in the event that the couple decided to separate. In any event, it would be essential as a minimum for the mediator to discuss fully with the clients the nature of the prior involvement and would require the express consent of both participants prior to continuing with mediation. The mediator should clarify the differences between his or her prior involvement and the specific tasks to be performed in mediation. Some codes of conduct expressly prohibit mediators from acting when there has been any form of significant prior involvement, either as a mental health professional or as a lawyer. Other codes of conduct are more flexible, but in every case, it is essential that the mediator make full disclosure of prior involvement and obtain the consent of both parties in writing.

Another area that needs consideration is whether the mediator can change from the role of mediator into the role of counsellor for one or both parties following the mediation process. It is probably inappropriate for the mediator, once he or she has taken on an impartial role, subsequently to take on any form of partial role in dealing with the parties. There are several issues that should be considered. For example, it is important for the client and for the general public to maintain a distinction between the role of the mediator and the role of the therapist. By changing from one role to another, the mediator may create a confusion of roles and give the clients contradictory messages about the mediation process. In the event that the clients need the assistance of the mediator to deal with subsequent disputes, the mediator would be unable to assist if, following mediation, he or she had offered counselling services to one of the parties.

There are some circumstances where it may be appropriate for the mediator to continue assisting the couple in an impartial capacity following the mediation. For example, if the parties wish further assistance in developing communication skills so as to carry out effectively the mediation agreement, the mediator is probably in a very good position, given his or her knowledge of the parties and their communication problems, to assist in this matter. This is unlikely to be in the form of long-term therapy, but rather is directed at implementing effectively a mediation plan. This could also be seen as preventing a breakdown of the mediation agreement because the parties lack the essential skills to carry it out.

It may also be appropriate for the mediator to assist in monitoring how the parents are carrying out their agreement and its impact on the children from time to time. Again this is an impartial role, and if the mediator did not carry out this function, then the parties would have to go to a totally new professional at considerable expense and further emotional turmoil for them and the children. Also, it would take some time to develop a sufficient relationship with the new professional so that the individual could monitor their progress. The key test is whether the mediator is maintaining an impartial role and whether the purpose of the assistance is to implement and stabilize the plan developed in mediation.

It is not appropriate for the mediator to represent either party as a lawyer, either prior to or subsequent to the mediation process. Some codes of conduct permit the mediator to act as a lawyer for one or both parties in uncontested matters or in matters that are totally unrelated to the divorce proceedings. Other codes of conduct prohibit not only the mediator, but also any partners or associates in the law firm, from acting on behalf of either party, either in contested or possibly even in uncontested matters in the future. It is probable that all codes of conduct would prohibit, as a minimum, acting on behalf of either party in a contested legal matter arising out of any of the issues discussed during the mediation. This would prohibit any representation of a party in a matter related to the divorce or separation and would probably prohibit a lawyer who had mediated financial and property issues from acting as the lawyer in real estate matters arising out of the divorce, such as the sale of the matrimonial home.

It is important for lawyers who are mediators to check not only the code of conduct for mediators in their jurisdiction, but also the code of conduct for their law society. The broadest rule is a prohibition against representing either spouse on any matter at any point in the future. As a minimum, it is essential that the lawyer disclose any prior involvement to the clients, either legal involvement or as a mediator, and that both clients consent, preferably in writing, to any subsequent involvement. It would be unwise and probably unethical for a lawyer to act in any contested family law matter once the lawyer has acted as a mediator.

The mediator should take constructive steps to ensure that the agreement will be fair and reasonable to both parties and the children. It is important that the mediator encourage both parties to have independent legal representation, preferably from the outset of mediation, so that both parties are aware of their legal entitlements and are making an informed decision. The mediator should ensure that both parties have full disclosure of all relevant information prior to reaching an agreement on any issue in dispute. This may mean referring one or both clients to an accountant, real estate appraiser, or business evaluator for expert advice as to valuations of property or the tax consequences of certain options. Or, it may mean consulting a doctor, teacher, or mental health professional about the children's health, educational progress, or emotional adjustment. The mediator can raise concerns about the fairness of settlement proposals directly with both parties together, as well as in individual caucuses. The purpose would be to ensure that each individual understood his or her rights and was making an informed decision without duress.

On the one hand, mediation is a voluntary process whereby parties reach an agreement that they have engineered. Mediation encourages private ordering, but on the other hand there is an obligation on the part of the mediator to prevent a grossly unfair result, particularly where children are involved. While the mediator should not interfere with most settlements arrived at by the parties, nevertheless the mediator may need to intervene in the following types of circumstances:

- where the mediator realizes that there is a considerable inequality of bargaining power between the spouses, such that one spouse appears to be under duress by the other spouse to reach a particular agreement;
- where one party is seriously emotionally disturbed and therefore unable to negotiate as an equal;
- where one party is withholding significant relevant information from the other and refuses to disclose this;
- where one party is feeling so guilty about the marriage breakdown or is so anxious to reconcile that he or she is unable to protect his or her own interests; and
- where one party is being coerced to give up certain rights in return for other benefits. For example, one spouse may be pressured into giving up the right to support in exchange for custody of the children.

In all of these circumstances, it is important for the mediator to discuss these issues with the clients and, if necessary, with their solicitors. If the mediator feels that the issue can be resolved by referring one or both clients out for additional assistance, from a therapist or an accountant, for example, then this should be done, and the mediation may need to be delayed until this occurs. If the situation cannot be remedied, then the mediator may have to withdraw from the mediation and should write a letter to the clients and their lawyers explaining the reason for this action.

(D) DUTY OF CONFIDENTIALITY

In both open mediation and closed mediation, the mediator should clarify from the outset that he or she will not voluntarily disclose to any third party information that is obtained during the mediation process except under the following circumstances:

- if both parties consent to the release of information in writing to a particular individual or organization;

- if the mediator is ordered to disclose information by an appropriate judicial authority or is required to disclose information by law;
- if the mediator has reasonable cause to believe that there may be an actual or potential threat to human life or safety;
- if non-identifying information is needed for research or educational purposes. If the clients are the subject of research, they should each have given their consent to participate.

The mediator should explain to the clients that even though the mediator will not voluntarily disclose information, he or she may be obligated to do so, for example, if the mediator learns information that creates a concern about physical or sexual abuse of children. In this case, the mediator would be under a statutory or ethical duty to provide the child welfare authorities with this information. In addition, even if the parties agree in writing that the mediator will not be called as an expert witness to testify in court, the court may decide that the mediator's testimony is essential to the issues in dispute and may require that the mediator testify.

It is important for the mediator to determine whether there are individuals whom the mediator should speak to with respect to the issues in dispute. For example, in a child custody dispute, the mediator may consider it essential to speak to the schoolteacher and the family doctor. In financial mediation, the mediator may wish to speak to the accountant or a property appraiser. The mediator should ask the spouses to sign a consent form permitting the mediator to receive and, if necessary, exchange information with specific individuals or agencies. In addition, the mediator will want permission to speak to the lawyers, new spouses, and significant caretakers for the children. In each case, it is important that both parents consent to these discussions.

(E) INDEPENDENT LEGAL ADVICE

It is the duty of every mediator to advise clients to obtain independent legal advice prior to commencing mediation and certainly before signing any agreement. The purpose of independent legal advice is to ensure that both clients are fully informed about:

- their legal rights and entitlements;
- alternative proposals for resolving the issues in dispute; and
- the consequences of an agreement under the law. For example, the clients must understand that the agreement will be binding unless the agreement was made under duress or without full disclosure of relevant information.

Lawyers can assist the clients to prepare and then swear their financial information forms.

(F) DUTY TO ENSURE NO HARM OR PREJUDICE TO PARTICIPANTS

The mediator is under a duty to suspend or terminate mediation whenever he or she believes that the process may be harmful or prejudicial to one or more of the participants. That is, the mediator should suspend or terminate the mediation when the mediator suspects that one or both parties are either unwilling or unable to participate effectively in the mediation process. For example, one party may be suffering from a serious emotional disorder and be unable to bargain in a reasonable manner. The mediator should also end mediation when he or she believes that the mediation is no longer useful, in order to avoid unnecessary expenses for the clients.

If the mediation process is suspended or terminated, the mediator should suggest additional professional services to the parties, if they are appropriate. For example, the mediator may recommend that one or both parties obtain individual counselling or that one or both parties have the assistance of an accountant or tax lawyer prior to resuming mediation.

The mediator has a duty to ensure that both clients are reaching agreement freely, voluntarily, and without duress. Despite the mediator's obligation to ensure that participants are not harmed or prejudiced by their participation in mediation, it is also a fundamental principle of mediation that the participants can design their own agreement, voluntarily, without being bound by statutes or common law. The mediator must walk a fine line between permitting the clients to design their own agreement and permitting an unreasonable agreement to occur. At a minimum, the mediator needs to draw the client's attention to possible areas of unfairness, and may need to discuss these with the client's counsel.

These are the principal issues that are generally addressed in professional codes of conduct. An example of such a code is the Code of Professional Conduct that has been adopted by the Ontario Association for Family Mediation.[2] This was the first code of conduct for family mediators in Canada. Family Mediation Canada has also adopted a federal code,[3] and several provinces have developed their own provincial codes.

3. Role of the Lawyer

The role of the lawyer in the practice of family law has changed considerably during the past two decades. According to the traditional role, each spouse selected a lawyer who would represent his or her interests against the other spouse. That often precipitated the entry of spouses into a system that made them adversaries even when there may have been no particular issue in conflict.

---

[2]   *Supra*, note 1, set out below in Appendix 10B.
[3]   *Supra*, note 1, set out below in Appendix 10D.

Conversely, the expanding use of family mediation has created at least three possible role options for lawyers when couples have made a decision to separate or divorce.

(A) INDEPENDENT LEGAL ADVOCATE

As an independent legal advocate, the lawyer performs the following functions:

- is familiar with the practice of law and supportive of family mediation;
- represents one of the spouses in conflict;
- where appropriate, recommends that clients try mediation and refers clients to a mediator; and
- consults on the terms of mediation with the mediator and other lawyer and is committed to same.

Specifically, Rule 10, paragraph 6A, of the Commentary in the Rules of Professional Conduct of the Law Society of Upper Canada, requires that:

> The lawyer should consider the appropriateness of ADR to the resolution of issues in every case and, if appropriate, the lawyer should inform the client of ADR options and, if so instructed, take steps to pursue those options.

(B) IMPARTIAL LEGAL CONSULTANT

This option is not accepted at present in Canada but is accepted in some jurisdictions in the United States.

As an impartial legal consultant, the lawyer performs the following functions:

- contracts carefully with both spouses to ensure that his/her functions preclude representing either spouse in any capacity during or after mediation;
- functions as an impartial consultant on legal issues and points of law to the couple;
- provides neutral input to both spouses about their rights and responsibilities before the law; and
- consults with the mediator as required, to remain informed on the progress of the couple and the issues resolved.

(C) MEDIATOR

This is a nontraditional role because lawyers usually represent one of the sides in a dispute.

As a mediator, the lawyer performs the following functions:

- places herself/himself in a non-adversarial position impartially between the two spouses;

- contracts carefully with both spouses to ensure their understanding that she/he is not functioning as a legal advocate for either spouse;
- encourages each spouse to obtain separate legal counsel (some lawyers as mediators will refuse to mediate unless separate legal counsel is arranged);
- establishes collaboration with both lawyers consistent with the professional practice of family mediation; and
- submits a report of resolutions reached to both clients and their lawyers when mediation is concluded.

The roles and functions now possible for lawyers specializing in family law are expanding. Lawyers should attend family mediation training programs that include specific reference to the knowledge and skills required by such roles.

4. Areas of Conflict for Lawyers Acting as Mediators

There is some concern that there may be conflicts between the requirements for lawyers when they are acting in a legal capacity and when they are acting as mediators. The most important concern is whether lawyers are violating their code of professional legal conduct by acting on behalf of parties who are in a conflict of interest. Virtually all codes of conduct for lawyers require that they act in a partisan fashion and clearly advocate their client's position. There are usually strong rules prohibiting or limiting any situations in which lawyers may be acting for parties who are adverse in interests.

Those jurisdictions that have addressed the issue of the lawyer as mediator generally have set out special rules in order to protect the public and preserve the traditional role of the lawyer. That is, most codes of professional conduct require that the lawyer acting as mediator must make the clients aware of the following:

- whether the lawyer has acted previously in some capacity for one or both parties. This matter must be disclosed to the other party and fully discussed. If the lawyer has acted in a legal capacity for one or both parties, the lawyer probably should not act as a mediator in the case;
- that the mediator will strongly recommend that both parties obtain independent legal advice throughout the mediation process and certainly before signing any agreement;
- that the lawyer who is acting as a mediator will not give independent legal advice to either party;
- that the mediator can give legal information, but cannot explain the implications of the law with respect to each party's specific position;
- that the mediator will require full disclosure of all relevant information prior to negotiating a settlement on any issue;

- that the mediator will not act on behalf of either or both clients in a legal capacity following the mediation. This is particularly true of any contested legal matters, especially if they arise out of issues referred to mediation; and
- that the mediator will not deal with issues that are beyond the mediator's special training as a lawyer. For example, if the lawyer who is acting as a mediator does not have special training in dealing with issues related to custody of and access to children, then these issues will not be included in the mediation process.

In Ontario, the Law Society of Upper Canada has a special rule governing lawyers acting as mediators.[4]

One amendment that the Law Society made to the existing Rules of Professional Conduct[5] for lawyers practising in Ontario is that Rule 5, Commentary 11 be expanded to include a specific reference to mediation. Rule 5, Commentary 11 now provides as follows:

> The Rule will not prevent a lawyer from arbitrating or settling, or attempting to arbitrate or settle, a dispute between two or more clients or former clients who are *sui juris* and who wish to submit the dispute to the lawyer.

It would be helpful if Commentary 11 were amended to include a reference to mediation. For example:

> The rule will not prevent a lawyer from arbitrating, mediating, or settling, or attempting to arbitrate, mediate, or settle a dispute between two or more clients or former clients who are *sui juris* and who wish to submit the dispute the lawyer.

The committee did take the position that the Law Society should provide guidelines to those lawyers who wish to practise family law mediation. They suggested the following guidelines:[6]

- A lawyer acting as a family law mediator should not provide legal advice, but rather should encourage the parties to obtain independent legal advice.
- The lawyer acting as mediator and any member of his law firm should not accept legal work arising from the mediation. The purpose of this guideline is to avoid a possible conflict of interest.
- The Law Society should encourage mediators to obtain additional academic and professional training in mediation.

---

[4] See Communiqué 13 (October 24, 1986), set out below in Appendix 10A. This Communiqué sets out the specific behavior required of lawyers who are acting as mediators in Ontario.

[5] Law Society of Upper Canada, Rules of Professional Conduct, adopted January 30, 1987 in *Professional Conduct Handbook*, set out below in Appendix 10A.

[6] *Ibid.*, "Family Law Mediation", Communique Plus, Number 13 (October 24, 1986).

- The lawyer acting as mediator should be aware, and should make the parties aware, that the mediator may not be able to keep the contents of any communication from either of the parties confidential or privileged. In addition, the lawyer acting as mediator should explain to the parties that the communications he or she receives as a mediator are not protected by solicitor-client privilege and there is a possibility that the mediator could be forced to reveal all or part of a communication if ordered by a court of law to do so.
- The Law Society should inform lawyers acting as mediators that professional liability insurance through the Law Society will cover a lawyer acting as a mediator. Non-practising lawyers or those who restrict their practice to mediation should be encouraged to obtain separate insurance coverage as mediators.

5. Qualifications for Mediators

This is an issue that is being discussed currently by a number of mediation associations. Most associations have not reached a consensus on the qualifications for practising as a mediator, the nature of training required, the requirements for being licensed or certified, and the mechanism for disciplining individuals who violate the code of conduct. However, a number of associations, such as the Academy of Family Mediators, the Ontario Association for Family Mediation, and the Alberta Family Mediation Society have made considerable progress in dealing with these issues. All of these associations have developed standards for practising mediators, and the Academy of Family Mediators and the Ontario Association for Family Mediation have adopted guidelines and training requirements for mediators. The standards for practising mediators adopted by the board of directors of the Ontario Association for Family Mediation in 1986, and amended from time to time, include the following:[7]

AREAS OF COMPETENCE

In order to qualify for and maintain membership in the Ontario Association for Family Mediation (hereinafter referred to as O.A.F.M.) as a "Practising Mediator", an applicant/member must satisfy the Association that he or she possesses the areas of competence set out below:

1. PROFESSIONAL EDUCATION: A graduate or law degree.

   A. To be a member in good standing in one's own professional organization is preferable, but not essential, because:

   (i) Some mediators may not wish to practise their own profession(s);

   (ii) Some professions (e.g. counselling) do not have their own professional organizations.

---

[7] Adopted from the Ontario Association for Family Mediation, application form for "Practising Mediator" status. Reproduced with permission.

B. An exception may be made at the discretion of the Membership Committee for a person not holding a professional degree, but who has demonstrated the ability to function at an academic level, and has had an exceptional amount of applicable personal experience.

2. <u>KNOWLEDGE OF MEDIATION THEORY AND SKILLS</u>

A basic knowledge of theory and skills as set out in the "Optimum Standards" appendix is essential, but for the purpose of application for membership, or continuing membership, an applicant/member must show that he or she has:

A.   Taken five days or 40 hours of mediation training taught by a recognized mediator or approved by the Ontario Association for Family Mediation, Family Mediation Canada, or equivalent.

The 40 hours of mediation training needs to include a minimum of five hours in each of the following categories:[8]

(i)   Conflict resolution theories;
(ii)   Psychological issues in separation, divorce, and family dynamics;
(iii)   Issues and needs of children in separation and divorce;
(iv)   Mediation process and techniques;
(v)   Family Law including custody, support, asset evaluation and distribution, and taxation as it relates to separation and divorce; and
(vi)   Family economics (not required if the basic training is limited to custody mediation).

OR

B.   Taught such a course him/herself; or

C.   Had an exceptional amount of applicable practical experience.

D.   Taken 20 additional hours of relevant mediation theory or skills including a minimum of 5 hours of domestic violence training (to include screening, safety measures, safe termination and alternatives to mediation).

An O.A.F.M. member must continue his/her mediation education through attending courses and workshops and reading about new developments in the field.

3. EXPERIENCE AND CONSULTATION/SUPERVISION IN THE ACTUAL PRACTICE OF MEDIATION

An O.A.F.M. practising mediator must:

A.   Have at least two years of relevant work experience in human service ; and

B.   Have mediated a minimum of five cases to the point of agreement. It is preferable that the mediator consult with or be supervised by a practising O.A.F.M. mediator.

---

[8]   These categories are those suggested by the Academy of Family Mediators as requirements of basic mediation training for people applying for full membership in that organization.

If the applicant lacks the minimum qualifications outlined in 1, 2 and 3 above, he/she shall submit a resumé and meet with the Membership Committee to discuss his/her acceptability for membership on an individual basis.

4. <u>STANDARDS OF PRACTICE</u>

Each applicant/member must

A.   Commit himself/herself and adhere strictly to the O.A.F.M. Code of Professional Conduct as a Standard of Practice. No mediator shall venture into an area of practice beyond his/her own area of expertise.

B.   Adhere to the O.A.F.M. Domestic Violence Policy.[9]

It is important to note that anyone can become a member of the Ontario Association for Family Mediation; however, in order to qualify for the membership category entitled "Practising Mediator", an individual would have to meet the criteria set out above. The Alberta Family Mediation Society has adopted a similar set of standards and in addition requires that a practising mediator have mediator liability insurance.

ANNOTATED BIBLIOGRAPHY

Baker-Jackson, M., Bergman, K., Ferrick, G., Hovsepian, V., Garcia, J., and Hulbert, R. "Ethical Standards for Court-Connected Mediators". In J.A. Lemmon, ed. "Making Ethical Decisions" (1985), 8 *Mediation Quarterly* 67. This article outlines the significant qualifications in terms of knowledge, training, and experience of public sector mediators.

Bernard, S.E., Folger, J., Weingarten, H., and Zumeta, Z. "The Neutral Mediator: Value Dilemmas in Divorce Mediation". In J.A. Lemmon, ed. "Ethics, Standards and Professional Challenges" (1984), 4 *Mediation Quarterly* 61. This chapter considers both a neutral and interventionist approach to mediation in the light of ethical considerations.

Bishop, T.A. "Mediation Standards: An Ethical Safety Net". In J.A. Lemmon, ed. "Ethics, Standards and Professional Challenges" (1984), 4 *Mediation Quarterly* 5. This article discusses the American Bar Association's Standards of Practice for Family Mediators and their implications for lawyers who are in practice as mediators.

Cooks, L., and Hale, C. "The Construction of Ethics in Mediation" (1994), 12 *Mediation Quarterly* 1, 55-75.

Cramer, C., and Schoeneman, R. "A Court Mediation Model with an Eye Toward Standards" In J.A. Lemmon, ed. "Making Ethical Decisions"

---

[9]   See the O.A.F.M. Abuse Policy set out below in Appendix 3B.

(1985), 8 *Mediation Quarterly* 33. This chapter looks at the typical stages of reaching an agreement and discusses how the mediator can follow accepted standards at each stage of the process.

Dibble, C. "Bargaining in Family Mediation: Ethical Considerations". In J.A. Lemmon, ed. "Ethics, Standards and Professional Challenges" (1984), 4 *Mediation Quarterly* 75. This article considers both the dangers and benefits of bargaining in family mediation and addresses the role of the mediator.

Engram, P., and Markowitz, J. "Ethical Issues in Mediation: Divorce and Labour Compared". In J.A. Lemmon, ed. "Making Ethical Decisions" (1985), 8 *Mediation Quarterly* 19. This article examines the ethical procedures for divorce mediators by comparing divorce mediation to labour mediation.

Folberg, J., and Taylor A. *Mediation: A Comprehensive Guide to Resolving Conflicts without Litigation*. San Francisco: Jossey-Bass Publishers, 1984. See particularly Part Four, "Mediation As a Profession — Educational, Ethical and Practical Dimensions", p. 233. See also Chapter 10, "Ethical, Professional and Legal Issues", p. 244. This chapter contains a comprehensive exploration of ethics, standards of practice, confidentiality, and mediator liability.

Gentry, D. "Mediator Attitudes and Preferences Concerning Mediator Certification" (1994), 11 *Mediation Quarterly* 4, 353-59.

Goldberg, S.D., Green, E.D., and Sander, F.E.A. "A Dialogue on Legal Representation in Divorce Mediation". In J.A. Lemmon, ed. "Making Ethical Decisions" (1985), 8 *Mediation Quarterly* 5.

Landau, B. "Identity Crisis: Mediation, Lawyers and Mental Health Professionals" (1985), 11 *Therapy Now* 9. This article explores the role conflicts experienced by lawyers and mental health professionals in relation to mediation and custody assessments.

Lande, J. "Mediation Paradigms and Professional Identities". In J.A. Lemmon, ed. "Ethics, Standards and Professional Challenges" (1984), 4 *Mediation Quarterly* 19. This article considers how mediation principles derived from general theories of dispute resolution may conflict with the American Bar Association's Standards of Practice for Family Mediators.

Milne, A. "The Development of Parameters of Practice for Divorce Mediation". In J.A. Lemmon, ed. "Ethics, Standards and Professional Challenges" (1984), 4 *Mediation Quarterly* 49. This article considers various practice principles that would best serve the client, the mediator, and the practice of mediation.

Milne, A. "Model Standards of Practice for Family and Divorce Mediation". In J.A. Lemmon, ed. "Making Ethical Decisions" (1985), 8 *Mediation Quarterly* 73. This chapter contains guidelines for practice for both court-connected and private family mediators. These are included in a draft code prepared by the Association of Family and Conciliation Courts in 1983-84.

Morris, C., and Pirie, A., ed. *Qualifications for Dispute Resolution: Perspectives on the Debate*. Victoria, B.C.: U Vic Institute for Dispute Resolution, 1994. This is an excellent collection of articles on mediator qualifications and other important practice issues. Of particular interest are the introduction by Catherine Morris, and Part Three: Critical Perspectives, including the articles by Michelle Lebaron Duryea, Cheryl Picard, and Andrew Pirie.

Perlmutter, F. "Ethical Issues in Family Mediation: A Social Perspective". In J.A. Lemmon, ed. "Making Ethical Decisions" (1985), 8 *Mediation Quarterly* 99. This article focuses in particular on mediation services for low-income families.

Pirie, A. "The Lawyer as Mediator: Professional Responsibility Problems or Profession Problems?" (1985), 63 *Canadian Bar Review* 279. This author outlines the important ethical issues for lawyers who are acting as mediators to consider and makes recommendations that the bar associations not overly regulate mediation by lawyers at this point in time.

Saposnek, D. *Mediating Child Custody Disputes*. San Francisco: Jossey-Bass Publishers, 1983. See Part V, "Challenges and Professional Issues", particularly Chapter 13, "Ethics, Values and Morals in Mediation", p. 257.

Saposnek, D. "What Is Fair in Child Custody Mediation". In J.A. Lemmon, ed. "Making Ethical Decisions" (1985), 8 *Mediation Quarterly* 9. This article examines the concept of fairness from different perspectives — individual, family, sociopolitical, cultural, and moral — and considers whether this would result in different recommendations.

Silberman, L.J. "Professional Responsibility Problems of Divorce Mediation" (1982), 16 *Family Law Quarterly* 107. This article outlines the response of the various bar associations in the United States to lawyers acting as mediators.

Taylor, A. "The Four Foundations of Family Mediation: Implications for Training and Certification" (1994), 12 *Mediation Quarterly* 1, 77-88.

Chapter Nine

Mediation in Practice: Conclusion

A. AGREEMENT BY PARTIES

If the parties reach an agreement on one or more issues, the mediator prepares a report containing the specific terms agreed to by the parties. The form of the mediator's report should be worked out in discussions with both counsel and the parties, preferably at the beginning of mediation, so that all parties are clear about what they will receive from the mediator. The report is usually called a *memorandum of understanding*.

If the parties have not initiated court proceedings and are hoping to arrive at a full separation agreement with respect to all of the issues in dispute, then the issues resolved in mediation can be incorporated into the separation agreement.

If one or both parties have initiated court proceedings, then the issues resolved in mediation can be incorporated into *minutes of settlement* that would be filed with the court on consent in order to terminate the legal proceedings.

1. Memorandum of Understanding

This document should outline in clear, unambiguous language the specific agreement reached on those issues sent to mediation.

One of the factors that contributes to couples returning to court to relitigate agreements is the lack of precision of the wording in the agreement. It is very important that the mediator state as clearly and specifically as possible what responsibilities or privileges each party will have. If the parties are to share responsibilities and privileges, it should be clear:

- what responsibilities each party will bear;
- what privileges each party will have;
- under what circumstances a party will have such responsibilities and privileges;
- what notice one party is required to give to the other party;
- whether the responsibility is something that a particular spouse is required to do or whether it is something that the spouse can be requested to do, if he or she is available; and
- what will happen if one party is unable or unwilling to fulfil a responsibility or accept a privilege.

In general, it is preferable to set out:

- specific times for access visits on weekends, during the week, on statutory holidays, during school breaks, and at other times;
- specific times and locations for pickup and delivery; and
- whether the parties intend to permit additional access time on request and whether this will trigger an expectation for compensatory time.

The mediator can explain to the parties that in the future, once they are more comfortable with each other's involvement, they can behave in a more flexible way with respect to access times. However, at the beginning, particularly with clients who do not trust each other, a schedule that clarifies their respective rights and obligations is usually helpful.

It is very important to include the parties' intentions with respect to changes in custody or access arrangements in the event that the parties move more than a certain distance apart. Families are very mobile, and one or both spouses may move due to a job, a new relationship, for economic or other reasons. An arrangement that has worked well for a number of years may suddenly grind to a stop because a party wishes to move out of the city or even out of the province or country. It is important to anticipate that this may happen and to include a provision to cover this possibility. Many cases end up in litigation when this situation is not anticipated.

In cases of financial mediation, it is important to consider material changes in the parties' circumstances, such as:

- the loss of a job;
- obtaining employment for a previously unemployed spouse;
- the effect of illness or long-term disability;
- the death of a spouse; or
- the remarriage of one or both spouses.

All of these factors could constitute a material change of circumstances that should trigger a re-examination of the original agreement The process that the parties wish to follow when there is a material change in circumstances should be included in the agreement.

If the parties have agreed to mediate a new arrangement in the event that there is a material change in circumstances (such as remarriage or a move to a new province), the agreement should state how the mediator will be chosen and how the mediator's fees will be shared. That is, will one party pay the full cost, will the fees be shared 50-50, or will the fees be paid in proportion to gross income at the time?

It may be desirable to have an interim agreement, possibly for three to six months, before completing a final agreement. This would give the parties a chance to evaluate whatever plan they have chosen, both in terms of the best interests of the child and their own needs. An interim agreement would also give the parties an opportunity to adjust to the separation. At the time set for termination of the agreement, the parties could return to mediation to review the contents of the interim agreement and decide whether to continue with it indefinitely, for a further period of time, or whether to make appropriate changes. A time-limited agreement may be preferable in the following circumstances:

- if the child's needs, wishes, and/or stage of development change, and it is desirable to reconsider the previous parenting plan;
- if the parties' circumstances change such that a review is warranted;
- if the parties do not have independent legal advice, and a time-limited agreement would limit the effect of any adverse legal consequences.

If one or both parties refuse to obtain independent legal advice, the mediator should not witness the signature of the parties on the memorandum of separation. If both parties have solicitors, it is recommended that the memorandum of understanding be signed in the respective lawyers' offices.

Unless the mediator is a trained lawyer, the mediator should not attempt to draft a separation agreement for the parties. This is because:

- the mediator could be charged under provincial legislation with the unauthorized practice of law;
- the mediator may not appreciate the implications of certain clauses dealing with custody, financial matters, and releases in terms of their legal significance for the parties;
- the mediator could be sued if one or both parties are prejudiced as a result of clauses that are included in or omitted from the agreement; or
- the legal position of one or both clients could be adversely affected because of the mediator's lack of legal training.

Some lawyers hold the view that even if the mediator is a lawyer, he or she should not draft the complete separation agreement because:

- the mediator may only be dealing with some of the issues in dispute and therefore not have adequate information with respect to all of the issues and their implications for both parties that normally would be included in a complete agreement;
- drafting a separation agreement may create some role confusion in the client's mind about whether the mediator is acting as a mediator or a lawyer; and
- the solicitors for the clients may feel the mediator is usurping their role.

This issue should be fully discussed with both the clients and their solicitors in advance to clarify the expectations of all parties and avoid future confusion or problems. In fact, the lawyer and clients may wish to have the mediator draw up specific clauses of the separation agreement relating to mediation because:

- the mediator who is legally trained both understands the nature of the agreement reached and can express the client's wishes most clearly;
- the parties are saved the expense of having one or both lawyers who were not present during the discussions try to draft these particular clauses.

The authors recommend that even mediators who are lawyers draft a memorandum of understanding which could be changed into a separation agreement once the parties have received independent legal advice. The mediator should not witness the parties' signatures to the separation agreement.

In addition to the memorandum of understanding, the mediator should prepare a brief report. If the parties have initiated legal proceedings, then the brief report would be sent to the judge along with the minutes of settlement and a copy of the memorandum of understanding.

The memorandum of understanding should be sent to the parties and to their legal counsel, prior to signing, so that the clients can obtain independent legal advice. Both in the memorandum of understanding and in the brief report, the mediator should indicate that the parties have been strongly advised to obtain independent legal advice prior to signing any agreement.

This brief report should contain the following types of information:

- a statement of the issues that were sent to mediation;
- a statement of which issues were resolved and which issues are still in dispute;
- who was seen during the mediation, how often, in what combinations, and for what total period of time;
- a summary of the terms of the memorandum of understanding and some additional explanation or encouragement for the parties with respect to implementing the memorandum of understanding;
- the intention of the parties when arriving at an agreement;
- the basic responsibilities and privileges of each parent in the context of the best interests of the children;
- any significant concerns or possible obstacles that were identified during the mediation that may affect the ability of one or both parties to carry out the terms of the agreement, along with any suggestions for handling these difficulties if they should arise.

The mediator should indicate that he or she would be available to assist the parties should there be some initial difficulties in implementing the agreement or should difficulties arise in the future due to a material change in circumstance or developmental changes in the children. The covering report should also encourage the parties to overlook their own differences as spouses in order to cooperate in the best interests of their children. This is particularly important in situations where both parents want to maintain a close and loving relationship with the children.

2. Separation Agreement

The mediator should review the memorandum of understanding with the clients to be sure it accurately reflects their wishes and then should send counsel a copy of the memorandum of understanding, which can be incorporated into a full separation agreement. Unless the parties were engaged in comprehensive mediation, a separation agreement usually takes into consideration a number of issues that were not discussed during the mediation process.

Once certain issues have been agreed upon during mediation, the clients and their counsel usually continue to negotiate other related issues. For example, if the mediation involved custody and access issues, the lawyers might deal with financial matters, and would then draft a separation agreement including clauses with respect to:

- child support;
- spousal support;
- cost-of-living increase in support;
- division of property;
- possession and ownership of the matrimonial home;
- division of debts;
- material change in circumstances;
- share of pension funds; and
- releases with respect to future claims and liabilities.

It is hoped that the mediation process will set the tone for cooperative and reasonable bargaining with respect to issues that are not covered by mediation. The mediator should communicate to the lawyers any approaches that might prove helpful in maintaining a cooperative atmosphere. If the remaining issues are dealt with in an adversarial manner, it may undermine the parties' trust in each other and their willingness to fulfil their agreement on the issues that were sent to mediation.

Under the Ontario Rules of Civil Procedure,[1] the parties are encouraged to disclose information to each other fully and at an early stage. This is to minimize suspicion and distrust and encourage settlement. It is important to note that there is no onus on a spouse residing in Ontario to request disclosure of relevant financial information; rather there is an obligation on both spouses to provide the other spouse with full and complete disclosure. The penalty for failing to disclose is that any domes-

---

[1] R.R.O. 1990, Reg. 194.

tic contract, such as a separation agreement, can be set aside by a court because one party failed to disclose significant assets, debts, or liabilities to the other. In addition, certain procedural steps are now required in civil cases, particularly family law cases, to encourage a negotiated settlement rather than an adversarial battle. For example, all contested matters must be heard in a pre-trial conference or by a "dispute resolution officer" prior to proceeding to litigation. These rules should encourage new practices among lawyers and should make the approach of family law lawyers more compatible with the type of approach and objectives used by mediators.

3. Minutes of Settlement

If one or more parties have initiated litigation, then those issues that have been resolved in mediation can be finalized in minutes of settlement. This document is filed with the court, and in most cases, the judge will sign an order in keeping with the terms of the minutes of settlement.

In the event that there are still outstanding issues that have not been resolved, partial minutes of settlement can be filed with the court that deal with only those issues that have been settled.

B. PARTIAL AGREEMENT OR NO AGREEMENT BY PARTIES

In the event that the parties fail to agree on one or more of the issues in dispute, the mediator or one or both parties may terminate the mediation process. One or both lawyers may recommend that mediation terminate, but the decision is made by the clients or mediator.

1. Termination by Mediator

The mediator may decide to terminate the mediation process, prior to an agreement, for various reasons, for example:

- Unequal bargaining power can arise because of many factors, such as the following: one party has achieved an emotional divorce, while the other party is still longing for reconciliation; one party has a good grasp of relevant information with respect to the issues in dispute, but the other party has very little knowledge or information about the issues in dispute (this arises particularly with financial matters); one party uses duress on the other party (for example, physical violence, threats, harassment, refusal to pay support, threatened legal action for custody, or withholding of access); differences in education; differences in financial status; differences in emotional stability; differences in motivation for ending the marriage (for example, desire to remarry, or guilt regarding marriage breakdown).

- The mediator feels that one party is delaying the mediation in order to take advantage of a status quo situation (that is, one party may have *de facto* custody of the children and believe it is to his or her advantage to delay mediation).
- The parties may be so hostile to each other that the mediation is unlikely to be productive and may even be destructive of the emotional health of one of the parties.
- One party may be willing to enter an agreement that the mediator feels is detrimental to the wellbeing of the children. The mediator should exercise this discretion carefully. In mediation, the emphasis should be on private ordering, that is, allowing the parties to arrive at a bargain that they feel is reasonable and acceptable. However, if a mediator participates in what is really an unconscionable transaction, then the mediator, on ethical grounds, should withdraw. This is particularly true when there is a risk to children. In any event, if the mediator suspects abuse or neglect of children, the mediator has a statutory duty to report to the child welfare authorities. This duty should be explained to the parents.
- One party fails to make proper financial disclosure or in fact misleads the other party with respect to finances.
- One party refuses to pay the mediator's fees within a reasonable period of time.

In the event that the mediator plans to terminate mediation without agreement by the parties, the mediator should inform the parties of the decision to terminate and should then contact counsel. The mediator should explain to both the parties and counsel the basis for the termination.

If the mediation is open mediation, then the mediator could prepare a report with respect to the mediation process, at the request of one or both parties. If the mediator has been asked for recommendations, then the mediator should include recommendations with respect to the issues in dispute as was agreed upon. In preparing the report the mediator should indicate:

- the amount of time spent in mediation;
- who was seen and the reasons for termination;
- a statement as to whether it would be desirable for the mediation to continue at a future date and under what circumstances (for example, once one or both parties have participated in counselling); or
- constructive suggestions as to how to deal with the major obstacles to a mediated solution.

2. Termination by Party(ies)

One or both parties may decide to terminate the mediation process because of:

- perceived bias by the mediator, for example, with respect to the sex, age, ethnic or racial group, socio-economic status, or religious preference of a party;
- a lack of confidence or trust in the mediator or the other party;
- a personality conflict with the mediator;
- discomfort during the mediation process, particularly in meetings with the other party;
- threats, abuse, or a perceived inequality of bargaining power;
- a belief that the mediator is not acting in an impartial manner;
- a belief that the mediator does not have a sufficient understanding of the children's needs; or
- a belief that the other party is using the delay to his or her advantage.

If one or both parties decide to terminate, this should be discussed directly with the mediator to see whether the issue(s) can be resolved. If the party still has some concerns, the party should discuss the matter with his or her lawyer.

The mediator should be open to hearing comments and criticisms about his or her process, and where the concerns are justified, the mediator should endeavour to change his or her behaviour in order to meet the needs of the parties, but this should not be done so as to please one party over another. If the mediator believes that certain changes would be desirable, these changes should be discussed first with the other spouse, so that it will not appear that one spouse is manipulating the mediator.

If the party is still not satisfied, then he or she can terminate the mediation. The party or the party's lawyer should draft a letter to the mediator and the opposite lawyer indicating the reasons for the withdrawal. The letter should also contain an indication of circumstances, if any, under which mediation could be resumed.

3. Termination Suggested by Lawyer(s)

Mediation can only be terminated by a client or the mediator. The lawyer can advise his or her client to terminate and raise concerns with the mediator, but it is not the lawyer's prerogative to make that decision. Certainly, it would be responsible conduct for the lawyer to voice his or her concerns with the client and the mediator if:

- the lawyer believes that the mediator has a bias on an issue that is highly relevant to the mediation (for example, with respect to the sex of the custodial parent, the age of the custodial parent, religious preference, sexual orientation, racial or ethnic group, or socioeconomic status, *etc.*);
- the lawyer is concerned that the other party is taking advantage of the mediation process either for delay or for initiating legal proceedings that are in direct conflict with the mediation process. For

example, one lawyer might suspect that the other spouse is dissipating or transferring assets to prevent them being shared with the other spouse; or

- the lawyer loses confidence in the procedure followed by the mediator.

In the event that the lawyer wishes the mediation process to terminate, the lawyer should first discuss his or her concerns with the client. The lawyer should attempt to determine whether the concerns he or she has are in fact perceived by the client or perceived by other individuals who are involved in the mediation process. If the lawyer is not satisfied, the lawyer should discuss the concerns directly with the mediator. Prior to taking any action to terminate the mediation, the lawyer should obtain instructions from the client on the client's wishes.

C. REPORTS

1. Closed Mediation

In closed mediation, the mediator only reports on the issues that were resolved during mediation. In this case, a memorandum of understanding is drawn up by the mediator specifying the issues that were agreed to.

For those issues where agreement was not reached, the mediator simply states "agreement was not reached on the following issues", and lists the issues.

In closed mediation, the mediator does not report on the process and does not make any recommendations.

In closed mediation cases, the mediator usually has an agreement with the parties or a court order specifying that he or she would not be called to court as an expert witness to give evidence on behalf of either party.

2. Open Mediation

If requested by one or both parties or the court, the mediator can report on all issues sent to mediation, whether or not they were resolved.

The content of the report depends on the open mediation agreement. This report may contain one or more of the following:

- a report on issues that are resolved;
- for those issues that are not resolved, a statement by the mediator about the process followed, the parties' positions on these issues, and the obstacles to an agreement; and/or
- if requested by one or both parties, recommendations by the mediator about the resolution of the issues that are still in dispute.

The mediator should discuss the nature of the report requested with the parties prior to beginning the mediation. That is, is the mediator expected to prepare a report with recommendations in the event that mediation is not completely successful?

For those issues that were resolved by the parties, the mediator would usually not make a personal comment about the agreement reached. Exceptions to this would be if the court has ordered the mediator to provide an opinion on the adequacy of the settlement reached or if the mediator is concerned that the agreement creates some danger for the children. The report would usually focus on those issues where agreement was not reached. In these cases, if the mediator has been requested to make recommendations, the mediator should set out a fair, reasonable, and workable plan for the parties and the court to consider.

ANNOTATED BIBLIOGRAPHY

Coogler, O.J. *Structured Mediation and Divorce Settlement: A Handbook for Marital Mediators*. Toronto: Lexington Books, D.C. Heath and Company, 1978. See particularly Chapter 7, "The Marital Settlement Agreement", at p. 63.

Folberg, J., and Taylor, A. *Mediation: A Comprehensive Guide to Resolving Conflicts without Litigation*. San Francisco: Jossey-Bass Publishers, 1984. This book contains a discussion about preparing the settlement agreement. See particularly Part Two "Mediation Stages, Concepts and Skills", Chapter 3, "Stages in the Mediation Process", at p. 38.

Gold, L. *Between Love and Hate: A Guide to Civilized Divorce*. New York: Plenum Press, 1992. See *supra*, Chapter 4, Annotated Bibliography.

Haynes, J.M. *Divorce Mediation: A Practical Guide for Therapists and Counsellors*. New York: Springer Publishing Company, 1981. See particularly Part IV, "Conclusion", Chapter 7, "Some Implications for Practice", at p. 127.

Ricci, I. *Mom's House, Dad's House: Making Shared Custody Work, How Parents Can Make Two Homes for their Children After Divorce*. New York: Collier Books, Macmillan Publishing Co., 1980. See *supra*, Chapter 4, Annotated Bibliography.

Saposnek, D. *Mediating Child Custody Disputes*. San Francisco: Jossey-Bass Publishers, 1983. This book contains a helpful discussion with respect to drafting a mediation agreement. See particularly Part II, "Structuring the Mediation Process", Chapter 5, "Drafting the Mediation Agreement", at p. 97.

Chapter Ten

Custody Assessments

A. ASSESSMENT PROCEDURE

1. Mediation — The First Step

A chapter on custody assessments has been included in this book because the authors take the position that the clients should be offered an opportunity to find a mediated solution to the issues in dispute. Except in cases of serious abuse, a mediative approach should be tried first for the following reasons:

- Parents should be encouraged to take responsibility for their children, and parents are in the best position to know their children and understand what parenting arrangement would be in the best interests of their children.
- If the assessor does not attempt mediation as a first step, then the parties are almost inevitably headed for an adversarial court battle. Such a battle is not in the children's best interests, nor in the parent's best interests.
- If the parties do succeed in reaching a settlement with the assistance of a mediator, they are more likely to accept the result and not to relitigate in the future.
- A mediated settlement is likely to save the parties considerable emotional strain as well as considerable expense.

2. Purpose of Custody Assessment

In conducting a custody assessment, it is important to decide what is the purpose of the assessment. Is the purpose to determine who is the best parent? Or, is the purpose to develop a parenting plan that would be in the best interests of the children? There is a fundamental difference in attitude between these two initial starting points. If the assessor considers the purpose to be determining the best parent, then the following assumptions might apply:

- The assessor probably presumes that the result will be sole custody to one of the two parents (as opposed to a joint custody or a shared parenting arrangement).

- The assessor will attempt to determine which parent is better than the other (for example, with respect to financial status, educational achievement, job security, or personality strengths).
- The assessor probably emphasizes a clinically oriented assessment process. Information gathering is likely to be through psychological testing and individual interviews, as opposed to joint meetings of both parents.
- The assessor will probably spend very little time with the spouses together trying to mediate a cooperative parenting plan.
- The assessor will probably place more emphasis on the stated or perceived preference of the children for one parent over the other.
- It is highly likely that the assessor will prepare a full custody assessment report, which will be submitted to the parties and the court.
- The case is likely to proceed to trial with the assessor called as a witness by the parent who is "preferred" in the assessment report.

On the other hand, if the assessor starts from the premise that the purpose of an assessment is to develop a cooperative parenting plan that is in the best interests of the children, then the assumptions are somewhat different, namely:

- The assessor is likely to place considerable emphasis on attempting to reach a mutually agreeable settlement.
- In the absence of serious abuse issues, the assessor is likely to take the position that it is important for the children to have a warm and loving relationship with both parents and that a desired outcome is an arrangement that maximizes the children's opportunity to spend time with both parents in an atmosphere of reduced tension. This outcome presumes two competent and caring parents.
- The assessor is likely to spend considerable time with the children to observe the ways in which they relate to both parents, and then with both parents together to consider various alternatives for cooperating so as to meet the children's needs, interests, and wishes.
- The assessor is likely to focus more on the future of the parenting relationship than on the past or even the present. That is, the assessor will be interested in determining to what extent both parents are willing to share parental responsibilities and are competent to carry these out.
- The assessment will focus on the communication between the parents and their ability and willingness to cooperate in the interests of their children.
- The assessor is likely to explore the possibility of a joint custody or shared parenting arrangement, particularly in cases where there are two reasonably competent parents who have the ability to set aside their individual differences in the interests of the children. In some cases, the parents dislike each other intensely, live very different life-

styles, but respect each other's parenting ability, recognize that they both love the children and are loved by the children, and on this basis are prepared to cooperate in their parenting.

- The assessor is likely to focus on factors that might undermine the cooperation or make a shared parenting arrangement more difficult, such as considerable distance between the parents, unwillingness to share the transportation, the attitude of a new spouse that may obstruct cooperation, a poor parent-child relationship, distrust or fears of abuse between the spouses or directed at the children.

- The assessor will encourage the parties to reach their own settlement so that they can avoid an adversarial battle, and in many cases the assessor will not need to prepare a detailed assessment report. The more usual result would be a memorandum of understanding by the assessor followed by minutes of settlement prepared by the solicitor.

3. Differences Between Mediation and Assessment

In what way is an assessment different from mediation?

In an assessment, unlike closed mediation, the assessor is asked to prepare a report containing his or her observations, opinions, and recommendations. This may occur whether or not the parties reach an agreement. In closed mediation, the mediator prepares a report only with respect to those issues resolved in mediation. The mediator does not include his or her observations, opinions, or recommendations. In open mediation, the mediator may prepare a report that is similar to an assessment, although possibly not as detailed, and will only include recommendations if this is specifically requested by the parties. A report in open mediation could include the mediator's observations with respect to issues that were not resolved.

Mediation is a process that essentially emphasizes the private ordering of dispute resolution. That is, the parties are expected to resolve their own difficulties by arriving at a voluntary settlement. An assessment is a process whereby an impartial expert makes recommendations (where these are requested by the parties or the judge) which are then considered by a judge who makes a decision for the parties as to how their dispute will be resolved. There is no requirement that the parties accept the assessor's recommendations, and the final resolution is imposed by the court.

The assessment report will carry considerable weight with the court, and for this reason the assessor must spend additional time, which would not be needed in mediation, learning about the special needs, interests, wishes, and stages of development of the children, and about the capacity of the parents to parent and to cooperate with each other.

An assessment focuses on what information an assessor needs in order to arrive at a recommendation, whereas mediation focuses on what information the parties need in order to resolve their dispute on their own.

An assessor must do a complete and thorough investigation, including contacts with a number of collateral sources to ensure that the procedure followed meets acceptable professional standards and to ensure that his or her report is considered credible by the court. A mediator who is not being asked for recommendations does not need to carry out an extensive investigation.

4. Assessment Interviews

The following are basic guidelines for the types of interviews and data collection procedures that are usually carried out in an assessment.

(A) MEETING OF ASSESSOR AND BOTH COUNSEL

The objectives of this meeting are the same as those set out in Chapter 4 with respect to mediation. However, there are some additional purposes.

It is important for the assessor to clarify with counsel that he or she will be attempting to arrive at a settlement as a part of the procedure. The assessor also needs to make clear with counsel what will be expected of him or her if the mediative approach is successful. Will the assessor still be expected to prepare a full custody assessment, or will a memorandum of understanding with a brief report be adequate?

It is recommended that an assessor not prepare a full assessment report unless it is required by the court for the following reasons:

- The assessment report is likely to be lengthy and more costly than the memorandum of understanding and a brief report.
- A full custody assessment often includes information that could be upsetting to one or both parties and will likely weaken rather than encourage cooperative parenting. Many parents feel defensive, somewhat humiliated, and often considerably distressed at having their weaknesses exposed.
- The information contained in a full assessment report may be used by one or both parties as further ammunition for their continued battle with each other.
- If a settlement is reached, it is best to emphasize the positive results and state what the parties did that was good, rather than expose their weaknesses. The settlement itself may be undermined by disputes over details in an assessment report.

The assessor should clarify the fact that if an assessment report is prepared, the assessor would agree to be called as a witness by either party and would be willing to be cross-examined by both.

The assessor should clarify the payment of fees during the assessment process, and for the preparation of a report or agreement. It is desirable to have all fees shared throughout, so that there is no suggestion that the assessor has produced a favourable report for the party who is paying his or her fees. This is also in keeping with the assessor's position that he or she is concerned with the best interests of the children and is impartial as between the parties. However, it is likely that the parent who is favoured in the report will pay for the assessor to appear in court as an expert witness.

(B) MEETING OF ASSESSOR AND BOTH PARTIES TOGETHER

See Chapter 4 for a discussion of the objectives of this meeting. The following aims should also be considered.

- The assessor should explain to the parties that they will be encouraged to develop a cooperative parenting plan on their own rather than leave the decision with respect to their children to strangers such as the assessor or a judge.
- The assessor should clarify with the parents what will happen in the event that they do reach an agreement. That is, the assessor may prepare a memorandum of understanding and a brief report rather than an assessment report, unless the assessment report is required by the court.
- The assessor should explain the implications with respect to fees if the parties settle versus if the parties fail to settle and an assessment report and expert witness testimony are required. If at all possible, the assessor should ask the parties to share his or her fees for the entire process. If this is not possible, or if one party will pay the majority of the fees, the assessor should obtain an agreement in writing that the other party will not raise the issue of who paid the fees to allege bias by the assessor in favour of the spouse who paid.

(C) MEETING OF ASSESSOR WITH EACH PARTY SEPARATELY

Some assessors prefer to meet initially with the parties separately and then hold a joint meeting at some other time. This is a preferred approach in cases of domestic violence where one party feels intimidated or at risk.

This issue was discussed in Chapters 3 and 4 with respect to mediation, and the discussion is relevant to assessments.

(D) HOME VISIT

In a custody assessment, it is recommended that the assessor meet the children in their home environment. While some assessors prefer to see children in their offices, and in some cases this is necessary (for example, if the family lives a considerable distance away), nevertheless a home visit is important for the following reasons:

- Children are far more comfortable in a familiar setting, and communication with the assessor will be enhanced.

- It is more likely that a child will show normalized behaviour in a family setting than in the assessor's office. Also the child is likely to be far less anxious and more communicative.
- A home visit provides the assessor with considerable information about the family's lifestyle and the extent to which the family is child-oriented. This information is more difficult to obtain in an office setting.
- The assessor is able to evaluate parenting ability more accurately in a home setting than in an office interview. For example, the assessor has an opportunity to observe the type of nutrition given the children, the adequacy of stimulation available, the appropriateness of the living arrangements, and the desirability of the neighbourhood. In addition, it is more likely that the assessor will observe typical family patterns and discipline techniques in a home setting.
- The assessor should visit with the children in each parent's home in order to observe differences in the home environment and parent-child relationships.

The assessor may choose to hold a number of meetings in the home on the day of each home visit, for example, with both parents and the children, with one parent and the children, with all children together, with each child separately, with each parent separately, with the children with one parent and a new partner, with the new partner alone, with a regular babysitter alone, or with extended family members who are directly involved in the care of the children alone. Meetings with the parent alone, the new partner, the babysitter, or extended-family caregivers could be held at the office on a different day, if preferred, or if necessary because of time constraints.

It is recommended that the first home visit be in the home where the children spend the majority of their time. The aim is to make the children feel as comfortable as possible when meeting the assessor and engaging in the assessment interviews. The same procedure should be followed during the second home visit with the non-custodial parent.

(E) MEETING WITH PARTIES TOGETHER ON ONE OR MORE OCCASIONS

Additional meetings with both parties may be necessary, prior to reaching an agreement or preparing a report, for such reasons as the following:

- to offer the parents information as to the children's response to the separation;
- to improve the parents' ability to communicate about parenting issues; and
- to determine whether the parents can work out their own parenting plan for sharing responsibilities and time with the children.

Additional meetings may be needed with the children with one or both parents or with one child and a particular parent, with parents and their new partners, or with the entire family.

In difficult cases, a second evaluator could be used to provide independent observations of the children, parents, new partners, or other significant figures.

5. Comments with respect to Home Visits

The assessor should discuss with both parents prior to a home visit how the visit will be explained to the children. The children should be told essentially that the assessor is a professional person whom the parents have asked to help them work out a parenting plan that will be in the best interests of the children. During the visit, the assessor will be spending time with both the parents and the children.

Prior to speaking to the children, it is important to ensure that the children have been told by both parents that they are free to say whatever they wish to the assessor, that the parents' feelings will not be hurt by what they may say, and that there will be no negative repercussions for them. The children should also be told that while their views will be considered, their parents or, in the alternative, a judge will be making the final decision.

It is usually best to hold a meeting of both parents together with the children, or at least one parent with the children, prior to seeing the children individually. The children need some time to become comfortable in the presence of the assessor, and the assessor needs some context of family interaction before beginning the individual sessions with each child. The assessor should ensure that the meetings with each child are held in private and in a setting where the child is most comfortable.

During the home visit the assessor needs to be tuned into such things as:

- whether there is affection shown between the parents and each child;
- whether there are appropriate toys and educational stimulation;
- the standard of cleanliness in the home;
- whether nutritious meals and snacks are served;
- whether there are pictures of the children, trophies, or other items that indicate the value of the children to the parent;
- the daily routines for the children;
- whether the children are fearful, clinging to the parent, or independent and confident in meeting strangers;
- the parent-child interaction, that is, whether the parent gives each child praise, encourages independence, sets reasonable limits, values the child's suggestions and opinions, or is critical or control-

ling, uses lax or excessive discipline, and minimizes the child's contribution.

The assessor should observe the interaction between the siblings to determine whether the siblings are supportive of each other or vying for attention. Do they include or exclude each other? Do they bicker or get along reasonably well? Does the parent intervene in an appropriate way when necessary with the children?

The assessor should eat one meal with the family, if possible, and observe:

- how nutritious the meal is;
- the types of limits and expectations with respect to table manners;
- whether the children are comfortable and participate in the conversation, or are ignored and uncomfortable.

The assessor should observe the quality of interaction between the children and other significant figures who are to be interviewed, in terms of how they are greeted by the children, whether there is any display of affection, or whether they are largely ignored.

At the end of the day, before the assessor leaves, it is desirable to hold a brief meeting between the children and the parent(s) just to sum up the day and ensure that everyone is clear about the next step in the process. The next step may be a home visit at the other spouse's home, and the children should be informed about when this will occur and what the purpose of the meeting will be. This will make the children more relaxed for the second visit.

6. Collateral Sources

In addition to interview information, the assessor needs to collect information from external sources that have relevant and, it is hoped, reliable information with respect to the needs, interests, and stages of development of the children, as well as the parenting capacity of both parents. Such information can be collected through reports, telephone conversations, and, if necessary, direct visits with such sources as:

- the school;
- the family doctor;
- other mental health professionals;
- the Children's Aid Society;
- the public health nurse; or
- the employer.

7. Standards of Practice

As with mediation, it is important for the assessor to establish that he or she:

- has appropriate qualifications with respect to education, training, and experience;
- adheres to a professional code of conduct as set out by his or her professional discipline; and
- adheres to a code of conduct established by a recognized professional organization for mediators and/or assessors.

The credibility or weight given to an assessment report will be determined by its thoroughness and its conformity with ethical standards. The court will be particularly interested in the following types of information:

- the amount of time spent in the total assessment process;
- who was interviewed, what combination of persons, for how long, and on how many occasions;
- what collateral sources were contacted;
- whether significant allegations were followed up (for example, with respect to alcohol, drug, or physical abuse, emotional disturbance, or criminal behaviour);
- whether the assessor attempted to resolve the dispute through mediation prior to making recommendations;
- whether the assessor explained the nature of the recommendations to the parties and counsel prior to submitting the report to court (and possibly prior to preparing the report);
- whether the report was up to date (that is, did the assessor update his or her observations close to the time of the trial?);
- whether the report was thorough; and
- whether the assessor presented a fair and balanced account of the parties in the report and in the testimony given in court.

B. PREPARATION OF CUSTODY ASSESSMENT REPORTS

If the parties reach agreement or substantial agreement, the assessor should summarize the areas of agreement reached. Where the parties reached an impasse or where the plan was below a reasonable standard of care for a child, the assessor should set out his or her recommendations. For each recommendation, the assessor should provide a rationale focusing on why that recommendation was in the best interests of the child.

This report should also contain a brief outline of the topics described below. However, a lengthy family history or evaluation of the parties is usually not necessary and could provoke feelings of resentment which could undermine a cooperative parenting plan.

In the event that the parties fail to resolve their dispute and a full assessment report is required, the following types of information should be included:

Referral sources

The report should state whether this is a court-ordered assessment or one that is being conducted on the consent of the parties. The report should indicate whether the parties jointly selected the assessor or whether the assessor was selected by one of the parties over the opposition of the other. If the recommendation for an assessment was made by an external agency, such as the Children's Aid Society, this should be indicated.

Reasons for Referral

The report should indicate whether the referral was made to help the parents develop a cooperative parenting plan, select one parent in preference to the other, investigate allegations of child abuse, alcoholism, or mental disorder, or for some other reason(s). The events leading to the referral should be stated clearly.

It should also be clear whether the report was prepared for a contested custody trial, a child welfare trial, or because one or both parents wished to review existing custody and access arrangements.

Objective(s) of Assessment

The report should set out the questions to be answered by the assessment. For example, is the primary concern the best parenting arrangements, or is the issue restricted to the most appropriate access schedule or the involvement of a new partner in the children's lives?

Qualifications of Assessor

The report should contain a brief summary of the assessor's qualifications and a full *curriculum vitae* should be attached to the report.

Assessment Process

The report should state who was seen or spoken to and for how long, and what materials, reports, or court documents were reviewed. This information can be included in paragraph or chart format.

Family History

The report should contain relevant family history, that is, information pertaining to the objectives of the assessment. This may include a history of the marriage, the early parenting of the child, the reasons for the marriage breakdown, if relevant, the present parenting plan, and any difficulties or positive features of the present plan.

History of the Child and Assessor's Observations

This section should include information with respect to the child's physical, psychological, social, emotional, and educational development. Included should be information with respect to the child's strengths and weaknesses, as well as special needs and abilities.

Summary of Observations of Family and of Information from Other Sources

The report should contain a summary of family dynamics in relation to possible parenting arrangements, and should summarize the relevant information from such sources as the school teacher, family doctor, and other involved professionals.

Discussion of Alternative Parenting Arrangements

The report should discuss viable parenting options in light of the objectives of the assessment. The relative strengths and weaknesses of the alternatives should be considered.

Recommendations

The assessor may then wish to set out in specific terms the final recommendations with respect to the involvement of each parent in the child's life. This can include such recommendations as:

- sole versus joint custody;
- the primary residence of the child (if any);
- the amount of time to be spent with each parent, including the specific days and times for access;
- the manner in which parental responsibilities and privileges should be shared. such as health care, educational planning, religious training. and access to information;
- what should occur if one parent moves out of the jurisdiction or far enough away such that the access arrangements are no longer feasible;
- the method of dispute resolution to be used if the parents have a further dispute with respect to custody of or access to the children.

It is important for the assessor to indicate to both the parties and counsel that he or she will be available to meet with one or both parties prior to the trial date for the following purposes:

- to discuss the recommendations;
- to make a further attempt at settlement;
- to refer one or both parties for professional assistance, such as counselling or treatment for alcohol abuse; and
- for additional information with respect to the needs of the children and how both parents can meet these needs.

The assessor should maintain a position of impartiality as between the parents and should remember throughout this process that the primary task is to devise a parenting plan that will be in the best interests of the children. A good assessment report is not one that helps one parent win and destroys the other parent, but rather one that makes constructive, reasonable recommendations that will eventually lead to a reduction of tension and an improvement in relationships between the children and both parents.

Rationale for Recommendations

The assessor should set out in this section the criteria that he or she is applying in making recommendations. Also, the assessor should summarize those key facts and observations with respect to each criterion that is relevant to a recommendation. For example, if the stability of the child's living arrangements is an important factor to the assessor, the report should make this clear. A summary should be given of the relevant facts and observations with respect to how each parent would affect the stability of the child's living arrangements. For example, one parent might be a professional musician and plan to take the child on extended world tours with nannies and tutors available. The other parent might be engaged in employment that does not require travelling and that would result in the child growing up in a familiar community, near friends and extended family members. The assessor should indicate how the different parenting plans would impact on the child's stability.

ANNOTATED BIBLIOGRAPHY

"Association of Family and Conciliation Courts Model Standards of Practice for Child Custody Evaluation" (1994), 32 *Family and Conciliation Courts Review* 4, 504-513.

Brown, C. "Custody Evaluations: Presenting the Data to Court" (1995), 33 *Family and Conciliation Courts Review* 446-461.

Chisholm, B., and MacNaughton, C. *Custody/Access Assessments: A Practical Guide for Lawyers and Assessors*. Toronto: Carswell, 1990. A comprehensive description of practical procedures and post-assessment issues from authors trained in social work and the law respectively.

Custody/Access Assessment Guidelines: Report of the Interdisciplinary Committee for Custody/Access Assessments. Toronto: The Ontario Psychological Foundation, 1987. These guidelines were revised in 1996 by the Ontario Interdisciplinary Association of Custody and Access Assessors and reprinted by the Psychology Foundation of Canada. Toronto, 1996.

Gardner, R. *Family Evaluation in Child Custody Litigation*. New Jersey: Creative Therapeutics, 1982. This is a practical guide to performing custody assessments and includes a very useful discussion about the interview process, including who to interview, what information to collect, and also how to prepare a report.

Haynes-Seman, C., and Baumgarten, D. "Improvement of Clinical and Legal Determinations in Cases of Alleged Child Sexual Abuse" (1995), 33 *Family and Conciliation Courts Review* 472-483.

Hysjulien, C., Wood, B., and Benjamin, G.A. "Child Custody Evaluations: A Review of Methods Used in Litigation and Alternative Dispute Resolution" (1994), 32 *Family and Conciliation Courts Review* 4, 466-489.

Keeney, B. P., ed. *Diagnosis and Assessment in Family Therapy*. Rockville: Aspen Publications, 1983. A collection of papers by some of the foremost family therapists and diagnosticians in the United States and Canada, describing how to make family assessments more comprehensive.

Parry, R., Broder, E., Schmitt, E., Saunders, E., and Hood, E. *Custody Disputes: Evaluation and Intervention*. Toronto: Lexington Books, 1985. This book contains a number of interesting chapters written by experienced professionals with respect to the theory and practice of custody assessments.

Skafte, D. *Child Custody Evaluations: A Practical Guide*. California: Sage Publications Inc., 1986. This book is an informative, highly readable guide for those preparing custody evaluations.

Stahl, P. *Performing Child Custody Evaluations: A Guide Book*. Thousand Oaks, California: Sage Publications, 1994. An in-depth integration of case history and procedures for custody evaluators. Other issues include professional liability and burnout, with appendices providing sample forms and ethical standards.

Taylor, A., and Bing, H."Settlement by Evaluation and Arbitration: A New Approach for Custody and Visitation Disputes" (1994), 32 *Family and Conciliation Courts Review* 4, 432-444.

Chapter Eleven

The Mediator/Assessor as Expert Witness

A. WHEN EXPERTS REQUIRED TO TESTIFY

Prior to beginning the mediation process, it is important to consider the circumstances under which a mediator or an assessor might have to appear in court. It should be clear to the clients and the mediator that the mediator could be subpoenaed to court to testify if he or she was involved in one of the following procedures:

- *Open mediation or an assessment where the mediation or assessment has been court ordered.* Pursuant to ss. 30(7) and 31(5) of the Ontario *Children's Law Reform Act,*[1] the mediator/assessor is required to submit a report to court, he or she can be summonsed by one or both parties as a witness, and the other party or parties may cross-examine the mediator/assessor on the contents of the report. In this case, the mediator/assessor might be called to appear in court even if the parties have come to an agreement on all issues. This would occur if the judge wanted additional information on how the agreement was arrived at, whether the clients appeared to have equal bargaining power, and, therefore, whether the agreement was reached voluntarily. The mediator/assessor might be asked to comment on the fairness of the agreement by either counsel or the judge.

- *Open mediation or an assessment where the parties do not reach an agreement on one or more issues.* The mediator/assessor may be summonsed by one or more parties to appear in court. The other party or parties may then cross-examine the mediator/assessor on the mediation process and the contents of any report that was written. This could occur whether or not the mediation or assessment was court ordered.

- *Closed mediation, where the mediation was court ordered pursuant to a statute that permitted closed mediation.* In this case, it is unlikely that the mediator would be summonsed to appear in court. For example, a statute such as the Ontario *Children's Law Reform Act,* ss. 31(4)(*b*) and 31(7), permits closed mediation and establishes a statutory privilege for any communication made during the course of mediation. Sec-

---

[1] R.S.O. 1990, c. C.12.

tion 31(7) states with respect to closed mediation that

> 31(7) . . . evidence of anything said or of any admission or communication made in the course of the mediation is not admissible in any proceeding except with the consent of all parties to the proceeding in which the order was made under subsection (1).

It is not clear whether the mediator could be summonsed to give evidence in a proceeding that was not under the statute that permitted closed mediation. For example, it is not clear whether the mediator could be required to testify in child welfare proceedings or in proceedings under the *Criminal Code*.[2] These statutes do not confer any special statutory privilege on the discussions held in mediation. Similarly, unless there is an order pursuant to s. 10(4) or (5) of the *Divorce Act*,[3] there is a remote possibility that the mediator could be called as a witness in divorce proceedings and compelled to reveal what would otherwise be confidential communications. Section 31(7) of the Ontario *Children's Law Reform Act* does say that any admission or communication made in the course of mediation is not admissible in any proceeding except with the consent of all parties to the proceeding, but to date there has been no case law to indicate whether that statutory privilege would be respected in proceedings under another statute. While the discussions in mediation might be protected at common law as settlement negotiations, this privilege might not apply to other proceedings, particularly a child welfare case, where the primary concern is the best interests of the child. It is important for mediators to understand and to communicate to clients any limitations on the confidentiality they can promise their clients.

- *Closed mediation arranged by agreement, that is, not pursuant to a court order for closed mediation.* The mediator may have an oral or written agreement with the parties and/or their counsel that the mediation is to be closed. This means that any admission or communication made during the course of the mediation is to be confidential and the mediator is not to be called as an expert witness in any proceeding. If this agreement is not made pursuant to an order under a statute such as the Ontario *Children's Law Reform Act*, which has provision for closed mediation, then the communications may not be kept confidential in subsequent litigation. In these circumstances, it is possible that the mediator could claim a privilege based on the common law protection extended to settlement negotiations that take place when litigation is pending or contemplated. However, the mediator could not guarantee clients that he or she would not be required to testify if subpoenaed. It is important for media-

---

[2]   R.S.C. 1985, c. C-46.
[3]   R.S.C. 1985, c. 3 (2nd Supp.).

tors to explain to clients that they cannot guarantee confidentiality, particularly if it is believed that the mediator has relevant information about the safety of children or threats of harm to the parties or their families.

1. Subpoena

A mediator/assessor may appear in court on consent; that is, if the mediator/assessor has been called as a witness by one or more parties, the mediator/assessor may agree to appear without the need for a subpoena.

Regardless of whether the mediator/assessor is prepared to appear without a subpoena, the party or parties wishing to call the mediator/assessor may issue a subpoena, which is a court document that requires the mediator/assessor to appear on a particular day, at a particular time, at a particular place, in order to give testimony with respect to particular proceedings. The subpoena must be served personally on the mediator/assessor.

The subpoena usually requires that the mediator/assessor bring all relevant notes and documents with him or her. With respect to any notes made on the file, it is not permissible for the mediator/assessor to keep a separate personal file and an official office file. Any notes made during the course of the mediation/assessment process would have to be brought to court.

The party issuing the subpoena is usually under an obligation to provide conduct money to the mediator/assessor, and without the provision of conduct money, the subpoena is not valid.

If the mediator/assessor is served with a subpoena, then it would be a contempt of court if the mediator/assessor failed to appear. The consequences of being found guilty of contempt of court may be a fine and/or a jail sentence, depending on the particular statute or jurisdiction.

2. Privilege

The term "privilege" is often confused with "confidentiality". It is very important that both the mediator/assessor and the clients and their counsel understand the difference between these terms and are clear about whether the relationship is a privileged relationship or a confidential one. For the relationship to be privileged, at least one of the following conditions must be met:

- There must be statutory protection, such as under the Ontario *Children's Law Reform Act*, the British Columbia *Family Relations Act*,[4] or the *Divorce Act, 1985*. For a statutory privilege to apply, there must be a court order pursuant to the relevant statute.

---

[4] R.S.B.C. 1979, c. 121.

- There must be a relevant common law privilege. For example, there is a common law privilege that protects settlement negotiations when litigation is pending or contemplated. Several recent court decisions in Ontario and British Columbia, as well as in the United States and England, have ruled that mediation discussions entered into for the purpose of settling issues that were the subject of pending litigation were privileged. Recourse to the common law privilege may be available in cases where no statutory privilege applies.
- The court may make a finding that it is in the public interest to protect certain communications. Wigmore has established four fundamental conditions that must be met before privilege will be extended to communications. These are:[5]

    1. The communications must originate in a *confidence* that they will not be disclosed.

    2. This element of *confidentiality must be essential* to the full and satisfactory maintenance of the relation between the parties.

    3. The *relation* must be one which in the opinion of the community ought to be sedulously *fostered*.

    4. The *injury* which would inure to the relation by the disclosure of the communications must be *greater than the benefit* thereby gained for the correct disposal of the litigation.

If the relationship is privileged, then any communications or admissions made during the course of the mediation may only be disclosed if all of the parties to the communication consent to the disclosure.

The privilege belongs to the clients, rather than the mediator. Therefore, if both clients wish to waive the privilege, they may do so, and the mediator may disclose the contents of their communication.

3. Confidentiality

Confidentiality is a legal, moral, and ethical duty to keep certain matters secret or confidential. Most mental health professionals and other professionals have an ethical duty, often set out in professional codes of conduct, to maintain a confidential relationship with their clients. That is, they are bound not to disclose any communications made during professional contacts, with certain exceptions.

There may be a conflict between privilege and confidentiality in that professional communications may not be privileged, even though the professional has promised to keep information confidential. For example, a doctor, psychologist, or social worker may be compelled to testify, even though his or her professional relationship is based on confidentiality. Only the solicitor-client relationship is protected by privilege. However,

---

[5]   8 *Wigmore on Evidence* § 2285.

the court has the discretionary power to exclude confidential communications if the court concludes that there are strong public policy reasons for doing so. It should be made clear to clients that there can be no protection for confidential communications if there is a concern about possible abuse to children.

It is very important for the mediator, the clients, and their counsel to consider the issues of confidentiality and privilege prior to the mediation beginning. The following issues should be clarified:

- whether the appointment of the mediator is pursuant to a statute that confers privilege or whether it is by agreement of the parties; and
- whether the mediation is open or closed. If it is closed mediation pursuant to a statute that confers privilege, then the communications will be privileged.

Once these issues are decided, then if the mediation is by agreement of the parties (not pursuant to a court order), the agreement should include a specific reference to a "without prejudice" relationship based on the common law privilege afforded settlement negotiations. If the mediation is open or if an assessment is requested, the agreement should indicate that the communications will not be privileged. However, the relationship would still be confidential in the sense of most professional-client relationships.

The confidentiality belongs to the clients, rather than the mediator. Therefore, if both clients wish to waive the confidentiality, they may do so and the mediator may disclose the contents of their communication.

B. QUALIFICATIONS OF EXPERT WITNESS

The general rule in litigation is that the judge is the trier of fact. That is, the judge draws inferences from the evidence presented in court and reaches a decision on the issues in dispute.

In making decisions in cases involving custody of or access to children, the court often relies on opinion evidence given by expert witnesses. These expert witnesses are not bound by the same evidentiary restrictions as ordinary witnesses. That is, expert witnesses (those who establish special qualifications for dealing with the issues in dispute) are permitted to include hearsay in their evidence. In addition, the expert witness is permitted to draw inferences based on facts, hearsay, research findings, and other sources for arriving at an opinion. The process used by an expert in drawing inferences is very similar to the judicial role and is very much broader than the usual role of a witness. Because of the special latitude given the expert, it is important that the expert have the necessary qualifications for giving opinion evidence. The more qualified the mediator/

assessor, the more likely the trier of fact (the judge) will permit the witness to give an expert opinion and will give weight or credibility to that expert opinion.

The expert has to establish his or her expertise in the following areas: education, training, experience, and methods of conduct and code of practice.

1. Education

The mediator/assessor should have:

- a post-graduate degree in a mental health field, such as psychology, social work, psychiatry, or counselling;
- ongoing attendance at relevant educational programs and conferences to upgrade skills and information with respect to mediation and assessments; and
- up-to-date knowledge of the mediation/assessment literature, as well as literature on child development, parenting skills, and the impact of separation and divorce on families.

2. Training

The mediator/assessor should have:

- completed a training program conducted by recognized authorities on mediation and assessments or taught such a program; and
- ongoing contact with a peer group of competent professionals for the purpose of case consultation, sharing of information, and supervision.

3. Experience

The mediator/assessor should:

- have an ongoing professional practice with mediation and/or assessment cases;
- belong to a recognized professional organization for mediators and/or assessors; and
- have published articles or research findings in professional newsletters, journals, or books for mediators and/or assessors or have spoken at conferences or seminars attended by other professionals.

4. Methods of Practice and Code of Conduct

The mediator/assessor should:

- conduct the mediations and/or custody assessments according to well-recognized standards of practice within the profession;

- be prepared to outline the methodology used and be able to justify this methodology on the basis of the generally accepted standards of practice in the field and the needs of the particular case; and
- subscribe to a code of conduct set out by his or her professional discipline (for example, psychology, psychiatry, or social work), and in addition adhere to a code of conduct for mediators and/or assessors as set out by a recognized professional organization for mediators and/or assessors.

The mediator/assessor should provide the clients, their counsel, and the court (if relevant) with an up-to-date *curriculum vitae* that outlines all of the qualifications as set out above that are relevant for conducting mediation or assessments.

In the event that the parties are unable to agree on an individual to conduct an assessment, the court should have sufficient information to determine which individual is most qualified for the task.

C. GUIDELINES FOR GIVING TESTIMONY IN COURT

In mediation/assessment cases, the expert is usually attempting to determine what is in the best interests of the children, and does not view himself or herself as acting for any of the parties. The expert performs something of an *amicus curiae* role, that is, a friend of the court. Given the impartial role of the mediator/assessor, he or she should be very careful to maintain that neutral stance and not be drawn into taking particular positions because they are of benefit to one of the parties.

Prior to trial, it is important that the mediator/assessor offer the parties and counsel an opportunity to meet with him or her in order to give the mediator/assessor any relevant, up-to-date information. This opportunity should be offered to both sides.

In a number of cases that go to court, a settlement can be reached during the course of the trial by one or both counsel or the judge asking for a brief recess for the parties to meet and discuss whether any of the issues can be resolved. The mediator/assessor should indicate to the judge and to the parties and their counsel that he or she will be available, during the course of the trial, if this might prove helpful in reaching a settlement. This again underlines the impartial role of the mediator/assessor.

If the expert is to testify, the first task is to determine whether the expert is qualified to give opinion evidence. Opposing counsel may argue that the court should not accept a witness's report or testimony as that of an expert. If counsel's argument is successful, then the mediator/assessor will not be able to give opinion evidence and will not be able to rely on any hearsay in his or her testimony. It is important that the mediator/assessor bring an up-to-date *curriculum vitae* to court and be prepared to respond to questions about why, in general and specifically in this case, he or she should be permitted to give expert testimony.

The judge will weigh the mediator/assessor's credibility and this credibility will depend on such factors as:

- the qualifications of the mediator/assessor;
- the methodology used in the case and how closely this methodology approximates the standards in the field;
- the code of ethics followed;
- the factual basis from which the mediator/assessor drew his or her conclusions;
- the mediator/assessor's appearance (the mediator/assessor should always appear in court well dressed and well groomed); and
- the impression of impartiality as opposed to partiality. Was the mediator/assessor paid exclusively by one side? If so, was this agreed to by the parties in advance? Did the mediator/assessor see both sides in the dispute, and did the mediator/assessor spend approximately equal amounts of time with each? Were the mediator/assessor's facts gathered from a variety of sources, including independent sources, or were the facts gathered primarily from those with a stake in the proceedings, that is, supporters of one party?

The mediator/assessor must be prepared to testify in court if a report has been submitted, and to be cross-examined on this report. Unless there is a statutory exception to being called, the mediator/assessor should expect to be called as a witness and give *viva voce* evidence.

Following establishment of the credentials of the professional, the party who called the mediator/assessor will ask questions. This is known as the examination-in-chief. The counsel conducting the examination is not permitted to ask leading questions. That is, the counsel cannot ask questions suggesting a particular answer. The questions must be open ended, and it is wise for the mediator/assessor to meet with the counsel who will be doing the examination-in-chief in advance of court in order to determine those areas that will be covered.

The mediator/assessor will next be cross-examined by the opposing counsel. The purpose of cross-examination is to reduce the credibility of the expert's opinion. It is permissible when cross-examining for the counsel to suggest answers or to lead the witness, but it is not permissible to badger the witness.

When being cross-examined, it is important for the expert to remain professional and unemotional. He or she should not take the questions personally and should not respond with sarcasm or hostility. It is always permissible to ask for a question to be repeated. If the answer to a question is unknown, or if a question is outside of the area considered by the mediation or assessment, it is wise to state that directly. The mediator/assessor should not argue with the questioner and not interrupt while the questions are being asked. The expert's answers will probably be cut short. The cross-examiner will try to stop the expert from talking when he or she is saying things that are not helpful to the opposing party. The counsel who conducted the examination-in-chief will have an opportunity to ask certain questions at a later time during the re-examination.

When giving testimony, the expert should speak slowly and clearly so that it is easier for the court reporter and the judge to make notes about the testimony. It is very irritating to the judge to have to keep reminding the expert witness to speak up and slow down.

It is required that the mediator/assessor take his or her entire file to court, that is, the report, as well as any notes made during interviews or telephone conversations. In addition, he or she should take all reports, documents, or other materials that were relied on as a basis for the mediation/assessment report. The expert's file will likely be examined by both counsel prior to asking questions in court.

If there are no notes made from interview conversations, the expert's report will likely have greatly reduced credibility. If memory is relied on for details of conversations and interviews, the judge is likely to put far less weight on the expert's ultimate report and recommendations than if careful notes were made during sessions.

When asked about opinions or recommendations, it is very important for the mediator/assessor to remember to state the factual basis for his or her recommendations. If the basis for the expert's opinion is solely hearsay, and if that hearsay information comes from a biased source, then again his or her recommendations will have little weight.

If the expert is asked a question and cannot remember the answer or the facts on which an answer would be based, it is permissible to use notes to refresh his or her memory. If the expert wishes to look at notes, then it must be established that the notes were made contemporaneously with the event; that is, the notes were made at the time or very close to the time of interviews or conversations and therefore are likely to be accurate. In addition, it must be established that the notes were made personally by the mediator/assessor.

If the mediator/assessor asks to see notes to refresh his or her memory, then counsel are likely to ask to see those notes. The notes should be in the mediator/assessor's personal handwriting, not dictated notes that were subsequently typed, because these notes may not be acceptable.

Many mental health professionals have a considerable fear of testifying in court. They are afraid of being humiliated, badgered, and asked questions they perceive to be irrelevant to the best interests of children. In addition, appearances at court are often inconvenient and disrupt a busy practice. Professionals often have to wait hours, if not days, to be called, and this causes further inconvenience and discomfort.

Many mental health professionals are critical of the legal system, because it appears that an adversarial approach is harmful, rather than helpful, to the family as a whole. It often appears to the mediator/assessor that the purpose of counsel is to cause psychological damage to the other party, rather than to find a solution to the problem that would be the most satisfactory for the children and even for the family as a whole.

It is important for the mediator/assessor to understand that the purpose of the court procedure is not to arrive at a therapeutic outcome. The purpose of the court system is to arrive at the truth, and the premise of our court system is that the truth is best obtained by a battle of two strongly partisan adversaries, namely, counsel. There is a growing awareness that the adversarial process is not the most suitable for family law matters, and therefore there is a gradual change in attitude and approach, both in the legislation and the actual court practice.

Both the legislation and courtroom procedure are moving away from matrimonial fault as a basis for deciding family law disputes. However, it is still the role of counsel for the party who is not satisfied with the mediator/ assessor's report to try to reduce the report's weight in the eyes of the court as a means of promoting his or her client's position.

Because of the great weight and latitude normally given to experts' reports, it is important that the report and expert opinion be capable of withstanding a strong test as to their credibility. Instead of looking at this as a personal attack, the mediator/assessor should welcome the opportunity to have his or her facts and opinions tested thoroughly by the court process as a safety check. In the event that the report is based on poorly researched facts, on biased opinions, or on insufficient time with the parties, it is important for the family to have a weak report exposed. Similarly, if a report has been prepared on the basis of a thorough examination and the recommendations are carefully thought out, then the mediator/assessor and all of the parties concerned are likely to have more confidence in it. It is in the public interest to have these reports, which are given such great weight by the courts, thoroughly tested.

ANNOTATED BIBLIOGRAPHY

Brown, C. "Custody Evaluations: Presenting the Data to Court" (1995), 33 *Family and Conciliation Courts Review* 446-461.

Kirkpatrick, G.J. "Should Mediators Have a Confidentiality Privilege?" In "Legal and Family Perspectives in Divorce Mediation" (1985), 9 *Mediation Quarterly* 85. This article examines the question of the limitations on the expert refusing to testify in court. It considers the balance between the right to privacy and the court's need to know.

Moir, D. "The Clinician As a Witness." Paper presented at the Association of Conciliation Courts Conference, Toronto, 1983.

Sopinka, J. and Lederman, S. *The Law of Evidence in Civil Cases*. Toronto: Butterworths, 1974. This is the leading text on the law of evidence in civil cases.

Weisman, N. "The Admissability of Hearsay Evidence: Defining and Applying Necessity and Reliability Since R. v. Kahn" (1995), 13 *Canadian Family Law Quarterly* 2, 67-87.

Ziskin, J. *Coping with Psychiatric and Psychological Testimony*, Volumes 1 and 2. California: Law and Psychology Press, 1981 (Supplement, 1983). This book offers a strong critique of expert evidence in child custody cases, as well as in criminal and personal injury cases. The author is a psychologist and a lawyer, and uses both professional backgrounds to prepare the lawyer for cross-examination of the mental health expert. This book would be very valuable for both mental health professionals and lawyers dealing with contested custody cases.

List of Appendices

Appendix 1A

Letter from Mediator: Willingness to Act — Mediation

LETTER TO LAWYERS
(Referral Source)

(*Date*)

(*Mediator's Name and Address*)

(*Lawyer's Name and Address*)

Dear Solicitor,*

<u>Re: Mediation — (*Client's Name*)</u>

I am writing to indicate that I would be willing to offer mediation services in this case.

I would like to explain briefly the service I would offer. I would be retained by both parents, and my goal will be to help them arrive at a voluntary agreement on those issues that they wish to submit to mediation. My experience and that of my colleagues indicates that when a solution is reached by the parties themselves, they are more likely to carry it out in practice.

I would be prepared to offer either open or closed mediation, depending on the wishes of both parties. In either case, if the parties reach an agreement on all issues sent to mediation, I would prepare a Memorandum of Understanding outlining the agreement reached.

If the parties select open mediation and they do not reach agreement on one or more issues, I would prepare a Memorandum of Understanding on those issues that were resolved and a report reviewing the mediation process for those issues that were not resolved. This report could be submitted to court and, if necessary, I could be called as a witness by either party to testify about the report.

If closed mediation is selected and the parties do not reach agreement on one or more issues, I would prepare a Memorandum of Understanding on those issues that were resolved and a statement specifying which issues were not resolved. There would be no report and I would not be called as a witness in a court proceeding.

Please find attached my *curriculum vitae* and an outline of the general procedure I follow in mediation. If I am retained I would hold an initial meeting with both counsel to clarify the issues to be mediated and whether open or closed mediation is desired, and to determine the specific procedure that would be most helpful given the issues to be mediated and the circumstances of the particular case.

My fee is $ ___ per hour for interviews, preparing a Memorandum of Understanding and/or a report. An additional fee is required for preparation for court and attendance as an expert witness, should this be necessary.

With respect to payment of my fees, my policy is that both spouses share the cost equitably (not necessarily equally), if possible, because I want to ensure that both of them perceive me as objective and impartial. I will ask for a retainer in the amount of $ ___ before beginning and a refresher when the retainer is depleted.

I am looking forward to assisting both clients in arriving at a satisfactory resolution of the issues submitted to mediation.

Yours sincerely,

_____

MEDIATOR

Encl.
* *This letter could be adapted for use with clients.*

Appendix 1B

Letter from Mediator/Assessor: Willingness to Act — Custody Assessment

LETTER TO LAWYERS
(Referral Source)

(*Date*)

(*Assessor's Name and Address*)

(*Lawyer's Name and Address*)

Dear Solicitor,*

<u>Re: Custody Assessment — *(Client's Name)*</u>

I am writing to indicate that I would be willing to carry out a custody assessment in this case.

I would like to explain briefly the service I would offer. I would be retained by both parents, and my goal will be to arrive at a parenting plan that would be in the best interests of the child(ren). To the extent possible, I will encourage the parents to contribute to the design of a parenting plan that they are both comfortable with and that reflects the needs and interests of their child(ren). My experience and that of my colleagues indicates that when a solution is reached by the parties themselves, it is more likely to be followed. If the parties do reach an agreement, I would draft a Memorandum of Understanding outlining the agreed-upon plan and send copies to both counsel and both parties. In addition, I would prepare a brief report outlining some suggestions for implementing and maintaining the agreed-upon plan.

If the parents cannot reach agreement on some or all issues, then I would prepare a full custody assessment report containing my recommendations for the plan that would best meet the child(ren)'s needs. This report would be submitted to counsel and to the court, and I would be willing to be called to court to testify.

Please find attached my *curriculum vitae* and an outline of the general procedure that I follow in conducting custody assessments. Of course, the procedure would have to be modified to cover the needs of the particular case.

My fee is $ ___ per hour for interviews and preparation of a report. I charge an additional fee for preparation for court and attendance as an expert witness, should this be necessary.

With respect to payment of my fees, my policy is that both spouses share the cost equitably (not necessarily equally), if possible, because I want to ensure that both of them perceive me as objective and impartial. I will ask for a retainer in the amount of $ ___ before beginning and a refresher when the retainer is depleted. If I am retained, I would hold an initial meeting with both counsel to clarify the scope of the assessment, to obtain relevant documents and background information and to clarify when the assessment report is required.

I am looking forward to assisting your client in arriving at a satisfactory resolution of the custody and access issues. Please feel free to contact me should you have any questions about my policies or procedures.

Yours sincerely,

_____

ASSESSOR

Encl.
* *This letter could be adapted for use with clients.*

Appendix 2A

Outline of Mediation Procedure

As a general outline, the procedure in mediation is as follows:

(a) *Intake call(s) and pre-mediation screening:*
- clarify how clients were referred and why;
- collect basic background information, including whether clients are living together or separately (addresses and phone numbers), ages of children, and issues to be mediated;
- conduct preliminary screening for abuse;
- explain the mediation process, fees, *etc.*;
- obtain names, addresses, and phone numbers of solicitors; and
- send out an information package re mediation and client questionnaire (include questions about abuse, control, comfort level negotiating with the other party, demographic information, and position on issues).

(b) *Meet with counsel for the parties* in order to:
- establish whether mediation will be open or closed;
- clarify what issues are to be mediated;
- clarify payment of fees;
- review and sign retainer contract;
- permit counsel, in each other's presence, to summarize the significant issues in the case and any legal steps taken;
- screen for abuse and control; and
- explain the mediation process.

(c) *Meet with the parties together* in order to:*
- explain the mediator's role as an objective, impartial professional as between the parents;
- encourage the parents to consider the best interests of the child(ren) in reaching a resolution to the issues in dispute;
- discuss the differences between open and closed mediation in order to determine the party's preference;
- review and sign retainer contract;

---

* If there is any concern about abuse or control, an individual screening meeting should take place at separate times before a joint meeting and before a decision is made to mediate. The victim of abuse (usually the woman) should be interviewed first.

- observe and try to improve the communication between the parents; and
- assist the parents to identify the issue and encourage them to work towards their own resolution of the issues in dispute, particularly where children are involved.

(d) *Meet with each parent individually* in order to:
- obtain relevant personal history;
- explore each parent's needs, interests, and concerns; and
- screen for abuse and control.

(e) *Meet with the child(ren) individually, with siblings (if any), and possibly with each parent* (this step is necessary for custody and access mediation only).

(f) *Meet with other significant adults* who are influential in decision making or who will be playing a caretaking role, such as new and common law spouses, grandparents, and other caretakers (this step is usually only necessary in custody and access mediation).

(g) *Request information from sources relevant to the issues in dispute*, such as schools, family doctors, mental health professionals, accountants, property appraisers, *etc.*

(h) *Prepare a Memorandum of Understanding and/or report:*
- If parents reach agreement, set out the agreement reached.
- If parents do not reach agreement, any report depends on whether it is "*open*" or "*closed*" mediation

In my experience, mediation takes approximately fifteen hours of interviews. It is difficult to judge the exact number of hours because this depends on the number of issues to be mediated, the type of issues, the complexity of the situation, the number of parties involved, the level of conflict between the parties, and their willingness to reach a voluntary agreement. Preparation of a Memorandum of Understanding and/or a report (in open mediation) requires additional time.

Appendix 2B

Outline of Custody Assessment Procedure

As a general outline, the procedure in custody assessments is as follows:

(a) *Meet with counsel for the parties in order to:*
- clarify what the assessor's role will be;
- establish whether open mediation is to be attempted at the outset of the assessment;
- permit counsel, in each other's presence, to explain which factors they feel are particularly significant in the case;
- ask counsel to provide affidavits, notices of motion, transcripts of evidence, professional reports, and other documents relevant to the assessment issues; and
- clarify the payment of fees, including fees for the preparation of a report, court preparation, and attendance as an expert witness.

(b) *Meet with the parties together in order to:*
- explain the assessor's role as an objective, impartial professional as between the parents;
- clarify whether mediation is to be attempted as an initial step;
- encourage the parents to develop a parenting plan whereby they share parental responsibilities and visitation with the child(ren) that is in the best interests of the child(ren);
- clarify the assessor's role, that is, to represent the best interests of the child(ren) in the event that the parents are not able to agree on a shared parenting plan;
- clarify the procedure to be followed in the assessment, including who is to be interviewed, in what location, and on how many occasions; and
- obtain the names of persons and agencies who have reliable and relevant information with respect to parenting capacity and the needs and interests of the child(ren).

(c) *Meet with each parent individually.*

(d) *Meet with the child(ren) individually, with siblings* (if any), *and together with each parent.*

(e) *Meet with other significant adults* who will be playing a caretaking role, such as new and common law spouses, grandparents, and other caretakers.

(f) *Request information from relevant sources* such as schools, family doctors, mental health professionals, *etc.*

(g) *Conduct home visits* to observe:
- the child(ren) interacting with each parent and stepparents, siblings, and step siblings;
- the neighbourhood setting of each home;
- the household routines as they pertain to the child(ren); and
- the standards of cleanliness, nutrition and disciplinary limits set.

(h) *Arrange for psychological testing* of the child(ren) and adults if necessary.

(i) *Prepare a Memorandum of Understanding and/or an assessment report.*

Custody assessments usually take approximately twenty to thirty hours of interviews and data collection. It is difficult to judge the exact number of hours because this depends on the complexity of the case, the seriousness of the concerns with respect to parenting capacity, the number of individuals involved, and the willingness of the parties to resolve the issues by agreement. Preparation of a Memorandum of Understanding and/or an assessment report requires additional time.

Appendix 3A

Client Questionnaire

Date: _____   Referred by: _____

HUSBAND

Name: _____
Home Address: _____   Business Address: _____
Mail to: Home _____   Business _____
Telephone: Home (   )_____   Business: (   )_____

Occupation: _____   Full time/Part time (number of hours ___)

Number of years at present place of employment: _____

Net income from employment: _____
Net income from other sources: _____

Date of birth: ___/___/___   Place of birth: _____

Length of residence in Ontario: _____   Canada: _____

Solicitor: _____   Telephone: _____
Address: _____

WIFE

Name: _____
Home address: _____   Business address: _____
Mail to: Home _____   Business _____
Telephone: Home ( )_____   Business: ( )_____

Occupation: _____   Full time/Part time (number of hours ___)

Net income from employment: _____
Net income from other sources: _____

Date of birth: ___/___/___   Place of birth: _____

Length of residence in Ontario: _____   Canada: _____

Solicitor: _____   Telephone: _____
Address: _____

MARITAL INFORMATION

Date of marriage/relationship: ___/___/___ City of marriage: _____

Date of present separation: _____
Date of previous separations: _____

Present marital status:
Married/Common law/Separated/Divorced/ Widowed/Single

Has a divorce petition been filed? Yes ___ No ___
(If yes, by: Husband/Wife)

Are you attending/did you attend marital/family counselling?
     Yes ___ No ___
     If yes, Name: _____ From: _____ (*date*) To: _____ (*date*)
     Address: _____   Telephone: _____

Are you interested in a reconciliation?
   Wife: Yes __ No ___
   Husband: Yes __ No ___

Are you interested in marital counselling? Yes __ No ___

Did you attend individual counselling?
   Wife: Yes __ No __ If yes, From: _____ (*date*) To: _____ (*date*)
   Name: _____   Telephone: _____
   Address: _____   Number of sessions: _____

   Husband: Yes __ No __ If yes, From: _____ (*date*) To: _____ (*date*)
   Name: _____   Telephone: _____
   Address: _____   Number of sessions: _____

CHILDREN OF PRESENT MARRIAGE/RELATIONSHIP

Begin with the oldest child:

	Name	Age	Birthdate	Grade	School	Primarily Residing With
1.	_____	___	_____	_____	_____	_____
2.	_____	___	_____	_____	_____	_____
3.	_____	___	_____	_____	_____	_____
4.	_____	___	_____	_____	_____	_____

FAMILY DOCTOR/SPECIALIST (FOR HUSBAND/WIFE/CHILD(REN))

Name: _____   Telephone: _____
Address: _____

BABYSITTER

Name: _____   Telephone: _____
Address: _____

COUNSELLOR/THERAPIST FOR CHILD(REN)

Name: _____   Telephone: _____
Address: _____

Previous Relationships

Have you been married before?

Wife: Yes __ No ___
If yes, Date of marriage/divorce/death: _____

Husband: Yes __ No ___
If yes, Date of marriage/divorce/death: _____

Children From Previous Marriage/Relationship

*Place an * beside any of the children involved in the present dispute.*

	Name	Age	Birthdate	Grade	School	Primarily Residing With
Wife:						
1.	_____	___	_____	_____	_____	_____
2.	_____	___	_____	_____	_____	_____
Husband:						
1.	_____	___	_____	_____	_____	_____
2.	_____	___	_____	_____	_____	_____

Parenting Issues

What we do best as parents is: _____

My significant concerns about parenting are: _____

My hopes/goals for parenting in the future are: _____

My reasons for separating are: _____

My significant concerns about my relationship with my spouse are:
_____

My significant hopes/goals for my relationship with my spouse are:
_____

During the relationship important decisions were made about:

		By My Spouse	By Me	Jointly
(a)	Household Finances	_____	_____	_____
(b)	Purchases of Family Property	_____	_____	_____
(c)	Children's Education	_____	_____	_____
(d)	Children's Health Care	_____	_____	_____
(e)	Children's Religious Training	_____	_____	_____
(f)	Children's Extracurricular Activities	_____	_____	_____

Are you able to make decisions about the children cooperatively?

_____

Have there been any incidents of verbal abuse?
    In the past six months?   Yes __ No ___
    At any time in the relationship? Yes __ No ___

Have there been any incidents of physical abuse?
    In the past six months?   Yes __ No ___
    At any time in the relationship? Yes __ No ___

Give specifics: _____

Are you able to discuss family issues openly with each other?
    Yes __ No ___

Give specifics: _____

PREVIOUS RELATIONSHIP(S)

Are you paying/receiving spousal support? Yes __ No ___
    If yes, Amount: _____
Are you paying/receiving child support? Yes __ No ___
    If yes, Amount: _____

NEW RELATIONSHIPS

Does husband have a new partner? Yes __ No ___
    If yes: residing together? Yes __ No ___
    Name: _____ Telephone: _____

Does new partner have children? Yes __ No ___
   If yes, residing with husband? Yes __ No ___

   Names of Children   Age

   _____   _____

   _____   _____

Are you paying/receiving financial assistance in the new relationship?
   Yes __ No ___
Does wife have a new partner? Yes __ No ___
   If yes: residing together? Yes __ No ___
   Name: _____   Telephone: _____

Does new partner have children? Yes __ No ___
   If yes, residing with wife? Yes __ No ___

   Names of Children   Age

   _____   _____

   _____   _____

Are you paying/receiving financial assistance in the new relationship?
   Yes __ No ___

POSSIBLE ISSUES IN DISPUTE

Do you anticipate a dispute regarding:
   Custody/Access/Child support/Spousal support/Possession of the
   matrimonial home/Division of property/Debts/Other? _____

Present custodial arrangement: Sole custody to: _____
                         Joint custody (shared parenting)
Desired custody arrangement: Sole custody to: _____
                         Joint custody (shared parenting)

Describe present visitation schedule:

Weekends #   1 / 2 / 3 / 4 / 5   With Mother/Father
           From: _____To: _____

Weekdays (Week 1)   M / T/ W/ T/ F /
With   __/__/__/__/__/
Weekdays (Week 2)   M / T/ W/ T/ F /
With   __/__/__/__/__/
Weekdays (Week 3)   M / T/ W/ T/ F /

With   ___/___/___/___/___/

Weekdays (Week 4)   M / T/ W/ T/ F/

With   ___/___/___/___/___/

Do you spend: Too much time/Too little time / The right amount of time /
     with each child?

Comment: _____

PRESENT RELATIONSHIP

Spousal Support

Are you presently: Paying / Receiving Spousal support? If yes, how much
     per month $ _____

Payments are made: Regularly/Irregularly

Child Support per Child

Are you presently: Paying / Receiving Child support. If yes, how much
     per month $ ___ per child. (Number of children: ___)

Payments are made: Regularly/Irregularly

Other Contributions To Living Expenses

Explain: _____

Matrimonial Home

I would like: Possession of the matrimonial home / Sale of the
     matrimonial home / Other

Other Assets

Have been divided / Have not been divided

Explain: _____

Debts

Significant Debts of Husband: _____

Explain: _____

Significant Debts of Wife: _____

Explain: _____

Appendix 3B

OAFM Policy on Abuse

Reproduced with the permission of the Ontario Association for Family Mediation

MEDIATION OF DISPUTES INVOLVING DOMESTIC VIOLENCE

Adopted at the OAFM Annual General Meeting, June 1994. Many of the concepts and recommendations come from the "Report from the Toronto Forum on Woman Abuse and Mediation, June, 1993".

INTRODUCTION (From Toronto Report)

1. History:

In June of 1991, the Ontario Association for Family Mediation launched an effort to involve North American professional dispute resolution associations in the development of joint policy statements regarding women abuse and mediation. This effort was a direct response to the concerns raised by women's and children's advocates. In May of 1992, 14 mediators representing officially and unofficially the Academy of Family Mediators, Family Mediation Canada, the Ontario Association for Family Mediation and the Society of Professionals in Dispute Resolution met with approximately 50 women's and children's advocates for the purpose of hearing their serious concerns about mediation in cases of abuse. Representatives of the black, native, immigrant and handicapped women's communities were invited to address the additional concerns of these groups. In March of 1993, representatives of most major family mediation associations met with several leaders and front line workers who assist abused women and children, including women of colour, immigrant woman and men who batter. Together they prepared joint recommendations for presentation at the 1993 meetings of the mediation associations.

It was agreed that these recommendations would address primarily:

* the education and training of mediators,
* the skilful screening of candidates for mediation,
* safety issues in mediation,
* alternatives to mediation for abused women.

The concern behind these recommendations was the alarming police statistics that show that more than 95% of complaints to police about abuse are made by women against male perpetrators. A recent survey by Statistics Canada revealed that approximately half of all women have experienced at least one incident of violence since the age of sixteen and 25% of all women have experienced violence at the hands of a current or past marital partner. This incidence is higher in separated or divorced women. The Toronto Forum concluded that "violence against women and its impact on children continue to pose serious questions for dispute resolution professionals and the practice of mediation. Women's advocates, mediators, mental health workers, lawyers and the judiciary are increasingly working together to understand the complex consequences of women abuse. In recent years, efforts at dialogue and collaboration have increased among mediators and women's advocates. They are starting, albeit cautiously, to address co-operatively and constructively the benefits and risks associated with mediation and the unique needs of abused women".

A Word about Language:

The Toronto Forum chose to use the phrase "Woman Abuse" to highlight the fact that complaints about physical abuse, stalking and endangerment in intimate relationships are made primarily by women against men. Where abuse is directed at men by women or where abuse occurs in same sex relationships, the same principles and safeguards should apply. Throughout the rest of this document the term domestic violence or abuse will refer to any woman, man or child who experiences the use or threat of physical, psychological, emotional or economic intimidation, coercion or force in an intimate relationship. The concern in mediation is the impact that abuse has on its victim. Abuse functions to secure power and control for the abuser and to undermine the safety, security, self esteem and autonomy of the abused person.

Abuse is defined broadly to include, but not be limited to:

- physical violence, including assault (pushing, shoving, slapping, choking, hitting, biting, kicking, etc);
- sexual assault;
- kidnapping, confining;
- use of or threat with a weapon;
- threats against children;
- unlawful entry;
- destruction or theft of personal property;
- violence against pets;

- stalking, harassment;
- psychological and verbal abuse including sarcastic, degrading and humiliating comments and name calling;
- contolling and/or manipulative behavior;
- withholding of economic and other resources;
- penalizing the abused person for asserting his/her independence or autonomy, etc.

The following standards of practice acknowledge that "parties to mediation must be able to negotiate safely, voluntarily, and competently in order to reach a fair agreement. Mediation cannot be fair if one of the parties is unable to mediate effectively and competently. "Abuse in intimate relationships poses serious safety risks and may significantly diminish a person's ability to mediate". For this reason, mediators need to identify "which cases are inappropriate for mediation, which are appropriate for specialized mediation and which may proceed in the usual way".

OAFM SAFETY STANDARDS

Assumption: Mediation in cases of Domestic Violence is probably inappropriate.

Family mediation cases in which there is or has been domestic violence are complicated and can be dangerous to the participants and the mediator. Therefore, beginning mediators and mediators not trained or experienced in domestic violence should not accept referrals of these cases, but rather should refer them for screening to a more appropriate resource (such as a lawyer or woman's advocate) or to an experienced mediator who has considerable professional experience in dealing with cases involving domestic violence. Another choice would be for an inexperienced mediator to co-mediate with someone who has considerable professional experience dealing with domestic violence in order to screen for appropriateness.

- Parties to mediation must be able to negotiate safely, voluntarily, and competently in order to reach a fair agreement. If the level of domestic violence is sufficient to jeopardize a party's ability to negotiate without fear or duress, the case should not be mediated. The criterion should be the victim's ability to participate effectively.

- There should be no mediation concerning the violence, itself. For instance, an offer to stop the abuse in exchange for something else should not be allowed in the mediation process.

- When safety is an issue, the mediator's obligation is to provide a safe environment for cooperative problem-solving or, when this does not seem workable, to help the clients consider more appropriate alternatives.

- Above all, the mediator must promote the safety of all participants in the mediation process and its outcome.

OAFM STANDARDS FOR ASSESSING WHETHER MEDIATION MAY BE APPROPRIATE

A. Prior to commencing mediation, all clients should be screened for any occurrences of abuse to determine which cases are inappropriate for mediation, which require additional safeguards, in addition to, or instead of mediation, and which should be referred to other resources.

   1. Conduct initial screening separately with the parties. This could be done a variety of ways. For example, preliminary screening could take place within a brief telephone contact. This should be supplemented by a face-to-face interview or a written questionnaire. Using a structured questionnaire, basic information can be gathered which includes details about any history of abuse. If screening is not done separately, a victim may be unwilling to reveal the presence of abuse and/or may be placed at risk for revealing the abuse.

   2. Screening should continue throughout the mediation process.

B. The issue of voluntariness is critical when it comes to creating a safe place for couples to meet and negotiate.

   OAFM recommends that mediation be voluntary on the part of the participants. It would be acceptable to mandate couples to orientation sessions at separate times during which information could be given about available options for resolving family law disputes (litigation, mediation, arbitration, custody assessments, lawyer assisted negotiation, etc. and about the impact of separation and divorce on parents and children). Inquiries about abuse should be made during the separate orientation sessions, before mediation is offered as an option.

C. Clients should be strongly encouraged to consult with attorneys prior to mediation and certainly before an agreement is finalized.

D.   Mediators must be knowledgeable about abuse:

Training for mediators should include the following:

1.   Issues related to physical and psychological abuse and its effect on family members;

2.   The impact that abuse (including witnessing abuse) has on children;

3.   Effective techniques for screening, implementing safety measures, and safe termination;

4.   Referral to appropriate resources, in addition to, or instead of mediation;

5.   Sensitivity to cultural, racial and ethnic differences that can impact the mediation process that may be relevant to domestic violence.

E.   Where a decision is made that mediation may proceed, mediators need to meet standards of safety, voluntariness, and fairness. When mediators have concerns, they should inform their clients that they are *not* neutral about violence or safety. Mediators should inform clients that they have a positive obligation to report past or present child abuse and threats of future abuse to any of the participants.

Procedural guidelines:

1.   Obtain training about abuse and become familiar with the literature.

2.   Never mediate the fact of the abuse.

3.   Never support a couple's trading non-violent behaviour for obedience.

4.   Set ground rules to optimize the protection of all parties.

5.   When appropriate and possible, arrange separate waiting areas and separate arrival and leaving times, permitting the victim to arrive last and leave first with a reasonable lag in time for safety purposes.

6.   Use separate meetings throughout the mediation process when appropriate, necessary, and/or helpful.

7.   Consider co-mediation with a male/female mediation team, as an option.

8.   Allow a support person to be present in the waiting room during screening, and/or during the mediation session.

9.   Maintain a balance of power between the couple, and, if this is not possible, terminate the mediation process and refer the couple to an appropriate alternative. Such alternatives might

include shelters, therapists, abuse prevention groups, and attorneys.

10. Where fairness of outcome may be an issue, the mediator should refer the clients to their counsel, financial advisor, support person, or other relevant resource for information and advice.

11. Terminate the mediation if either of the participants is unable to mediate safely, competently, and without fear or coercion. Precautions should be taken in terminating to assure the safety of the parties. For example, the mediator should not reveal information to one party or to the court that could create a risk for the other party.

12. Consider offering a follow up session to assess the need for a modification of the agreement.

THE OAFM BOARD AFFIRMED THE FOLLOWING GUIDELINES:

1. OAFM encourages its members to work with the diverse cultural and ethnic groups serving adults and children to improve public awareness and the development of a wider range of options and services for victims of abuse.

2. OAFM agrees to incorporate this policy within their standards of practice outlining the conduct expected of mediators in cases of abuse and clarifying that mediators must *not* be neutral with regard to violence or safety. The Standards of Practice should reflect that safety must take priority over neutrality.

3. OAFM agrees to work with government to develop standards to govern the practice of mediation.

4. OAFM requires all Practicing Members to participate in a minimum of five hours training on domestic violence including screening, safety measures, safe termination, and alternatives to mediation, when mediation is not appropriate.

Approved June 11, 1994

Appendix 3C

Do's and Do Not's Re: Safe Termination

Do's — Meeting With Victim (Statistics suggest that the victim will be a woman. Where this is not the case, substitute the appropriate gender.)

- Discuss with victim your concerns about mediation and alternatives that might better protect her and the children.
- Ask victim what would be a helpful approach for terminating safely.
- Tell victim what you will tell abuser and make a safety plan for her and the children in case abuser blames victim.

Do's — Meeting With Abuser

- Assist abuser to see that mediation is unlikely to be suitable or productive or meet his needs (*i.e.*, it is not likely to succeed and therefore there will be added delay and cost).
- Utilize abuser's language, information, and rationale if appropriate.
- State that mediator has a "gut feeling", based on his or her experience, that mediation is unlikely to succeed in this case, *i.e.*, take personal responsibility for termination.
- For "B) couples", if guidelines are set and not adhered to, focus on this as the basis for termination.
- Tell abuser that they are not ready for mediation. Suggest what needs to happen first (*e.g.*, counselling re effect of separation). They may be ready in the future.

Do Not's

- If abuse has not already been disclosed, don't reveal abuse to abuser's solicitor or to court because this could endanger victim.
- Don't blame or put down victim.

SAFETY PLANNING

Ask Victim

- Are you worried about your safety now? How will abuser react to mediation being terminated?

- Especially if they are still living together — do you feel safe in your present living arrangement? *If not,* have you talked to a woman's advocate or lawyer? Encourage her to do so — give names, addresses, and phone numbers. Help her make contact.
- Do you know of any emergency shelters in case you need to find a place of safety for you and the children? Give names and phone numbers.
- Do you have any other safe place to go? Do you have any money? Have you ever contacted the police?

Ask Abuser

- Do you have a lawyer? Encourage him to get one. Give names, addresses, and phone numbers.
- Do you have a counsellor? Encourage him to get one and to enter a Batterer's Treatment Program if appropriate.

Appendix 4A

Closed Mediation Retainer Contract

RE: (*Clients' Names*)

1. It is hereby agreed that (*name of Mediator*) is retained to act as the Mediator with respect to the following issues:

   (i)   parenting arrangements including custody of and access to the children;
   (ii)   child support and spousal support;
   (iii)   division of property;
   (iv)   possession of matrimonial home;
   (v)   other financial issues.

2. It is acknowledged that the Mediator is an impartial third party whose role is to assist the parties to negotiate a voluntary agreement.

3. In attempting to bring about an Agreement, the Mediator will meet with the parties for joint sessions and on occasion for individual sessions. The Mediator may include in the mediation process any other significant third party, such as a new partner, grandparents, other relatives, legal counsel, or other significantly involved persons following consultation with the parties.

4. It is acknowledged that (*name of Mediator*) will be acting as a Mediator and will not be acting as a lawyer. The parties are strongly advised to obtain independent legal advice, preferably before mediation commences, but in any event, before a final Agreement is reached, to ensure that they are fully informed of their legal rights and obligations and the legal implications of such an Agreement. In the event that the parties do not have independent legal advice prior to signing an Agreement, it is recognized that:

(i)   the parties may not be making fully informed choices in light of their respective legal rights;

(ii)   the Agreement they reach is less likely to be enforced by a court.

5. The Mediator may obtain information from relevant sources and may consult such persons and read such reports, records or documents as he/she deems necessary for arriving at an Agreement. It is agreed that the parties will:

(i)   make full disclosure of all relevant information reasonably required for the Mediator to understand the issues being mediated;

(ii)   execute any Releases of Information necessary for the Mediator to obtain relevant information.

6. If issues related to property or support are discussed during the mediation process, then the parties will:

(i)   make full financial disclosure to each other and the Mediator;

(ii)   undertake not to hide or dispose of any assets; or

(iii)   not cancel or change any beneficiaries of life insurance policies while the mediation is in process.

7. The parties understand that interim agreements with respect to custody of and access to the children or child or spousal support will be a factor to be considered by the courts, in the event that an agreement is not reached in mediation.

8. Neither party nor anyone acting on their behalf will take any fresh steps in the legal proceedings between the parties with respect to those issues that are being mediated.

9. If the parties reach agreement on some or all of the issues, the Mediator shall prepare a Memorandum of Understanding with respect to those issues for consideration by the parties and their respective counsel.

10. If the parties fail to agree on one or more issues it is understood that:

(i) anything said or any admission or communication in the course of the mediation is not admissible in any legal proceeding;

(ii) the Mediator will not be called as a witness by or on behalf of either party in any legal proceeding;

(iii) the Mediator may be required by the court to testify despite this agreement to the contrary;

(iv) if the parties do not reach an agreement through mediation on any specified issue, that will be so reported by the Mediator.

11. It is agreed that:

(i) the parties will each pay a retainer of $ _____ ($ _____ total) and will share the costs of the mediation equally;

(ii) interim accounts shall be sent out to the parties and payment shall be due when rendered;

(iii) the hourly rate will be $ _____ per hour and is subject to change upon notice by the Mediator.

(iv) from time to time an additional retainer will be requested to cover the anticipated next steps in the mediation. The mediation will not continue until the retainer is paid.

12. Interest will be charged at the Prime Rate on all accounts outstanding after 30 (thirty) days from the date the account is rendered.

13. The parties will be billed for an appointment in which there is less than 24 (twenty-four) business hours' notice prior to cancellation if the appointment is for 2 (two) hours. If an appointment is scheduled for more than 2 (two) hours, 48 (forty-eight) business hours' notice are required prior to cancellation. The parties will each be responsible for bills arising from his/her own cancellation. These charges are regardless of the reason for the cancellation, except at the Mediator's discretion. The parties will each be responsible for bills arising from his/her own cancellation.

14. Any report or Memorandum of Understanding will not be released until all outstanding professional fees and disbursements related to the mediation have been paid in full.

15. It is understood that either of the parties may terminate the mediation process at any time. The Mediator may suspend or terminate mediation whenever:

(i)   the process is likely to harm or prejudice one or more of the participants; or

(ii) the usefulness of the mediation process is exhausted; or

(iii) the Agreement being reached is unreasonable.

The Mediator will first advise the parties of the reason why he/she believes the mediation should be terminated.

16. Each of the undersigned acknowledges that he/she has read this Retainer and agrees to be bound by the terms herein.

DATED at _____, this _____ day of _____, 19 __.

_____	_____
WITNESS	FATHER'S NAME
_____	_____
WITNESS	MOTHER'S NAME
_____	_____
WITNESS	MEDIATOR

If both parties are represented by counsel, the Mediator should ask both counsel to review and sign the retainer contract to avoid future confusion with respect to the Mediator's role, whether it is "open" or "closed" mediation, the payment of fees, or other relevant matters. The following clauses should be substituted for clause 16 as set out above:

16. Counsel for the parties agree that they will assist the Mediator to obtain payment of his/her account in the same proportion as the parties are required to pay according to this Retainer. The Mediator agrees that he/she will notify the lawyers and the parties before the retainer is depleted and ask for a further retainer. The mediation will not continue until a further retainer is received.

17. Counsel acknowledges receipt of this document and agrees, subject to approval by their client, that the terms herein describe the nature of the Mediator's retainer.

DATED at _____, this _____ day of _____, 19 __.

_____	_____
WITNESS	FATHER'S NAME
_____	_____
WITNESS	MOTHER'S NAME
_____	_____
WITNESS	MEDIATOR

Appendix 4B

Open Mediation
Retainer Contract

RE: (*Clients' Names*)

1. It is hereby agreed that (*name of Mediator*) is retained to act as the Mediator with respect to the following issue:

    (i)   a parenting plan, including custody of and access to the children;

2. It is acknowledged that the Mediator is an impartial third party whose role is to assist the parties to negotiate a voluntary agreement.

3. In attempting to bring about an Agreement, the Mediator will meet with the parties for joint sessions and on occasion for individual sessions. The Mediator may include in the mediation process any other significant third party, such as a new partner, grandparents, other relatives, legal counsel or other significantly involved persons following consultation with the parties.

4. It is acknowledged that (*name of Mediator*) will be acting as a Mediator and will not be giving legal advice. The parties are strongly advised to obtain independent legal advice, preferably before mediation commences, but in any event, before a final Agreement is reached, to ensure that they are fully informed of their legal rights and obligations and the legal implications of such an Agreement. In the event that the parties do not have independent legal advice prior to signing an Agreement, it is recognized that:

    (i)   the parties may not be making fully informed choices in light of their respective legal rights;

    (ii)   the Agreement they reach is less likely to be enforced by a court.

5. The Mediator may obtain information from relevant sources and may consult such persons and read such reports, records or documents as he/she deems necessary for arriving at an Agreement. It is agreed that the parties will:

    (i)   make full disclosure of all relevant information reasonably required for the Mediator to understand the issues being mediated;

(ii)   execute any Releases of Information necessary for the Mediator to obtain relevant information.

6. The parties understand that interim agreements with respect to custody of and access to the children will be a factor to be considered by the courts, in the event that an agreement is not reached in mediation.

7. Neither party nor anyone acting on their behalf will take any fresh steps in the legal proceedings between the parties with respect to those issues that are being mediated.

8. If the parties reach agreement on some or all of the issues, the Mediator shall prepare a Memorandum of Understanding with respect to those issues for consideration by the parties and their respective counsel.

9. If the parties fail to agree on one or more issues it is understood that:

(i)   the Mediator will prepare a report outlining the Mediator's recommendation;
(ii)   anything said or any admission or communication made in the course of the mediation may be used in the report; and
(iii)   the Mediator may be called as a witness by either party in a legal proceeding and would be open to cross-examination by either counsel.

10. Copies of the report will be distributed to both counsel, both parties and the court at least two weeks prior to the court date.

11. It is agreed that:

(i)   each party will each pay a retainer of $ _____ ($_____ total) and share the cost of the mediation equally;
(ii)   interim accounts shall be sent out to the parties and payment shall be due when rendered;
(iii)   the hourly rate will be $ _____ per hour and is subject to change upon notice by the Mediator.
(iv)   from time to time an additional retainer will be requested to cover the anticipated next steps in the mediation. The mediation will not continue until the retainer is paid.

12. Interest will be charged at the Prime Rate on all accounts outstanding after 30 (thirty) days from the date the account is rendered.

13. The parties will be billed for an appointment in which there is less than 24 (twenty-four) business hours' notice prior to cancellation if the appointment is for 2 (two) hours. If an appointment is scheduled for

more than 2 (two) hours, 48 (forty-eight) business hours' notice is required prior to cancellation. These charges are regardless of the reason for the cancellation, except at the Mediator's discretion. The parties will each be responsible for bills arising from his/her own cancellation.

14. Any report or Memorandum of Understanding will not be released until all outstanding professional fees and disbursements related to the mediation have been paid in full.

15. In the event that the Mediator is called to court, a separate fee shall be required for preparation and attendance as an expert witness. This fee shall be paid in advance by the party who is calling the Mediator as an expert witness.

16. It is understood that either of the parties may terminate the mediation process at any time. The Mediator may suspend or terminate mediation whenever:

    (i)   the process is likely to harm or prejudice one or more of the participants; or
    (ii)   the usefulness of the mediation process is exhausted; or
    (iii) the Agreement being reached is unreasonable.

The Mediator will first advise the parties of the reason why he/she believes the mediation should be terminated.

17. Each of the undersigned acknowledges that he/she has read this Retainer and agrees to be bound by the terms herein.

DATED at _____, this _____ day of _____, 19 __.

_____
WITNESS

_____
WITNESS

_____
WITNESS

_____
FATHER'S NAME

_____
MOTHER'S NAME

_____
MEDIATOR

If both parties are represented by counsel, the Mediator should ask both counsel to review and sign the retainer contract to avoid future confusion with respect to the Mediator's role, whether it is "open" or "closed" mediation, the payment of fees, or other relevant matters. The following clauses should be substituted for clause 17 as set out above:

17. Counsel for the parties agree that they will assist the Mediator to obtain payment of his/her account in the same proportion as the parties are required to pay according to this Retainer. The Mediator agrees that he/she will notify the lawyers and the parties before the retainer is depleted and ask for a further retainer. The mediation will not continue until a further retainer is received.

18. Counsel acknowledges receipt of this document and agrees, subject to approval by their client, that the terms herein describe the nature of the Mediator's retainer.

DATED at _____, this _____ day of _____, 19 __.

_____
WITNESS

_____
WITNESS

_____
WITNESS

_____
COUNSEL FOR THE FATHER

_____
COUNSEL FOR THE MOTHER

_____
MEDIATOR

Appendix 4C

Assessment Retainer Contract

(RE: *Client's Names*)

1. It is hereby agreed that (*Assessor's name*), Mental Health Professional, is retained to act as the Assessor with respect to:

    (i)   a parenting plan, including, custody of and access to the children of the marriage.

2. It is acknowledged that the Assessor is an impartial third party whose role is to assist the parties to negotiate an agreement with respect to the outstanding issue.

3. In conducting the Assessment, the Assessor will meet with the parties for joint sessions and on occasion for individual sessions. The Assessor will have the right at any time to include in the assessment process any other significant third party, such as a new partner, grandparents, other relatives, legal counsel or other significant involved persons as he/she deems necessary.

4. The Assessor may obtain information from relevant sources and may consult such persons and read such reports, records or documents as he/she deems necessary for arriving at an Agreement.

It is agreed that the parties will:

(i)   make full disclosure of all relevant information reasonably required for the Assessor to understand the issues being assessed;

(ii)   execute any Releases of Information necessary for the Assessor to obtain relevant information.

6. The parties understand that any interim agreement with respect to custody of or access to the children will be a factor to be considered by the courts, in the event that an agreement is not reached in the Assessment.

7. Neither party or anyone acting on their behalf will take any fresh steps in the legal proceedings between the parties with respect to those issues that are being assessed.

8. If the parties reach agreement on some or all of the issues, the Assessor shall prepare a Memorandum of Understanding with respect to those issues for consideration by the parties and their respective counsel. The parties are strongly advised to obtain independent legal advice, preferably before the Assessment commences, but in any event, before a final agreement is reached, to ensure that they are fully informed of their legal rights and obligations and the legal implications of such an agreement.

9. If the parties fail to agree on one or more issues it is understood that:

(i)   the Assessor will prepare a report outlining the Assessor's recommendations;

(ii)   anything said or any admission or communication made in the course of the Assessment may be used in the report; and

(iii) the Assessor may be called as a witness by either party in a legal proceeding and would be open to cross-examination by either counsel.

10. Copies of the report will be distributed to both counsel, both parties and the court at least two weeks prior to the court date.

11. It is agreed that;

(i)   each party will pay a retainer of $ _____ each and will share the costs of the assessment equally;

(ii)   interim accounts shall be sent out to the parties and payment shall be due when rendered;

(iii)   the hourly rate will be $ _____ per hour and is subject to a change upon notice by the Assessor.

(iv)   from time to time an additional retainer will be requested to cover the anticipated next steps in the assessment. The assessment will not continue until the retainer is paid.

12. Interest will be charged at the Prime Rate on all accounts outstanding after 30 (thirty) days from the date the account is rendered.

13. The parties will be billed for an appointment in which there is less than 24 (twenty-four) business hours' notice prior to cancellation if the appointment is for 2 (two) hours. If an appointment is scheduled for more than 2 (two) hours, 48 (forty-eight) business hours' notice is required prior to cancellation. The parties will each be responsible for bills arising from his/her own cancellation.

14. Any report or Memorandum of Understanding will not be released until all outstanding professional fees and disbursements related to the Assessment have been paid in full.

15. In the event that the Assessor is called to court, a separate fee shall be required for preparation and attendance as an expert witness. This fee shall be paid in advance by the party who is calling the Assessor as an expert witness.

16. Each of the undersigned acknowledges that he/she has read this Retainer and agrees to be bound by the terms herein.

DATED at _____, this _____ day of _____, 19 __.

_____
WITNESS

_____
FATHER'S NAME

_____
WITNESS

_____
MOTHER'S NAME

_____
WITNESS

_____
MEDIATOR

If both parties are represented by counsel, the Assessor should ask both counsel to review and sign the retainer contract to avoid future confusion with respect to the Assessor's role, the scope of the assessment, the payment of fees, or other relevant matters. The following clauses should be substituted for clause 16 as set out above:

16. Counsel for the parties agree that they will assist the Assessor to obtain payment of his/her account in the same proportion as the parties are required to pay according to this Retainer. The Assessor agrees that he/she will notify the lawyers and the parties before the retainer is depleted and ask for a further retainer. The Assessment will not continue until a further retainer is received.

17. Counsel acknowledges receipt of this document and agrees, subject to approval by their client, that the terms herein describe the nature of the Assessment retainer.

DATED at _____, this _____ day of _____, 19 __.

_____
WITNESS

_____
WITNESS

_____
WITNESS

_____
COUNSEL FOR THE FATHER

_____
COUNSEL FOR THE MOTHER

_____
MEDIATOR

Appendix 5A

Consent to Release Information

To: (*Principal, School*) _____
FROM: Mr. and Mrs. _____
RE: (*Child's Name*) _____

I/WE HEREBY AUTHORIZE AND DIRECT YOU to release information relevant to school performance and adjustment respecting the above-named child(ren) to our Mediator/Assessor, (*name*) _____ (*address*) _____, as he/she may require.

AND FOR SO DOING this shall be your good and sufficient authority.

DATED at _____ this _____ day of _____ 19 __.

_____   _____

WITNESS

_____   _____

WITNESS

Appendix 5B

Covering Letter Re:
Consent to Release Information

(*Date*)

(*Address of Public School*)

Dear _____:

RE: (*Name*)

I have been retained by Mr. and Mrs. _____ as a Mediator/ Assessor to assist with respect to marital difficulties. Enclosed please find a Release of Information form duly signed by Mr. and Mrs. _____. I would greatly appreciate your contacting me by telephone as soon as possible to discuss information you may have with respect to the child's school performance and adjustment.

Yours sincerely,

_____

MEDIATOR/ASSESSOR

Encl.

Appendix 5C

Memo to File Re: Consents

CONSENT FORMS SENT TO:

Name: _____
Contact made: Yes __ No ___

Date Sent: _____

Telephone: _____

Name: _____

Contact made: Yes __ No __

Date Sent: _____

Telephone: _____

Appendix 6

Letter to Solicitors from Mediator

Dear Solicitors,

<u>Re: Tom Iam Perfect and Linda Norya Notte (Perfect)</u>

I am pleased to report that Linda and Tom have reached an agreement with respect to a Parenting Plan that outlines how they plan to share parental rights, responsibilities and time with their children, Jordy and Kathy. In addition, as we discussed, Linda and Tom asked to continue in mediation to deal with the issues of the matrimonial home, support, and other property and financial issues. Again I am pleased to report that they succeeded in reaching agreement on all issues.

By way of summary, Tom and Linda participated in the following process: They were seen in a combination of individual and joint sessions. In addition, each parent was seen with the children, and the children were seen both individually and in a sibling group. New partners were interviewed, the school, family doctor, and relevant mental health professionals were contacted with respect to information related to the needs and interests of the children.

During the mediation process, I met with counsel and held conference calls, particularly with respect to the financial issues. All documents and reports provided by the solicitors were reviewed by the mediator. Counsel were particularly helpful in preparing the client's sworn financial statements and an impartial accountant was jointly retained to value Tom's business. In addition, with the consent of Tom and Linda, I arranged for an impartial actuary to value Tom's pension.

I have enclosed a copy of the Memorandum of Understanding drafted with respect to those issues sent to mediation. Since I am a trained as a lawyer, I drafted the Memorandum so that it could be changed into a Separation Agreement quite easily once the parties have had independent legal advice. If one or both parties wishes to make some changes in the Memorandum, I would be more than happy to discuss this with both the parties and their lawyers. I would make any amendments that both parties agree on.

I have enjoyed working with both the parties and counsel and would be more than willing to offer assistance in the future should there be a change in circumstances or should some difficulty arise that might be best dealt with through mediation. I would appreciate receiving a copy of the final Agreement for my files, once the parties have had independent legal advice and have signed the Agreement.

Thank you for your cooperation in this matter.

Yours sincerely,

_____

MEDIATOR

Appendix 7

Sample: Parenting Plan

PARENTING RESPONSIBILITIES

1. Doctor appointments

2. Dentist appointments

3. Other appointments, *e.g.*, orthodontist, allergist, therapist, *etc.*

4. "Emergency" appointments:
   - medical care
   - child care
   - school/day care

5. Transportation to and from:
   - extracurricular activities
   - remedial programs
   - children's extended family (grandparents, cousins, aunts, and uncles)
   - friends (birthday parties, *etc.*).

6. Attendance at extracurricular activities:
   - parents
   - extended family
   - new partners

7. Transportation to and from visits with parent

8. Shopping:
   - for clothes
   - for sporting or other equipment
   - for gifts (for child's friends or family)

   Clarify payment for these items

9. Access to information:
   - medical, dental, mental health, educational, and how information to be shared

10. Attendance at school events:
    - parent/teacher meetings
    - other special events

11. Parental decision making with respect to:
    - education (including the type of school, location, cost, *etc.*)
    - health care (medical, dental, mental health, including counselling for child)
    - religion (including religious affiliation, attendance, education, *etc.*)
    - extracurricular activities, summer programs, remedial programs
    - other

    Clarify who has responsibility for decision making, registration, and payment of fees for children's needs.

12. Child's name (*Change of Name Act*)

13. Communication between parents re children's needs
    - process and guidelines.

14. Involvement of new partners or extended family:
  • with children
  • with parents
  Guidelines to minimize conflict and stress for children.

CHILDREN'S SCHEDULE:

The children will spend time with each parent as follows:

1. School breaks:*
  • Christmas School Break:
    — Christmas Eve
    — Christmas Day
    — Boxing Day
    — New Year's Eve
    — New Year's Day
  • March Break
  • Summer Break

2. Statutory holidays:*
  • Labour Day Weekend
  • Thanksgiving
  • Victoria Day
  • Canada Day
  • Civic Holiday (August)
  • Easter

3. Professional development days:*

4. Other special days:
  • Mother's Day
  • Father's Day
  • Child's birthday
  • Mother's birthday
  • Father's birthday
  • Religious observances

5. Regular schedule:
  • weekends
  • midweek
  • one-on-one contact

---

* Clarify responsibility for arranging and paying for children when parent not able to supervise children.

6. Telephone contact:
   * with children
   * with partners

7. Parental communication:
   * how
   * when
   * why

8. Out-of-province travel:
   * passports
   * letter of approval

9. Material change of circumstances, *i.e.*, Review parenting arrangements if:*
   * move by a parent (notice re when and where) so that present arrangements not feasible
   * children get older
   * new partner
   * illness/disability of a child
   * death or disability of a parent
   * other

10. Resolution of future disputes:
    * clarify process to be followed

Appendix 8

Sample Memorandum of Understanding Re: Custody and Access, Support and Property Division

This document is not intended to be a legally binding contract, but merely a statement of intention by the parties.

BETWEEN :

Tom Iam Perfect

(hereinafter the "Father/Husband")

Linda Norya Notte (Perfect)

(hereinafter the "Mother/Wife")

MEMORANDUM OF UNDERSTANDING

1. DEFINITIONS

In this Agreement:

1.1 *"Children's Law Reform Act"* means the *Children's Law Reform Act*, R.S.O. 1990, c. C.12, as amended, or its successor;

1.2 "Cohabit" means to live together in a conjugal relationship whether inside or outside of marriage;

1.3 *"Divorce Act"* means the *Divorce Act*, R.S.C. 1985, c. 3 (2nd Supp.), as amended, or its successor;

1.4 *"Family Law Act"* means the *Family Law Act*, R.S.O. 1990, c. F.3, as amended, or its successor;

1.5 "Father/Husband" means Tom Iam Perfect, who is one of the parties to this Agreement;

1.6 *"Income Tax Act"* means the *Income Tax Act*, R.S.C. 1985, c.1 (5th Supp.), as amended, or its successor;

1.7 "Matrimonial Home" means _____;

1.8 "Property" means property as defined by the *Family Law Act*;

1.9 *"Succession Law Reform Act"* means the *Succession Law Reform Act*, R.S.O. 1990, c. S.26, as amended, or its successor;

1.10 "Net Family Property" means net family property as that term is described in the *Family Law Act*;

1.11 "Mother/Wife" means Linda Norya Notte, who is one of the parties to this Agreement;

1.12 *"Trustee Act"* means the *Trustee Act*, R.S.O. 1990, c. T.23, as amended, or its successor;

1.13 *"Insurance Act"* means the *Insurance Act*, R.S.O. 1990, c. I.8, as amended, or its successor;

2. BACKGROUND

2.1 Tom and Linda were married to each other in the City of _____, in the Province of _____ , on the _____ day of _____, 19__.

2.2 Tom and Linda have two children of the marriage, namely Jordy, born on the _____ of _____ (12 years of age) and Kathy born on the _____ of _____ (9 years of age).

2.3 Tom and Linda have agreed to live separate and apart and have in fact lived separate and apart in the same home since the 1st of April, 19__ and plan to live separate and apart in different residences as of the 29th day of August, 19__. There is no reasonable prospect of reconciliation.

2.4 Tom and Linda have reached agreement, subject to advice from their lawyers, with respect to the following issues: a parenting plan for their children, Jordy and Kathy, child and spousal support, possession, ownership and division of their property, and equalization of their net family properties. This document sets out the agreements reached in Mediation and both parties agree to be bound by its terms.

3. FREEDOM FROM THE OTHER

3.1 Both Tom and Linda accept the fact of their separation and agree to respect each other's privacy and right to live separately. They will not annoy, harass, or in any way interfere with the other, or attempt to compel the other to cohabit or live with him or her.

4. PARENTING PLAN (CUSTODY)

4.1 STATEMENT OF PRINCIPLES

4.1.1   As the parents of Jordy and Kathy, we acknowledge that we are both devoted and loving parents and it is in the best interests of Jordy and Kathy to have a close relationship with both of us.

4.1.2   This Agreement sets out our commitment to provide Jordy and Kathy with the best parenting we are capable of from our separate homes. We will carry out our responsibilities and conduct ourselves as parents so as to enhance our children's growth and development within the spirit of this parenting plan.

4.1.3   We recognize that the level of tension between us during the past year has created an emotionally stressful situation for Jordy and Kathy. We both agree that in the future we will adhere to the following guidelines in order to reduce the level of conflict for our children and work toward an improved level of cooperation as parents:

(i)   We will encourage Jordy and Kathy to love both parents and their extended family.

(ii)   We will ensure that Jordy and Kathy participate in a Children of Divorce program and we will participate in counselling to deal with our own emotional issues related to the separation.

(iii)   We will discuss parenting issues directly with each other, without using Jordy and Kathy as messengers and these discussions will take place when Jordy and Kathy are not present. When Jordy and Kathy are present we will speak to each other in a respectful manner.

(iv)   We recognize that our parenting styles are different and agree to respect these differences. If a child complains about some aspect of parenting in the other parent's home, we will encourage that child to discuss the issue directly with the other parent. If the child is uncomfortable, we will help the child to communicate with the other parent. We will listen to such complaints without making judgments or interfering.

(v) If we have concerns about the children's safety or well being while in the other parent's home, we will discuss that directly with the other parent and if the situation is not resolved satisfactorily, we will seek the assistance of an appropriate professional for dealing with children or return to mediation.

(vi) We will hold weekly parenting telephone meetings at noon on Fridays and each of us will prepare an agenda of parenting issues to discuss. If we decide to change our present Agreement or to add new items, we will do so in writing and make sure we both have a signed copy.

(vii) We would both prefer to have the children continue attending the same church and therefore we agree to make all reasonable efforts to assist each other and the children to feel comfortable at this church.

(viii) We both agree that, if it is financially possible, we would like the children to continue to attend the Toronto French School. We both recognize that this means some financial sacrifices. If it is no longer possible or preferable for either child to attend, we will discuss this with each other before speaking either to the child or the school. We will try to work out a mutually acceptable alternative before enrolling the children in a different school and will return to mediation or speak to appropriate professionals at the school if we have difficulty resolving this issue.

4.1.4 Linda and Tom agree that they will have joint legal custody of the children and the children will reside in Linda's home and she will have the day-to-day care of the children.

4.2 PARENTING SCHEDULE

4.2.1 *Regular Times*

4.2.1.1 Jordy and Kathy will reside with their father at the following times:

(a) Each alternate weekend, a weekend to be defined as extending from Thursday after school until Monday morning. Tom will pick the children up after school and will return them to school. On the other week Tom will pick the children up after school on Thursday and return them to school on Friday morning.

(b)   Tom will take the children to church on the Sundays when the children are with him and Linda will take them to church on the alternate Sundays.

(c)   Each month Tom can arrange to spend one mid-week evening with each child individually. He will give Linda at least 48 hours' notice and, unless the children already have alternative plans, they will spend from after school until 7:30 p.m. with their father.

4.2.2   *Telephone Contact*

Kathy and Jordy will be permitted to have telephone contact with both parents at all reasonable times prior to their bedtime.

4.2.3   *School Breaks*

4.2.3.1 *Christmas School Break*

Unless the parents agree otherwise, the children will spend the first part of the Christmas School Break with their mother in odd-numbered years and from Boxing Day in the morning until New Year's Day with their father. In even-numbered years the children will be with their father from December 24th at 4 p.m. until December 31st at 4 p.m. The parents agree to meet by no later than November 15th of each year to finalize the specific dates.   If one parent wants to take the children on a vacation for more than the time provided by this schedule, then they will discuss that prior to November the 1st. If one parent takes the children for a vacation during one Christmas Break, then the other parent will have the right of first refusal the following Christmas.

4.2.3.2 *March School Break*

If the March Break is one week, the children will spend it with their father if he is able to take this time off work. He will let Linda know his plans no later than February 1st. Tom will return the children on the Sunday before school begins by 4 p.m. (unless both parents agree to a different return date).

If the March Break is two weeks, the children will spend one week with each parent, with the specific dates to be worked out between the parents by no later than February 1st.

4.2.3.3 *Summer School Break*

The children will spend up to three weeks with their father during the summer. Both Linda and Tom agree that the children should not be away from contact with the other parent for more than two weeks at a time until the youngest child is ten years of age. Both parents agree that they will decide no later than March 1st of each year about the children's summer activities, day camp, and vacation plans with each parent.

4.2.4　*Special Times*

4.2.4.1 *Statutory Holidays*

Kathy and Jordy will spend the statutory holidays with the parent with whom they are residing on that weekend according to the regular schedule. That is, an additional day will be added to the regular schedule.

4.2.4.2 *Professional Development Days*

The children will spend professional development days with whichever parent is able to take the day off work. This will be arranged two weeks before the P.D. Day. If neither parent is available, the parent who is scheduled to be with them according to the regular schedule will take the responsibility of arranging alternative care for that day.

4.2.4.3 *Birthdays*

Each parent will plan a celebration for each child's birthday at a time when that child is with that parent. Both parents can contact or see the child on his or her birthday if that is convenient.

4.2.4.4 *Parents' Birthdays*

The children will celebrate the parents' birthday when they are with that parent. The children can contact the parent on the actual birthday, if that is convenient.

4.2.4.5 *Mother's Day/Father's Day*

The children will spend time with their mother on Mother's Day and their father on Father's Day, with specific times to be arranged by mutual consent of the parents.

4.2.5 *Additional Access*

The parents will consult with each other with respect to additional time the children can spend one-on-one with each parent. Such arrangements will be made by mutual consent of the parents, taking into account the needs and interests of each child.

4.3 VARIATION OF PARENTING SCHEDULE

4.3.1   Tom and Linda agree that the terms of the parenting schedule may be varied upon at least 48 (forty-eight) hours notice to the other parent where it is shown that it would be in the best interests of the children to vary such parenting schedule. Such request for alteration of the parenting schedule will not be unreasonably withheld by either parent, unless it is in the best interests of the children not to accede to such a request.

4.3.2   In the event that a parent cannot be with the children during the time that the children are scheduled to be with that parent, then both parents wish to be offered an opportunity to be with the children before an alternative babysitting arrangement is made.

4.4   PARENTING RESPONSIBILITIES

4.4.1   Linda and Tom will consult with each other in advance with respect to significant decisions about the children's education, medical care, dental care, mental health care and religion and with respect to significant expenditures for the children where both parents will be contributing to such expenditures.

4.4.2   Both parents agree that Linda will arrange the doctor and dentist appointments and will consult in advance with Tom if she wishes assistance in taking the children to these appointments. Linda will continue to shop for the children's clothes. Tom will buy the sports items and equipment and will shop for clothing if Linda or the children request this.

4.4.3   Both parents agree to give their phone numbers and addresses to the children's school so that either can be contacted in the case of an emergency.

4.4.4   Both parents agree that they will take responsibility for the children if they are ill or injured while in that parent's care. Linda and Tom agree to notify the other parent if a child is ill or injured and either parent can ask the other parent for assistance, but if the other parent is unable or it is inconvenient, then the primary responsibility will remain with the parent with whom the children are residing at that time. This responsibility will include making alternative arrangements if neither parent is able to care for the children. Both parents agree that it is acceptable to call either Linda or Tom's extended family for assistance if neither parent can stay home with the children.

4.4.5   Both parents agree not to register the children for extra-curricular activities during the time the children are scheduled to be with the other parent. Linda and Tom agree to consult with each other at the beginning of each school semester before enrolling Jordy or Kathy in activities, particularly if they wish the assistance of the other parent in transporting the children or sharing the cost of the activity.

4.4.6 Both parents agree to share the transportation of the children to and from extracurricular activities, including birthday parties with specific times and arrangements to be determined by mutual consent of the parents. The parents will inform each other as soon as possible about invitations to birthday parties that take place when the children are with the other parent. The parent who will be taking the children will buy the birthday gift, unless the parents agree otherwise.

4.5 PARENTING RIGHTS

4.5.1 Both parents have a right to receive significant information with respect to the children's education, medical care, dental care, and mental health care, including the right to receive school report cards and to hold interviews with the children's teachers and school principals. Each parent will make arrangements directly with the school, doctor, or dentist for the information he or she wishes to receive.

Linda and Tom both have a right to attend any extracurricular activities involving the children. Extended family members may attend the children's extracurricular activities.

4.6 COMMUNICATION BETWEEN PARENTS

4.6.1 Linda and Tom agree to set aside a regular time for a "parenting meeting" by telephone (probably Friday at noon). Linda and Tom agree to establish an agenda of parenting issues to discuss at these times. Both parents agree that they will not use the children to carry messages between them, but rather will discuss parenting issues directly with each other. Linda and Tom also agree to exchange information in writing, *e.g.*, with respect to extracurricular activities, medical care, special events, *etc.* where this would be helpful and in the best interests of the children.

4.7 TRAVEL

4.7.1 Neither Tom nor Linda will remove the children from the Province of Ontario without the consent of the other parent, except for a brief vacation, and such consent will not be unreasonably withheld. Tom and Linda agree to give the other parent notice if the children are removed from the Province of Ontario for a brief vacation and such notice shall include the location and duration of the vacation [and/or the phone number of a contact person in case of an emergency]. Each parent shall give the other parent consent in writing if the children are to be removed from Canada for a brief vacation, for the purpose of satisfying the immigration authorities.

4.8 MOBILITY

4.8.1 Tom and Linda agree to give each other a minimum of sixty days' notice if this is possible, prior to moving his or her residence, and such notice shall include the address and phone number of the new residence. If either parent changes his or her residence such that the aforementioned parenting schedule cannot be followed, then they agree that any new parenting schedule will be based on the principle of maintaining a close relationship between the children and both parents. If this occurs, Tom and Linda agree to meet and discuss a revised parenting schedule. In the event that they cannot agree upon a revised schedule, they will attend mediation to discuss any changes prior to litigating such matters. Tom and Linda agree that neither of them will move his or her residence until the revised schedule has either been agreed upon or sixty days have elapsed from the date notice was given of the impending move.

4.9 CHANGE OF NAME OF CHILDREN

4.9.1 Tom and Linda agree that neither parent will change the name of the children without the written consent of the other parent. This provision shall be deemed to be a bar to any such application and may be filed with and shall be binding upon any officer of the Office of the Registrar General appointed under the *Vital Statistics Act,* R.S.O. 1990, c. V.4 who receives such application by either party in contravention of this provision.

4.10 DEATH/DISABILITY

4.10.1 Linda and Tom agree that if one parent predeceases the other or is unable to parent the children, then the other parent should become the sole custodial parent.

4.11 DISPUTE RESOLUTION

    4.11.1 In the event that Linda or Tom cannot agree on one or more significant issues in relation to the parenting arrangements or support:

        (a)   they agree to first give each other written notice of the nature of the disagreement;

        (b)   if no agreement has been reached within 30 (thirty) days after notice has been given, the parties agree to participate in mediation with (*name of Mediator*) or another mediator chosen on consent of the parties to resolve any dispute;

        (c)   Tom and Linda agree to share the cost of mediation in proportion to their gross income;

        (d)   if no agreement has been reached through mediation, Tom and Linda may then confer with their respective solicitors to settle what, if any, variation should be made;

        (e)   if no agreement has been reached through mediation or their respective solicitors within 90 (ninety) clear days after notice has been given, either parent may apply to a court to have any dispute with respect to custody or access or support determined pursuant to the *Children's Law Reform Act*, the *Family Law Act*, or the *Divorce Act*.

5. FINANCIAL PROVISION

5.1 SPOUSAL SUPPORT

    5.1.1   *Retroactive/Income Tax Payments*

        5.1.1.1 Tom made periodic payments of support to Linda for the benefit of her and the children in this calendar year totalling $7,500 ($2,500 per month) and last year totalling $47,840 ($920.00 per week). These payments shall be considered as having been made pursuant to this Agreement. They may be deducted by Tom and included by Linda in the calculation of their respective income taxes pursuant to the *Income Tax Act*, ss. 56.1(3)* and 60.1(3).

---

* Section 56.1(3) was re-enacted S.C. 1994, c.7, Sched VIII, s. 18.

5.1.1.2 Linda will provide Tom with a copy of her 1995 and 1996 tax returns by the 30th of April 1996 and 1997, and Tom will pay Linda's taxes that are attracted by the support payments, such tax to be calculated as if the support was in addition to all other income so that Linda will suffer no income tax consequence from such support payments.

5.2 CHILD SUPPORT

5.2.1 *Regular Support*

5.2.1.1 Commencing on the first day of April 1996, and on the first day of each subsequent month, Tom will pay to Linda for the support and maintenance of Jordy and Kathy the sum of $750 each ($1,500 total) per month in advance until one of the following occur:

(a) The child ceases to reside "full time" with Linda;

(b) Reside "full time" includes the child living away from the home to attend an educational institution, pursue summer employment, or take a vacation while otherwise maintaining his or her principal residence with Linda;

(c) The child becomes 18 years of age and ceases to be in full-time attendance at an educational institution. This would include a period of up to one year while the child was working and/or travelling;

(d) The child becomes 24 years of age;

(e) The child dies;

(f) The child is no longer a child of the marriage;

(g) Tom dies.

5.2.1.2 The quantum of child support was based on the fact that Tom agrees to pay all the costs associated with the children's schooling as set out in paragraph 5.3.5.1.

5.3 SPOUSAL SUPPORT

5.3.1 *Regular Support*

5.3.1.1 Commencing on the 1st day of April 1996, Tom shall pay to Linda, for her support, the sum of $1,000 per month until she:

(a) remarries;

(b) cohabits with another man and becomes a spouse pursuant to s. 29 of the *Family Law Act*. If this occurs it will be deemed a material change in circumstances, and Tom and Linda will return to mediation to discuss a reduction in her portion of support. See paragraph 6;

(c) dies.

5.3.1.2 If one of the conditions set out above occurs such that Linda is no longer entitled to support, the parties agree to review the quantum of child support according to the procedure set out in paragraph 6.

5.3.2 *Cost of Living Adjustment*

5.3.2.1 The amount of the monthly maintenance and support payments which Tom is required to make to Linda for the support and maintenance of her and the children pursuant to the provisions of this Agreement, will be increased with each unit of increase in the Consumer Price Index, provided that:

(i) The amount of increase in such payments will be directly proportionate to the increase in the Consumer Price Index published by Statistics Canada under the heading "All Items", Ontario Area (not seasonally adjusted), with base year 1981 equal to 100.

(ii) Any increase will be made once a year only and becomes effective on the first day of April of each year, commencing on the first day of April 1997, and will be based upon the Consumer Price Index published immediately prior to the effective date of adjustment.

(iii)   Any increase will be the lesser of:

(a)   The percentage increase in the Consumer Price Index as calculated above;

(b)   Tom's percentage increase in his total gross income from all sources. If Tom chooses to rely on this subsection he will, no later than March 1st in each year, produce to Linda a copy of his tax returns for the two immediately preceding years, which will form the basis of the calculation of the percentage increase in his gross income from all sources. If in the end Tom fails to provide the income tax returns for Linda, then the increase on April 1st of that year will be in accordance with the Consumer Price Index.

5.3.3   *Post-dated Cheques*

5.3.3.1   Tom shall forthwith deliver to Linda twelve post-dated cheques, dated for the first of the month from April 1st, 1996 to March 1st, 1997, inclusive, for the amounts payable to Linda pursuant to paragraphs 5.2 and 5.3. Thereafter in each year on or before April 1st, Tom shall provide to Linda a further twelve post-dated cheques for the next ensuing twelve-month period, and so on from time to time so long as he is obliged to make payments to Linda pursuant to paragraphs 5.2 and 5.3.

5.3.4   *Post-Secondary Education*

5.3.4.1   Tom and Linda will contribute in proportion to their gross income toward the costs of the post-secondary education for Jordy and Kathy, which costs include tuition, residence, supplies, equipment, and other incidental expenses. The parents shall provide each other with proof of their incomes.

5.3.5   *Additional Child Expenses*

    5.3.5.1 Tom will pay the children's tuition at Toronto French School for so long as one or both of the children attends. If one or both children transfer to the public schools, then Tom and Linda agree to review the quantum of child support according to the procedure set out in paragraph 6.

    5.3.5.2 Tom will pay for the children's extracurricular activities, camp fees, or other summer programs and remedial education. If Linda wishes Tom's contribution, she will consult with Tom before enrolling the children in activities and will obtain his consent, and this consent will not be unreasonably withheld. When Linda is earning more than $35,000, she will contribute in proportion to her gross income to these expenses.

5.3.6   *Medical/Dental Benefits*

    5.3.6.1 Tom is covered by Group Dental, Extended Health, and Drug Plans through his employment at ABC Creative Crafts Ltd. He will continue this coverage:

        (a) In the case of Linda, until one of the following occurs:
            (i) the marriage is terminated; or
            (ii) the benefit is no longer available to Tom through his employment.
        (b) In the case of each child, so long as Tom is obligated to support each child and the benefit is available to Tom through his employment.

    5.3.6.2 Where Linda is obligated to pay a fee directly to a dentist, hospital, health facility, or druggist in relation to any services which are covered in all or in part by Tom's plan, Tom will immediately endorse over to Linda any cheque he receives from the plan or plans in reimbursement for all or part of the services for which Linda has paid directly.

5.3.6.3 Tom and Linda will share in proportion to their gross income the cost of any medical, dental, and orthodontal expenses incurred by either parent for the children that are not covered by an insurance plan held by either parent. Tom and Linda shall provide each other proof of their incomes. If Linda wishes Tom's contribution, she will consult Tom in advance on any major dental or orthodontia treatment and obtain his consent, which consent will not be unreasonably withheld, before the commencement of the treatment.

6. MATERIAL CHANGE IN CIRCUMSTANCE

6.1 Tom and Linda intend paragraphs 4 and 5.3.1, 5.3.2, 5.3.4, 5.3.5, and 5.3.6 of this agreement to be final except for a variation because of a material change in circumstances, which shall include but not be limited to:

(i) a change in primary residence of the children;
(ii) a change in Linda's marital status as set out in paragraph 5.3.1 (a) and (b);
(iii) the parents' inability to work due to illness or disability;
(iv) a material change in income for either parent.

6.2 In the event that the parents cannot agree on issues of custody, access, child or spousal support, or medical and dental benefits, they agree to first give each other written notice of the nature of the disagreement and then to participate in mediation in order to resolve any disputes.

6.3 If no agreement has been reached 30 (thirty) clear days after notice has been given, the parties agree to participate in mediation with (*name of Mediator*) or another mediator chosen on consent of the parties to resolve any dispute. Tom and Linda agree to share the cost of mediation in proportion to their gross income.

6.4 If no agreement has been reached through mediation with respect to the issues of custody, access, child or spousal support, or medical and dental benefits, Tom and Linda may then confer with their respective solicitors to settle what, if any, variation should be made. If no agreement has been reached through mediation or their respective solicitors within 90 (ninety) clear days after notice has been given, either Tom or Linda may apply to a court to have any dispute with respect to custody, access, child or spousal support, or medical and dental benefits determined pursuant to the *Children's Law Reform Act*, the *Family Law Act,* or the *Divorce Act.*

7. MATRIMONIAL HOME

7.1   Tom and Linda purchased the "matrimonial home" in Linda's name after a decision to separate. They lived separate and apart under the same roof for 5 (five) months until Tom moved out. Linda and Tom acknowledge that title to the matrimonial home is held in Linda's name alone.

7.2   Tom hereby releases to Linda any and all interest he may now have or may afterwards acquire in the "matrimonial home", whether possessory or proprietary.

7.3   Linda will have exclusive possession of the "matrimonial home" hereafter.

7.4   Linda will pay all insurance premiums, monthly mortgage instalments, taxes and other expenses relating to the "matrimonial home", and will indemnify Tom from all such liability relating to the "matrimonial home".

7.5   Tom and Linda acknowledge that they have divided the contents of the "matrimonial home", in a manner satisfactory to both of them.

8. EQUALIZATION PAYMENT

8.1   Tom and Linda acknowledge that the husband's interest in his company, ABC Creative Crafts Ltd., and her interest in the "matrimonial home" are approximately equal. Tom and Linda acknowledge that the division of assets and liabilities as provided in this Agreement fully satisfies any and all entitlements each party has or may have to an equalization of their Net Family Properties.

9. LIFE INSURANCE

9.1   DOUBLE POLICY

9.1.1   Tom carries two policies of insurance on his life with

Good News Life Insurance Co., namely $350,000 (Policy Number 12345) and $50,000 (Policy Number 67890). Linda also carries two policies of insurance on her life with Good News Life Insurance Co., namely $175,000 (Policy Number 24680) and $50,000 (Policy Number 13579). Both Tom and Linda agree to maintain these policies with each other as sole, irrevocable beneficiary (in trust for the children) for so long as the children are entitled to support under the provisions of this Agreement.

9.1.2   Tom and Linda both warrant that they have irrevocably designated each other as the beneficiary (in trust for the children) under these policies and that both have filed a designation pursuant to the provisions of the *Insurance Act*.

9.1.3   Tom and Linda will each give the other a true copy of this designation within 14 days from the execution of this Agreement. Tom and Linda will maintain the policies in force, whether they do so through renewal from time to time or otherwise, and will pay or cause to be paid the premiums required on the policies as the premiums fall due. Tom and Linda agree that if they are no longer covered by the policies in force, they will immediately obtain replacement coverage for the plan or policies (ensuring that there is no gap in coverage beyond their control) to the extent available at similar cost, and will maintain the replacement coverage and will pay the required premiums as they fall due and so on for each succeeding policy. Tom and Linda agree that they will maintain the other parent as sole beneficiary (in trust for the children) of the policies for as long as Tom is required to support the children pursuant to the provisions of this Agreement.

9.1.4   Tom and Linda agree that when Tom is no longer required to support the children pursuant to the provisions of this Agreement, then both parties may deal with their respective policies as they wish free from any claim by the other or by their estate, and both parties or their personal representatives will give and execute any consent or other document then required to enable either party to deal with the policies.

9.1.5   Within 14 days of one party demanding it, that party will deliver proof to the other that the policies are in good standing. If Tom or Linda defaults in payment of the premiums and the policies are no longer in good standing, the other party may pay any premiums and may recover them from the other together with all of their costs and expenses including their solicitor/client costs.

9.1.6   If Tom dies without this insurance in effect, his obligation to pay support or maintenance pursuant to this Agreement will survive his death (notwithstanding section 5 of this Agreement) and will be a first charge on his estate.

10. PENSION FUNDS

10.1 CANADA PENSION PLAN

10.1.1   Both Tom and Linda may apply under the Canada Pension Plan for a division of pension credits earned from the date of marriage up to the date of separation.

11. RELEASES

11.1 PROPERTY

11.1.1   Except as provided in this Agreement, the parties agree that:

(a)   all of their property has been divided between them to their mutual satisfaction;

(b)   each releases all rights and interests in property owned by the other, which he or she had, has, or may acquire during his or her lifetime and upon his or her death under the *Family Law Act*, or the laws of any jurisdiction, including all rights to or interest in:

(i)   possession of property;
(ii)   ownership in property;
(iii)   division of property;
(iv)   compensation by payment of an amount of money, or by an award of a share of property or contribution of any kind, whether direct or indirect, made to property;
(v)   an equalization payment pursuant to the *Family Law Act*; and

   (vi) any resulting, constructive, or other type of trust.

  (c) none of the property that either now has or may have had in the past or may acquire in the future will be included in his or her net family property;

  (d) neither holds any property in trust for the other, whether by way of resulting trust or any other type of trust; and

  (e) they release all rights, possessory or otherwise, which either has or may acquire under Part II of the *Family Law Act*.

11.2 DEBTS AND OBLIGATIONS

11.2.1 There is an outstanding line of credit with the CIBC bank in the amount of $50,000 in the name of both parties, which line of credit is collaterally secured by the matrimonial home. On April 1, 1996, the balance owing on the line of credit is approximately $15,000.00. Tom agrees to assume sole responsibility for repayment of this indebtedness and shall indemnify and save Linda harmless with respect thereto. It is agreed that Tom will not utilize the line of credit for any further advances of funds, without Linda's knowledge and consent in writing. Should Linda utilize the line of credit after April 1, 1996, then she shall assume responsibility for such indebtedness.

11.2.2 Neither party will contract in the name of the other or bind the other in any way for any debts or obligations.

11.2.3 Except as provided in this Agreement, if debts or obligations are incurred by either party on behalf of the other, before or after the date of this Agreement, he or she will completely indemnify the other for all such debts or obligations or any related damages or costs.

11.3 ESTATE

11.3.1 Except as provided in this Agreement, and subject to any will, the parties each release all rights which he or she has or may acquire under the laws of any jurisdiction in the estate of the other, and in particular:

    (a)   under the *Succession Law Reform Act*, or the *Family Law Act*, or their successors:

        (i)   to share in the estate of the other upon dying intestate, or

        (ii)   to an allowance or payment as a dependent from the estate of the other; and

    (b)   under the *Trustee Act* to act as executor or administrator of the will or the estate of the other; and

    (c)   under the *Family Law Act* or any other statute to his or her entitlement thereunder on the death of the other.

12. FULL AND FINAL SETTLEMENT

12.1 The support and property provisions of this Agreement are inextricably intertwined and constitute a full and final financial settlement.

13. GENERAL RELEASE

13.1 Each of the parties accepts the provisions of this Agreement in full satisfaction of all claims and causes of action each now has or may acquire including, but not limited to claims and causes of action for custody, child maintenance or child support, maintenance, support, interim maintenance or interim support, possession of or title to an interest in property, or equalization of net family property or equalization payments of any kind, or any other claim arising out of the marriage of Linda and Tom except for a decree of divorce. Nothing in this Agreement bars any action or proceeding by either party to enforce any of the provisions of this Agreement.

14. SEPARATION AGREEMENT TO SURVIVE DIVORCE

14.1 If a divorce judgment is obtained, all the terms of this Agreement will continue in force.

15. AGREEMENT TO PREVAIL

15.1 This Agreement prevails over any matter that is provided for:

    (a)   in the *Family Law Act*;

    (b)   any succeeding legislation; and

    (c)   any subsequent domestic contract between one of the parties and another person where the Agreement makes provision for such matter.

16. PROPER LAW

16.1 The proper law of this Agreement is the law of Ontario.

17. SEVERABILITY OF TERMS

17.1 All of the terms of this Agreement are severable from each other and will survive the invalidity of any other term of this Agreement.

18. GENERAL

18.1 The parties will each execute any document or documents reasonably required from time to time to give effect to the terms and intent of this Agreement.

18.2 There are no representations, collateral agreements, warranties, or conditions affecting this Agreement.

18.3 The terms of this Agreement are binding on the respective heirs, executors, and assigns of the parties.

18.4 This Agreement may be amended only by a further Agreement in writing which is witnessed.

18.5 If any provision of any statute of any jurisdiction invalidates or voids this Agreement, or any amendments to it, as a domestic contract, it is the intention of the parties that each provision of this Agreement or any amendments to it be construed as a separate contract under ordinary contract law and enforceable as such.

19. COHABITATION

19.1 If at any future time, the parties, with their mutual consent, cohabit as husband and wife for a period or periods totalling not more than ninety (90) days with reconciliation as the primary purpose of the cohabitation, the provisions contained in this Agreement will not be affected except as provided in this section. If the parties with their mutual consent cohabit as husband and wife for a period of, or periods totalling more than, ninety (90) days with reconciliation as the primary purpose of cohabitation, the provisions contained in this Agreement will become void, except that nothing in this section will affect or invalidate any payment, or conveyance or act made or done pursuant to the provisions of this Agreement.

20. FINANCIAL DISCLOSURE

20.1 Tom and Linda acknowledge that each of them:

(a) has been given a reasonable opportunity by the other to obtain full disclosure, and has disclosed to the other all of his or her assets, debts, and other liabilities, existing at the time this Agreement was made;

(b) has made such investigation of the financial circumstances of the other as he or she considers reasonable; and

(c) is satisfied with the information furnished and disclosure made.

21. INDEPENDENT LEGAL ADVICE

21.1 Tom and Linda acknowledge that each of them:

(a) has had independent legal advice, or has been encouraged to obtain legal advice;

(b) understands his or her rights and obligations under this Agreement and the nature and circumstances of this Agreement; and

(c) is signing this Agreement voluntarily, without undue influence or coercion from the other.

22. COSTS

22.1 Tom and Linda will each pay his or her own legal fees and disbursements incurred by him or her and will share equally the Mediator's fees and disbursements.

To Evidence Their Agreement Tom and Linda have signed this Agreement under seal before a witness.

DATED this _____ day of _____, 19____.

SIGNED, SEALED, AND DELIVERED)

   in the presence of   )

)

)

)

)

_____) _____

WITNESS   ) Tom Iam Perfect

)

_____) _____

WITNESS   ) Linda Norya Notte

[**Note:** The clients should *not* sign the Memorandum of Understanding in the Mediator's office. This signature page should be sent to the lawyer for each party so that the clients can receive independent legal advice and then sign the Agreement in their lawyers' offices.]

Appendix 9A

Ontario Interdisciplinary Association of Custody/Access Assessors

Custody/Access Assessment Guidelines*

PREFACE

The original *Custody / Access Assessment Guidelines* (1988) provided assessors with a detailed outline of the essential steps involved in conducting assessments in this challenging area. The authors ensured that consultation came from diverse professional perspectives resulting in a generic set of "commonly understood norms . . . [which] could then serve as the basis for future professional standards." Eight years later, this document still is the basic standard for providing parents, their lawyers and the court with important information and guidance in planning the care of children in separated families. It also has been employed by the various professional Colleges in making judgements about their members' performance in this emotionally charged area.

As assessors incorporated the *Guidelines* into their own practices, it became clear that aspects of the procedures could be clarified, expanded and rated for importance. The new *Guidelines* updates procedures with current practice, and includes two new sections, one on Court Testimony and another on the Maintenance and Release of File Information.

---

* **Authors**: Gary Austin Ph.D., C.Psych; Mario Bartoletti, Ed.D.; Barbara Chisholm, M.S.W.; Linda Chodos, M.S.W., C.S.W.; Barbara Landau, Ph.D., LL.B., LL.M.; Andrea Litvack, M.S.W., C.S.W.; and Howard Waiser, Ph.D., C.Psych. These Guidelines represent a revision of the original Custody/Access Guildelines which were published by the Ontario Psychological Foundation (now known as the Psychology Foundation of Canada) in 1988. Endorsed by the Psychology Foundation of Canada. Reproduced with the permission of the Ontario Interdisciplinary Committee on Custody/Access Assessment.

Most important, the new *Guidelines* classifies all of the procedures as either "mandatory" or "discretionary" to define a primary base of necessary activities and some areas of flexibility. The meaning of these terms is as follows:

Mandatory: Procedures which must be done to provide an adequate custody and access assessment for the parents or the court. If a procedure is not done, then a comparable one should be done or a rationale should be provided.

Discretionary: Procedures which are recommended but which are subject to the clinical judgement of the assessor depending on such factors as variations in professional practice, case requirements, financial limits, time limits and so forth.

The Committee would like to emphasize that the *Guidelines* is not a manual that details all the clinical techniques, assessment criteria, ethical dilemmas etc. that This information can be found in a number of textbooks or training programs on custody and access assessments. Furthermore, the *Guidelines* do not set out the specific qualifications of an assessor, although the Committee recognizes the broad set of skills this area of forensic practice requires.

The Committee hopes that these guidelines assist assessors to offer parents, lawyers and the court, a quality service that leads to sound parenting plans for children experiencing separation and divorce.

(June 10, 1996)

I. PURPOSE AND PRESUMPTIONS

A. PURPOSE

The purpose of a custody/access assessmen[1] is to advise parents, their lawyers and the court about those parenting arrangements which would be in the best interest[2] of the children[3] and within the capabilities of the family.

---

[1] These guidelines do not address specific issues in relation to child welfare assessments or cases in which there is physical or sexual abuse.

[2] The term "best interests" is defined, for example, in the Ontario Children's Law Reform Act, R.S.O., 1990, Chapter 12, Section 24(2).

[3] Throughout this report, the term "children" will be used to refer to either "child" or "children".

B. Presumptions

1[M]. that an assessment will only be undertaken by a mental health professional who is qualified to conduct custody and access assessment[4];

2[M]. that the parent[5] be strongly advised to have independent legal advice;

3[M]. that a complete and impartial custody/access assessment cannot be conducted on a one-sided basis (i.e., not on behalf of one parent alone, but only on behalf of the family as a whole[6];

4.[M] that an assessor must disclose any prior relationship between the assessor and any member of the family and, in most cases, should not perform an assessment if there is a prior relationship of any kind unless with written consent.

5[M]. that the parties to the assessment be informed that the assessment process is not confidential, and that any information received by the assessor is subject to subpoena;

6[M.] that evidence of child abuse or imminent harm to an adult or child will be reported to the appropriate authoritie[7];

7[M]. that, in cases where issues arise that are beyond the scope of the assessor's expertise, the assessor will seek consultation with a professional in the area of concern.

8[D]. that joint sessions should be considered cautiously in cases of domestic violence and always with safeguards and on a voluntary basis;

9[D]. that the assessor explore the possibility of a settlement by encouraging the active participation and mutual cooperation of the parents.

10[D]. that parents contribute, whenever possible, to the development of the parenting plan that is in the best interests of their children;

---

[4] "Qualified" means that the assessor meets the standards set out in Section 30 (1) of the Children's Law Reform Act, R.S.O.,1990, Chapter 12, or the relevant family law legislation in the jurisdiction where the assessment is being conducted.

[5] The term "parents" in these guidelines includes foster parents, guardians, adoptive parents or any other people who may function as parents to the child.

[6] One-sided assessments are partial, by definition, and therefore inadequate for determining the most appropriate parenting arrangements. In addition, when conducted on behalf of one parent, instead of both parents, they tend to exacerbate conflict within the family. Clinical contact with only one parent and the children in a treatment context may provide some limited understanding of the family, but does not constitute a complete custody/access assessment and therefore no recommendations with respect to custody and access issues should be made.

[M] Mandatory - those activities that ought to occur (see Preface)

[D] Discretionary - those activities that may occur (see Preface)

[7] If disclosure of abuse occurs during the assessment, the assessor should consider suspending the assessment until the matter has been addressed.

11[M]. that, if ordered by the court, the assessor is obliged to prepare a report which may contain recommendations, to be submitted to the parents and lawyers, and to be filed with the court;

12[M]. that, after the completion of the assessment, the assessor and the parents should avoid switching the role of an assessor to a role that would render any possible future testimony and/or re-assessment invalid (c.f. closed mediation, therapy for one party)

II. PROCEDURE

A. REFERRAL AND CONTRACTING

Although most referrals are made by lawyers, they may be made by other people such as parents, social service or court personnel and other professionals. The assessor should first contract with the lawyers, if they have been retained, and then with the parents.

1[M]. Contracting with the Lawyers:
the assessor should communicate (meeting, letter or telephone) with all the lawyers prior to commencing the assessment, in order to accomplish the following:

a. to review the assumptions stated above;

b. to affirm that the assessor will act in an impartial and unbiased manner;

c. to identify the specific issues and questions to be addressed in the assessment;

d. to discuss the assessment procedure and rationale;

e. to determine the reporting procedure:
(1) when the report is due,
(2) the scope and distribution of the report, and
(3) whether specific recommendations are required;

f. to agree on the fees, including an estimate of the total anticipated cost, the hourly rate, the proportion to be paid by each party and the method of payment (for example, by way of retainer or on account with the lawyers[8];

---

8   It may be advisable to obtain a retainer which should be held in a trust account pending provision of services.

g.   to receive materials such as affidavits, court documents, reports and other relevant documents;

h.   to clarify the nature of the communication process with the lawyers throughout the assessment process;

i.   to clarify that the assessor will request of all referring lawyers that all pertinent written materials are copied to the other lawyer; and

j.   to clarify that all written material from the assessor will be copied to all lawyers.

2^M.   Contracting with the Parents:

The assessor shall arrive at a contractual agreement with the parents. This process can be accomplished in individual or joint meetings at the discretion of the assessor. In cases involving domestic violence, a joint meeting may not be advisable.

The objectives of the contractual process are:

a.   to review and confirm all of the contracting issues agreed to by the lawyers;

b.   to discuss the assessment procedure, including:

(i)   who may be seen or contacted;
(ii)   what may take place during the sessions;
(iii)   whether home visits will be conducted;
(iv)   the lack of confidentiality of the assessment process; namely, that any information obtained or opinions formed, during the assessment may be included in the assessment report, which in turn may be filed with the court to become part of the public record;
(v)   how long the process is likely to take.

c.   to determine other relevant professional sources of information regarding the children's needs (for example, school teachers, the family doctor, mental health professionals, etc.), and to obtain signed consent forms to gather information from these source[9].

d.   to clarify that all materials submitted to the assessor will be reviewed with both parents at the discretion of the assessor.

---

[9]   As a fee may be required to obtain such information from a professional, it should be explained that such fees will be treated as disbursements on the assessor's account.

3^D.   Confirming letter or retainer contract:

The assessor may choose to summarize in writing the terms of reference and any contractual issues which have been agreed upon with the lawyers and the parents.

B. ASSESSMENT PROCESS

In the assessment process itself, the following contacts may be made. The type of contact, the order in which they are made and the amount of time spent on any one of them, will vary according to the individual case and the judgement of the particular assessor.

1^D.   In meeting with the parents together the following objectives should be considered:

   a.   to provide education regarding the effects of separation and divorce on children and parents, and regarding alternative parenting arrangements;

   b.   to observe the interaction between the parents and to attempt to improve the parents' communication;

   c.   to assess the parents' ability and willingness to cooperate with each other;

2^M.   Meeting with each parent individually:

   a.   to explore any issues such as: individual, marital and family history, spousal or child abuse, mental health, addictions, parenting ability, special concerns about the children, personal future plans, etc.;

   b.   to learn about their children, including any special needs they may have;

   c.   to discuss each parent's proposal with respect to parenting arrangements;

   d.   to consider each parent's willingness to cooperate with the other parent in sharing parental responsibilities.

   e.   to determine areas of agreement with respect to parenting arrangements.

3^M.   Meeting with each parent and the children together:

   a.   to observe the interaction between each parent and the children with respect to emotional responses, discipline and the overall quality of their family relationships, including sibling interaction.

b.   this meeting can be contraindicated in some exceptional cases, for example, in cases of abuse.

4[M].   Interviewing the children:

a.   to ascertain each child's level of maturity, particular interests, aptitudes, abilities, special needs, daily routines etc.;

b.   to assess the relationship among the children and each child's perception of his or her relationship and involvement with family members;

c.   to assess each child's views regarding possible parenting arrangements where they can be reasonably ascertained;

d.   to explore issues of safety among family member[10];

e.   to assess how each child is coping in all respects (for example, emotionally, socially and academically).

5[D].   Meeting with the family as a whole:

a.   to familiarize oneself with the family as a whole and to form an impression of them as a group.

6[M].   Interviewing significant other caregivers\collaterals:

(Such as partners, grandparents, nannies, extended family members, step-siblings or others at the discretion of the assessor.)

a.   to ascertain the nature of their relationships with the children and\or parents;

b.   to determine their perspectives on the family and their views on possible parenting arrangements; and

c.   to see how they might contribute to and\or participate in any new parenting plan.

7[D].   Home visits:

The assessor may choose to visit each parent's home so as to enable the assessor:

a.   to assess the family's behaviour in their own natural setting and

---

[10]   If there are reasonable grounds to suspect that a child is or may be suffering, or may have suffered abuse, the assessor must report the suspicion and the information on which it is based to the local child protection agency (cf. the Ontario Child and Family Services Act, R.S.O.,Section 68, 1990).

    b.   to observe the environment of each proposed home.

8[M].   Communication with relevant professionals (for example, mental health, physicians, educators, police, etc.):

    a.   to acquire from relevant professionals (usually by telephone or report) specific information about, as well as their general impression of, family members.

9[D].   Psychological testing:

Where the assessor has been trained and is qualified in this area, psychological testing may be used.

C. ANALYSIS AND FORMULATION

At this stage in the assessment, the assessor reviews all of the data collected and impressions formed in light of the nature and the objectives of the particular assessment.

1[M].   In those cases where the parents have reached agreement, the purpose of the analysis and formulation is:

    a.   to clarify and elaborate the parenting plan;
    b.   to evaluate the soundness of the plan especially with respect to the children;
    c.   to approve those aspects of the plan that are appropriate; and
    d.   to make any recommendations that may be necessary.

2[M].   In those cases where the parents have not reached agreement, the purpose is:

    a.   to formulate recommendations for a parenting plan (incorporating the parents' plan, where appropriate) based on a review of the entire assessment process.

D. VERBAL PRESENTATION OF FINDINGS

1[D].   Verbal presentation to the Lawyers:

    a.   to inform the lawyers as to the outcome of the assessment;
    b.   to explain the process of the assessment and the rationale for the findings;
    c.   to allow the lawyers to ask questions, offer comments or

make factual corrections;

d. to give the lawyers an opportunity to achieve a settlement regarding a parenting plan;

e. to facilitate the acceptance and implementation of the plan; and

f. to advise the lawyers, should the matter be proceeding to trial, of the assessor's availability to meet with them, preferably together, to prepare for trial and of the assessor's willingness to be cross-examined by the lawyers.

2^D. Presentation to the Parents (separately or together):

a. to inform the parents as to the outcome of the assessment;

b. to explain the rationale for any recommendations;

c. to allow the parents to ask questions or to offer any comments as well as to make any factual corrections;

d. to invite the parents to cooperate in an agreement, based on the assessment findings; and

e. to discuss implementation of the plan.

III. WRITTEN REPORT

A. REPORT OF PARENTAL AGREEMENT

1^D. When the parents have been able to develop a complete parenting plan that the assessor thinks is not contrary to the best interests of the children, the assessor may:

a. prepare a report describing the parenting plan;

b. provide a limited commentary on the plan;

c. recommend that it be implemented; and

d. assist the lawyers in preparing Minutes of Settlement.

B. REPORT IN THE EVENT OF PARENTAL DISAGREEMENT

If parental agreement has not been reached, the assessor should:

1^M. prepare a report containing relevant information and the assessor's recommendations;

2^M. include in the report sufficient information and rationale for the recommendations so as to assist the court in arriving at a judgment; and

3^M. ensure that any potentially damaging material is presented in such a manner as to take into account its impact on family members and their relationships (bearing in mind who might read the report both now and in the future).

C. COMPREHENSIVE ASSESSMENT REPORT

The following headings identify the important information to be contained in a report; however, there may be individual differences in style and format depending on the assessor's judgement and the circumstances of the case.

1[M].   Referral Sources:

The report should state whether it is a court-ordered assessment or one that is being conducted on the consent of the parties, and the referral source.

2[M].   Reasons for Referral:

The report should set out the circumstances leading to the referral and the reasons given by the referral sources.

3[M].   Objectives of the Assessment:

The report should set out the issues to be addressed by the assessment; for example whether the primary concern is the best parenting arrangement or whether the issue is restricted to the most appropriate access schedule or the involvement of a new partner in the children's lives.

4[D].   Qualifications of the Assessor:

The report could contain a brief summary of the assessor's qualifications and a curriculum vitae should be attached to the report or provided prior to a trial.

5[M].   Assessment Process and Sources of Information:

The report should state who was seen or spoken to and the relevant reports and materials reviewed.

6[D].   Family History:

The report could contain relevant family history; that is, information that pertains to the objectives of the assessment.

7^M. The Children:

The report should summarize the assessor's understanding of the children, including information and observations that are relevant to the objectives of the assessment.

8^M. The Parents:

The report should identify the parents' issues and summarize the assessor's understanding of the parents, including information and observations that are relevant to the objectives of the assessment.

9^M. Summary:

The report should contain a summary of the relevant information including the assessor's clinical opinions.

10^D. Discussion of Alternative Parenting Arrangements:

The report may discuss viable parenting options in light of the objectives of the assessment. The relative strengths and weaknesses of the alternatives may be presented.

11^M. Rationale for Recommendations:

The assessor should set out the criteria, which may include legislated criteria, used in making any recommendations and should summarize the key factors, with respect to each criterion, that are relevant to a recommendation.

12^D. Recommendations:

The report may contain the assessor's specific recommendations about parenting arrangements and their implementation including the involvement of professionals or agencies.

IV. COURT TESTIMONY

Usually one parent's lawyer subpoenas the assessor to a trial, often the parent who is most supported by the report's recommendations. Usually this parent or the lawyer pays the assessor for the trial preparation and appearance. If the assessor is asked to testify, the following events may occur:

1.^D Communication with Lawyers before court to provide:

    a.   an acknowledgement of the trial appearance notice;

b.   an estimate of the costs for preparation, travel, and court testimony;

c.   the conditions for consultation before the trial;

d.   a curriculum vitae, if not provided earlier.

2.^{D} Submission of the Clinical File:

a.   if a lawyer wants to subpoena the clinical file, the assessor should receive a notice of motion and may wish to argue in motions court that parts of the file should not be open to the parents.

3.^{D} Materials to bring to Court:

a.   the entire clinical file and supporting documents.

V. MAINTENANCE AND RELEASE OF FILE INFORMATION

Custody and access files are a special case in that they contain information on conflicting parties whose interests likely differ and yet whose rights need to be protected. While it is indicated that some information should be released to parents, clinical judgement must be employed to determine if harm may result.

Policies for the release of file information may vary across disciplines and individual assessors should consult with their regulatory organization if they are uncertain how to proceed.

VI. COMMENTS ON THE *GUIDELINES INVITED*

A. COMMENTS

The Committee would be pleased to receive any comments on the *Guidelines* and any suggestions as to possible improvements. Also, should you wish to receive notification of any future work of the Committee, kindly send your name and address.

Persons wishing to receive further information about the association may write to:

Ontario Interdisciplinary Association of Custody/access Assessors
c/o LITVACK & CHODOS ASSOCIATES
40 Sheppard Avenue West
Suite 610
Toronto, Ontario
M2N 6K9

(June 10, 1996)

Appendix 9B

Outline of Custody Assessment Report

1.   Referral Sources

2.   Reasons for Referral

3.   Objectives of the Assessment

4.   Qualifications of the Assessor

5.   Assessment Process

6.   Family History, Including Relevant Marital History, Child Development, and Family Dynamics

7.   Summary of Observations of the Family and of Information from Other Sources

8.   Summary of Important Issues

9.   Alternative Parenting Arrangements

10. Rationale for the Recommendations

11. Recommendations of Assessor

Appendix 10A

The Rules of Professional Conduct of the Law Society of Upper Canada

Reproduced with the permission of the Law Society of Upper Canada.

The following are specific rules for lawyers who act as mediators in Ontario:

INTEGRITY

Rule 1

The lawyer must discharge with integrity all duties owed to clients, the court, the public and other members of the profession.

COMMENTARY

1. Integrity is the fundamental quality of any person who seeks to practise as a member of the legal profession. If the client is in any doubt as to his lawyer's trustworthiness, the essential element in the true lawyer-client relationship will be missing. If personal integrity is lacking, the lawyer's usefulness to the client and reputation within the profession will be destroyed regardless of how competent the lawyer may be.

2. Dishonourable or questionable conduct on the part of the lawyer in either private life or professional practice will reflect adversely upon the integrity of the profession and the administration of law and justice as a whole. If the conduct, whether within or outside the professional sphere, is such that knowledge of it would be likely to impair a client's trust in the lawyer as a professional consultant, the Society may be justified in taking disciplinary action.

3. Generally speaking, however, the Society will not be concerned with the purely private or extra-professional activities of a lawyer which do not bring into question professional integrity or competence.

IMPARTIALITY AND CONFLICT OF INTEREST

Rule 5

The lawyer must not advise or represent both sides of a dispute and, save after adequate disclosure to and with the consent of the client or prospective client concerned, should not act or continue to act in a matter when there is or there is likely to be a conflicting interest.

COMMENTARY

1. A conflicting interest is one which would be likely to affect adversely the lawyer's judgment on behalf of, or loyalty to a client or prospective client, or which the lawyer might be prompted to prefer to the interests of a client or prospective client.

COMMENTARY

11. The Rule will not prevent a lawyer from arbitrating or settling, or attempting to arbitrate or settle, a dispute between two or more clients or former clients who are *sui juris* and who wish to submit the dispute to the lawyer.

OUTSIDE INTERESTS AND THE PRACTICE OF LAW

Rule 17

The lawyer who engages in another profession, business or occupation concurrently with the practice of law must not allow such outside interest to jeopardize the lawyer's professional integrity, independence or competence.

COMMENTARY

1. The term "outside interest" covers the widest possible range and includes activities which may overlap or be connected with the practice of law, such as, for example, engaging in the mortgage business, acting as a director of a client corporation, or writing on legal subjects, as well as activities not so connected, such as, for example, careers in business, politics, broadcasting or the performing arts. In each case the question of whether and to what extent the lawyer may be permitted to engage in the outside interest, will be subject to any applicable law or rule of the Society.

2. The lawyer must not allow involvement in an outside interest to impair the exercise of independent professional judgment on behalf of the lawyer's clients.

3. Where the outside interest is not related to the legal services being performed for clients, ethical considerations will usually not arise unless the lawyer's conduct might bring the lawyer or the profession into disrepute, or impair the lawyer's competence as, for example, where the outside interest might occupy so much time that clients' interests would suffer because of inattention or lack of preparation.

LAW SOCIETY OF UPPER CANADA
COMMUNIQUE

24 October, 1986

* More and more members of the profession are serving as mediators primarily in the Family Law area but in other areas as well. Convocation adopted a new Rule 25 which was recommended by the Professional Conduct Committee. The Rule has been supplemented by guidelines which are set out in the Communiqué Plus. The new Rule reads: "The lawyer who functions as a mediator must ensure that the parties to the mediation process understand fully that the function being discharged is not part of the traditional practice of law and that the lawyer is not acting as a lawyer for either party. The lawyer as mediator acts to assist the parties to resolve the matters in issue."

The commentary that follows the Rule stresses that at the outset the parties to the mediation should be told that communications involved in the mediation are not covered by solicitor/client privilege and that the lawyer acting as mediator should not give legal advice, as distinct from legal information, but advise and encourage the parties to seek the advice of separate counsel, particularly with respect to a draft contract prepared by the mediator.

Kenneth Jarvis, Secretary.

COMMUNIQUE PLUS
Number 13   24th October, 1986

FAMILY LAW MEDIATION

The following are the Guidelines for Lawyer/Mediators:

1. The lawyer/mediator or any partner or associate of such lawyer/mediator, should not undertake mediation with any person whom he or she has previously represented or to whom he or she has given any prior legal advice relating to the matters to be mediated. If there has been any previous contact with either one or both of the parties on an unrelated matter, this should be disclosed to both parties and the mediation should proceed only on the written consent of both of them.[1]

2. The lawyer/mediator should inform the parties before the mediation commences that he or she will be functioning as a mediator and not as a

---

[1]   See Rule 5, Commentary 4, which contemplates dual "representation" on the written consent of the parties.

lawyer for either or both parties to mediation.[2] The differences between the two roles, i.e. as neutral facilitator and as advocate, should be fully explained. The parties should also be informed at this time that because no solicitor/client relationship exists, no solicitor/client privilege will attach to any communications made during the mediation process.[3] The parties should be asked to sign a written acknowledgement of the above.[4]

3. The parties to mediation should be encouraged to obtain independent legal counsel, preferably before mediation commences, but in any event, before a final agreement is reached.[5] Independent counsel should be asked to advise each spouse separately with respect to his or her legal rights and entitlements, give a legal opinion as to the range of probable dispositions by the court if the matters were litigated, to act as coaches for each party throughout the mediation process, to review and advise the spouses with respect to the adequacy of the financial disclosure received from the other spouse, to review and swear to the accuracy of their own client's financial disclosure, and finally, to review and advise with respect to the draft agreement and the effect of any release clauses contained therein. The spouses should be informed by the mediator of the risks of proceeding without independent counsel.

4. An agreement should be obtained by the mediator in the initial mediation session with respect to the confidentiality of the mediation sessions, including whether or not the mediator will be expected to submit a report or to testify in court if agreement is not reached by parties on some or all issues. If the mediation is open, the parties should agree as to whether the mediator's report will contain recommendations. If closed, the parties should be warned that no privilege exists for mediation unless, in Ontario, mediation has been ordered by a court on the consent of the parties. If so, the mediator may be required to testify despite the spouses' voluntary agreement to the contrary. Ideally, agreement with respect to the confidentiality of the mediation sessions should be made in writing.[6]

5. The mediating spouses should agree to make full financial disclosure to each other during mediation, and undertake not to hide or dispose of any assets, cancel or change any beneficiaries of life insurance policies, or take any further steps in legal proceedings while the mediation is in process. They should also be informed of and asked to acknowledge the risks

---

[2]   Rule 25.
[3]   Rule 25, Commentary 4.
[4]   See Standard Mediation Contract.
[5]   Rule 25, Commentary 2.
[6]   See paragraph 9, Standard Mediation Contract.

inherent in mediation, such as the development of a status quo with respect to custody, or the establishment of a standard for the level of spousal and/ or child support.

6. All of the above mentioned consents, undertakings and acknowledgements should be contained in a written mediation contract, signed by both spouses and the mediator.[7] The written contract should also contain a statement identifying the issues to be mediated, the conduct of the sessions, the terms and responsibility for payment, and the circumstances under which mediation can be terminated by either spouse or the mediator. A copy of the fully executed mediation contract should be given to each spouse and the original retained by the mediator.

7. In order to maintain an appearance of neutrality, the lawyer/mediator should avoid giving legal advice and should dispense only general legal information, in the presence of both spouses during the mediation process.[8] The spouses should be referred to their independent solicitors for any specific legal advice requested or required. Pamphlets and brochures on custody, support and the division of property, and the income tax consequences of separation and divorce may be made available by way of information in the mediator's office, if desired. The mediator should be available as a referral source for other experts who may be required from time to time in the course of mediation, such as accountants and appraisers.

8. The lawyer/mediator should stay within his or her own area of competence and should not attempt to mediate highly contentious child custody disputes without knowledge of child development and psychology, and training in counselling techniques, or unless co-mediating with a mental health professional.

9. Before holding him or herself out as a mediator, the lawyer/mediator should familiarize him or herself with mediation theory and techniques, preferably by enrolling in a course of mediation training led by qualified mediators and/or by a recognized mediation association.

10. The mediator should terminate mediation if, at any time, he or she believes that the conditions for mediation have been breached, or if, in the opinion of the mediator, one or more of the participants is being harmed or seriously prejudiced by the process.

---

[7]　See Standard Mediation Contract.
[8]　Rule 25, Commentary 5.

11. The lawyer/mediator may prepare a separation agreement in draft form, incorporating the terms of the agreement reached in mediation, but should refrain from discussing the legal effects and implications of the agreement which should be taken by each of the mediating spouses to their respective counsel for review and advice. The mediated agreement, if acceptable, should be executed in the offices of the independent solicitors wherever possible to avoid any appearance of coercion on the part of the mediator.

12. The lawyer/mediator or any partner or associate, should decline to represent either or both spouses in any subsequent legal matter related to the issues mediated. Rather, the mediator should keep him or herself available as a neutral to assist the parties in future in the event that any modifications are required to the mediated settlement.

13. If the lawyer co-mediates with a mental health professional, he or she should bill separately for his or her individual services.[9]

14. To avoid confusion in the minds of mediation clients between lawyer and mediator roles, the lawyer/mediator might consider having separate letterhead, business cards and account stationery for his or her legal and mediation practices. Separate offices, telephone numbers and office signs would be even stronger evidence of the separation of the two roles but are not required.

[**Note:** The Law Society in British Columbia has established very different rules for lawyer mediators. The Law Societies of Alberta, Saskatchewan, and Manitoba are likely to enact rules in the near future that are similar to the British Columbia model.]

THE LAWYER AS ADVOCATE

The following is paragraph 6A of the Commentary under Rule 10 (The Lawyer as Advocate). It addresses the lawyer's duty with respect to alternative dispute resolution (ADR). It reads:

> The lawyer should consider the appropriateness of ADR to the resolution of issues in every case and, if appropriate, the lawyer should inform the client of ADR options and, if so instructed, take steps to pursue those options.

---

[9] Rule 10, Commentary 6.

Appendix 10B

Code of Ethics
Ontario Association for Family Mediation
Code of Professional Conduct

Reproduced with the permission of the Ontario Association for Family Mediation.

1. Foreword

The following rules are intended to govern the relations of family mediators with their clients, their professional colleagues, and the general public so that all will benefit from high standards of practice in family mediation. The rules are to be observed in spirit as well as in practice.

2. Definition of Terms

For the purposes of this Code, family mediation is defined as a non-adversarial process in which a qualified and impartial third party (the mediator) helps family members resolve their disputes. The resolution is voluntary and is based on sufficient information and advice for each participant.

In open mediation, if the parties fail to agree voluntarily on one or more issues, the mediator may prepare a report on the mediation and/or make recommendations. In open mediation, such a report may be used in subsequent court proceedings.

In closed mediation, there is no such report or recommendations and the process is entirely confidential.

3. Competence

It is the obligation of anyone acting as a family mediator to ensure that he or she is fully qualified to deal with the specific issues involved.

(a) It is acknowledged that family mediators will have a diversity of education and training, but the obligation to refrain from rendering services outside the limits of the family mediator's qualifications and capabilities remains.
(b) Family mediators shall co-operate with and endeavor to involve other competent professionals where the situation requires it.
(c) Family mediators shall engage in continuing education to ensure that their mediation skills are current and effective.
(d) Family mediators shall perform their service in a conscientious, dili-

gent, and efficient manner in accordance with this Code of Conduct.

4. Duty of Confidentiality

The mediator shall not voluntarily disclose to anyone not a party to the mediation any information obtained through the mediation process except:

(a) non-identifying information for research or educational purposes; or

(b) with the written consent of the parties to the mediation contract; or

(c) where ordered to do so by an appropriate judicial authority or required to do so by law; or

(d) where the information discloses an actual or potential threat to human life or safety or a proposed breach of the Criminal Code of Canada.

If mediation is open, communications made in the course of the mediation and the mediator's report and recommendations may be disclosed to a third party only for the purposes of resolving the dispute whether by litigation or otherwise.

While closed mediation imposes the intention and the duty of confidentiality on the mediator, it cannot confer privilege, and the mediator should advise the parties that the intended confidentiality cannot be guaranteed.

5. Impartiality

The mediator has a duty to be impartial in relation to the participants. Impartiality requires that the mediator shall not have preconceived opinions in favour of or against one person or the other.

(a) The mediator shall disclose to the participants any biases he or she may have relating to the issues to be mediated.

(b) The mediator will refrain from mediating in cases where the mediator knows there has been any significant prior involvement by the mediator or any partner or associate of the mediator with one of the participants except after full disclosure of the involvement to, and express consent by, the other participant(s). The role of the mediator should be distinguished from the earlier relationship.

(c) A lawyer-mediator, or any partner or associate of such lawyer-mediator, should decline to represent either or both spouses in any subsequent legal matter related to the issues mediated.

Rather, the mediator should keep him or herself available as a neutral to assist the parties in future in the event that any modifications are required to the mediated settlement.

(d) The perception of partiality on the part of the mediator by one or both participants does not in itself require the mediator to withdraw. In these circumstances, it is only the duty of the mediator to advise the participants of their right to terminate the mediation.

6. Agreement to Mediate

The mediator has a duty to explain the mediation process clearly to the participants before reaching an agreement to mediate. In particular, the mediator shall do the following:

(a) define mediation, distinguishing it from other methods of dispute resolution and from therapy and marriage counselling;

(b) determine the appropriateness of mediation for the participants in light of their particular circumstances;

(c) discuss the differences between closed mediation, open mediation and assessment, and the implications of each, and require the parties to choose open or closed mediation;

(d) advise participants that either of them or the mediator has the right to suspend or terminate the process at any time;

(e) explain the cost of mediation and reach an agreement with the participants regarding payment. It is inappropriate for the mediator to charge a contingency fee or to base the fee on the outcome of the mediation process;

(f) advise the participants of the role of independent legal advice in accordance with paragraph 9 of this Code. In the event the mediator is a lawyer, the lawyer-mediator shall inform the participants that he or she cannot represent either or both of them in any subsequent legal matter related to the issues mediated;

(g) discuss with the participants the mediator's specific procedures and practices;

(h) recommend that the agreement to mediate be written and signed by the parties and the mediator.

7. Potential Problems in Mediation

It is the duty of the mediator to advise the participants of potential problems that may arise during mediation. Some of these problems include:

(a) the possibility that one or both spouses may use the time during the mediation to dissipate or conceal assets;

(b) the fact that a status quo may be developing with respect to the custody of the children so that the non-custodial parent may be prejudiced in any future custody claim in the courts, notwithstanding any agreement to the contrary;

(c) the fact that information disclosed during the mediation may be used against a participant in the event of subsequent legal proceedings.

    i) Even if the information disclosed directly in the mediation is confidential, it may open up lines of inquiry and/or reveal other information which might not otherwise have come to light in any subsequent litigation.

    ii) A judicial authority may require disclosure of information revealed during mediation.

8. Information, Disclosure and Advice

It is the duty of a mediator to actively encourage the participants to make decisions based upon sufficient information, knowledge and advice:

(a) Every family mediator has an ongoing obligation to advise participants of the desirability and availability of independent legal advice. While neutral legal information may be made available to the parties, each should be encouraged to obtain legal advise.

(b) Where financial or property issues are involved, the mediator shall obtain an undertaking from the parties to make frank and full disclosure of their financial and related circumstances at the appropriate time in the mediation process. The mediator will assist the parties and their advisors to achieve such disclosure. A mediator has an ongoing obligation to advise both parties to obtain legal and other professional advice and assistance in this respect.

9. Independent Legal Advice

It is the obligation of every family mediator to advise clients:

(a) of the availability of independent legal advice for each spouse;

(b) of the advisability of obtaining it from the outset of the mediation;

(c) to obtain independent legal advice prior to signing the mediated agreement.

10. Duty to Minimize Harm or Prejudice to Participants

It is the duty of the mediator to suspend or terminate mediation whenever continuation of the process would harm or prejudice one or more of the participants.

(a)   The mediator shall suspend or terminate mediation where the ability or the willingness of either of the participants to effectively participate in the process is lacking

(b)   The mediator shall suspend or terminate mediation when its usefulness is exhausted so that there is no unnecessary expense to the participants from unproductive mediation.

(c)   If the mediator has suspended or terminated the process, he or she may suggest that the participants obtain appropriate professional services.

(d)   When the mediator believes the agreement being reached is unreasonable, he or she shall so advise the participants.

(e)   Notwithstanding impartiality, the mediator has the duty to promote the best interests of the children and to assist the parents to examine the separate and individual needs of each child.

(f)   While the mediator has an obligation to minimize the harm or prejudice to participants in the process, it is a fundamental principle of mediation that competent and informed participants can reach an agreement which may not correspond to legal guidelines contained in the relevant statutes or case law or that does not correspond to general community expectations and standards.

(g)   The mediator shall see that the participants are reaching agreement freely, voluntarily and without undue influence.

11. Public Communications

(a)   The purpose of public statements concerning family mediation should be:

    i)   to educate the public generally about the process; and

    ii)   to present the process of mediation objectively as one of several methods of dispute resolution in order to help the public make informed judgments and choices.

(b)   When advertising professional services, mediators should restrict themselves to matters which educate and inform the public. These could include the following to describe the mediator and the services offered: name, address, telephone number, office hours of the particular mediation service, highest relevant academic degree, relevant training and experience in mediation, appropriate professional affiliations and membership status, and any additional relevant or important consumer information.

(c)   Public Communications should not imply that membership in the Ontario Association for Family Mediation constitutes certification as a mediator.

12. Duty to Encourage Reporting of Breaches of Code

It is the obligation of family mediators to encourage clients to report in writing real or apparent breaches of this Code forthwith to the Chairman of the Standards and Ethics Committee and/or to the President of the Ontario Association for Family Mediation.

―――――――

Appendix 10C

Model Standards of Practice for Family and Divorce Mediation

Reproduced with the permission of the Academy of Family Mediators.

Symposium on Standards and Practices for Family and Divorce Mediation
May 22-23, 1984
Denver, Colorado

Introduction

Mediation offers families a means of resolving disputes through a cooperative decision making process. Family and divorce mediation has evolved without the benefit of established standards or guidelines tailored for this distinct new service.

The Association of Family and Conciliation Courts has facilitated the formulation of Model Standards of Practice for Family and Divorce Mediation by serving as the convenor for three symposiums on Divorce Mediation Standards and Ethics. Over forty individuals representing thirty professional organizations attended the first symposium held December, 1982 in San Diego, California.

It was the consensus of the delegates attending this symposium that it was premature to establish a certification procedure for family and divorce mediation but that the development of parameters of practice would assist individual mediators and the development of the practice.

A second symposium was convened in May, 1983, in Toronto, Ontario, Canada to begin to develop a draft of parameters of practice for family and divorce mediators. With the aid of resource materials from participating organizations, delegates discussed the ethical issues of family and divorce mediation as they relate to the client, the mediator, the practice of mediation and its relationship to community and colleagues.

A subcommittee reflecting the field and settings of family and divorce mediation was subsequently appointed to draft model standards of practice. The drafting committee consisted of Christopher Moore, chairperson, Director of Training, Center for Dispute Resolution, Denver, Colorado; Thomas Bishop, member of the ABA Family Law Section Mediation and Arbitration Committee, and in private practice, New London, Connecticut; Clarence Cramer, Director Pinal County, Conciliation Court, Florence, Arizona and President Mediation Association of Southern Arizona; Jay Folberg, President AFCC and Professor of Law, Lewis & Clark Law School, Portland, Oregon; Lois Gold, Vice President Academy of Family Mediators and Director Family Mediation Center, Portland, Oregon; Ann Milne, Chairperson, AFCC Mediation Committee and in private practice, Madison, Wisconsin; and Patrick Phear, representative of the American Arbitration Association and Director Children's Judicial Resource Council, Cambridge, Massachusetts.

With the financial assistance of the National Institute for Dispute Resolution, the drafting committee met and using resource materials and standards and ethical statements from 18 other organizations prepared a draft of Model Standards of Practice for Family and Divorce Mediation. This draft was distributed to 130 individuals and organizations for comment. Thirty invited delegates attended the third and final symposium in Denver, Colorado May 22-23, 1984 and completed the drafting process.

The development of these Model Standards of Practice reflects the diversity of mediation practices while manifesting the need to provide principles of practice that cross settings and disciplines. They are being distributed to courts, organizations, agencies and individuals for subscription, endorsement or adoption. The Model Standards may also serve as a foundation document for those organizations that must develop their own standards to fit unique services not specifically addressed in this model. The Model Standards of Practice are presented as a means of furthering the practice of family self-determination and embody the principle of mediation as a process of consensus.

Ann Milne, ACSW
Chairperson, AFCC Mediation Committee

Preamble

Mediation is a family centered conflict resolution process in which an impartial third party assists the participants to negotiate a consensual and informed settlement. In mediation, whether private or public, decision making authority rests with the parties. The role of the mediator includes reducing the obstacles to communication, maximizing the exploration of alternatives, and addressing the needs of those it is agreed are involved or affected.

Mediation is based on principles of problem solving which focus on the needs and interests of the participants, fairness, privacy, self determination, and the best interests of all family members.

These standards are intended to assist and guide public and private, voluntary and mandatory mediation. It is understood that the manner of implementation and mediator adherence to these standards may be influenced by local law or court rule.

I. Initiating the Process

A. Definition and Description of Mediation.

The mediator shall define mediation and describe the differences and similarities between mediation and other procedures for dispute resolution. In defining the process, the mediator shall delineate it from therapy, counselling, custody evaluation, arbitration, and advocacy.

B. Identification of Issues.

The mediator shall elicit sufficient information from the participants so that they can mutually define and agree on the issues to be resolved in mediation.

C. Appropriateness of Mediation.

The mediator shall help the participants evaluate the benefits, risks, and costs of mediation and the alternatives available to them.

D. Mediator's Duty of Disclosure.

1. Biases.

The mediator shall disclose to the participants any biases or strong views relating to the issues to be mediated.

2. Training and Experience.

The mediator's education, training, and experience to mediate the issues should be accurately described to the participants.

E. Procedures.

The mediator shall reach an understanding with the participants regarding the procedures to be followed in mediation. This includes but is not limited to the practice as to separate meetings between a participant and the mediator, confidentiality, use of legal services, the involvement of additional parties, and conditions under which mediation may be terminated.

F. Mutual Duties and Responsibilities.

The mediator and the participants shall agree upon the duties and responsibilities that each is accepting in the mediation process. This may be a written or verbal agreement.

II. Impartiality and Neutrality

A. Impartiality.

The mediator is obligated to maintain impartiality toward all participants. Impartiality means freedom from favoritism or bias either in word or action. Impartiality implies a commitment to aid all participants, as opposed to a single individual, in reaching a mutually satisfactory agreement. Impartiality means that a mediator will not play an adversarial role.

The mediator has a responsibility to maintain impartiality while raising questions for the parties to consider as to the fairness, equity, and feasibility of proposed options for settlement.

B. Neutrality.

Neutrality refers to the relationship that the mediator has with the disputing parties. If the mediator feels or any one of the participants states that the mediator's background or personal experiences would prejudice the mediator's performance, the mediator should withdraw from mediation unless all agree to proceed.

1. Prior Relationships.

A mediator's actual or perceived impartiality may be compromised by social or professional relationships with one of the participants at any point in time. The mediator shall not proceed if previous legal or counseling services have been provided to one of the participants. If such services have been provided to both participants, mediation shall not proceed unless the prior relationship has been discussed, the role of the mediator made distinct from the earlier relationship and the participants have been given the opportunity to freely choose to proceed.

2. Relationship to Participants.

The mediator should be aware that post-mediation professional or social relationships may compromise the mediator's continued availability as a neutral third party.

3. Conflicts of Interest.

A mediator should disclose any circumstance to the participants which might cause a conflict of interest.

III. Costs and Fees

A. Explanation of Fees.

The mediator shall explain the fees to be charged for mediation and any related costs and shall agree with the participants on how the fees will be shared and the manner of payment.

B. Reasonable.

When setting fees, the mediator shall ensure that they are explicit, fair, reasonable, and commensurate with the service to be performed. Unearned fees should be promptly returned to the clients.

C. Contingent Fees.

It is inappropriate for a mediator to charge contingent fees or to base fees on the outcome of mediation.

D. Referrals and Commissions.

No commissions, rebates, or similar forms of remuneration shall be given or received for referral of clients for mediation services.

IV. Confidentiality and Exchange of Information

A. Confidentiality.

Confidentiality relates to the full and open disclosure necessary for the mediation process. A mediator shall foster the confidentiality of the process.

1. Limits of Confidentiality.

The mediator shall inform the parties at the initial meeting of limitations on confidentiality such as statutorily or judicially mandated reporting.

2. Appearing in Court.

The mediator shall inform the parties of circumstances under which mediators may be compelled to testify in court.

3. Consequences of Disclosure of Facts Between Parties.

The mediator shall discuss with the participants the potential consequences of their disclosure of facts to each other during the mediation
process.

B. Release of Information.

1. The mediator shall obtain the consent of the participants prior to
releasing information to others.

2. The mediator shall maintain confidentiality and render anonymous all
identifying information when materials are used for research or training
purposes.

C. Caucus.

The mediator shall discuss policy regarding confidentiality for individual
caucuses. In the event that a mediator, upon the consent of the participants, speaks privately with any person not represented in mediation,
including children, the mediator shall define how information received
will be used.

D. Storage and Disposal of Records.

The mediator shall maintain confidentiality in the storage and disposal of
records.

E. Full Disclosure

The mediator shall require that there is disclosure of all relevant information in the mediation process as would reasonably occur in the judicial
discovery process.

VI. Self Determination

A. Responsibilities of the Participants and the Mediator.

The primary responsibility for the resolution of a dispute rests with the
participants. The mediator's obligation is to assist the disputants in
reaching an informed and voluntary settlement. At no time shall a mediator coerce a participant into agreement or make a substantive decision for
any participant.

B. Responsibility to Third Parties.

The mediator has a responsibility to promote the participants' consideration of the interests of children and other persons affected by the agree-

ment. The mediator also has a duty to assist parents to examine, apart from their own desires, the separate and individual needs of such people. The participants shall be encouraged to seek outside professional consultation when appropriate or when they are otherwise unable to agree on the needs of any individual affected by the agreement.

VII. Professional Advice

A. Independent Advice and Information.

The mediator shall encourage and assist the participants to obtain independent expert information and advice when such information is needed to reach an informed agreement or to protect the rights of a participant.

B. Providing Information.

A mediator shall give information only in those areas where qualified by training or experience.

C. Independent Legal Counsel.

When the mediation may affect legal rights or obligations, the mediator shall advise the participants to seek independent legal counsel prior to resolving the issues and in conjunction with formalizing an agreement.

VIII. Parties' Ability to Negotiate

The mediator shall assure that each participant has had an opportunity to understand the implications and ramifications of available options. In the event a participant needs either additional information or assistance in order for the negotiations to proceed in a fair and orderly manner or for an agreement to be reached, the mediator shall refer the individual to appropriate resources.

A. Procedural.

The mediator has a duty to assure balanced negotiations and should not permit manipulative or intimidating negotiation techniques.

B. Psychological.

The mediator shall explore whether the participants are capable of participating in informed negotiations. The mediator may postpone mediation and refer the parties to appropriate resources if necessary.

IX. Concluding Mediation

A. With Agreement.

1. Full Agreement.

The mediator shall discuss with the participants the process for formalization and implementation of the agreement.

2. Partial Agreement.

When the participants reach a partial agreement, the mediator shall discuss with them procedures available to resolve the remaining issues.

B. Without Agreement.

1. Termination by Participants.

The mediator shall inform the participants of their right to withdraw from mediation at any time and for any reason.

2. Termination by Mediator.

If the mediator believes that participants are unable or unwilling to meaningfully participate in the process or that a reasonable agreement is unlikely, the mediator may suspend or terminate mediation and should encourage the parties to seek appropriate professional help.

3. Impasse.

If the participants reach a final impasse, the mediator should not prolong unproductive discussions that would result in emotional and monetary costs to the participants.

X. Training and Education

A. Training.

A mediator shall acquire substantive knowledge and procedural skill in the specialized area of practice. This may include but is not limited to family and human development, family law, divorce procedures, family finances, community resources, the mediation process and professional ethics.

B. Continuing Education.

A mediator shall participate in continuing education and be personally responsible for on-going professional growth. A mediator is encouraged to join with other mediators and members of related professions to promote mutual professional development.

XI. Advertising

A mediator shall make only accurate statements about the mediation process, its costs and benefits, and about the mediator's qualifications.

XII. Relationships with Other Professionals

A. The Responsibility of the Mediator Toward Other Mediators.

1. Relationship with Other Mediators

A mediator should not mediate any dispute which is being mediated by another mediator without first endeavoring to consult with the person or persons conducting such mediation.

2. Co-Mediation.

In those situations where more than one mediator is participating in a particular case, each mediator has a responsibility to keep the others informed of developments essential to a cooperative effort.

B. Relationship with Other Professionals.

A mediator should respect the complementary relationship between mediation and legal, mental health, and other social services and should promote cooperation with other professionals.

XIII. Advancement of Mediation

A. Mediation Service.

A mediator is encouraged to provide some mediation service in the community for nominal or no fee.

B. Promotion of Mediation.

A mediator shall promote the advancement of mediation by encouraging and participating in research, publishing, or other forms of professional and public education.

Parameters of Practice for Family and Divorce Mediation

Resource List

> Academy of Family Mediators — Standards of Practice
> American Arbitration Association — Family Mediation Rules
> American Association for Marriage and Family Therapy — Membership Standards

American Association of Pastoral Counselors — Code of Ethics

American Bar Association, Family Law Section, Standards of Practice for Divorce Mediators, adopted in principle by the Council of the Family Law Section, 7/29/83

American Bar Association, 1982 Annual Meeting, Rule 2.2 Intermediary Comment

American Psychological Association — Ethical Standards of Psychologists

Arizona State Bar Family Law Section — Standards of Practice for Family Mediators

Association of Family and Conciliation Courts — Task Group Report, Education and Training of Mediators

Center for Dispute Resolution, Denver, Colorado, Code of Professional Conduct for Mediators

Family Mediation Association — Proposed Code of Professional Responsibility for Practicing Family Mediators

Massachusetts Council on Family Mediation — Draft Standards

Mediation Association of Southern Arizona — A Proposed Code of Ethics

Mediation Consortium of Washington State — Proposed Standards of Practice for Mediators

Mediation Council of Illinois — Professional Standards of Practice

Michigan Council for Family and Divorce Mediation — Statement of Ethics

National Association of Social Workers — Code of Ethics, Professional Standards

Participating Organizations

Academy of Family Mediators

American Academy of Matrimonial Lawyers

American Arbitration Association

American Association for Mediated Divorce

American Association of pastoral Counselors

American Bar Association Family Law Section, Mediation & Arbitration Committee

American Bar Association Special Committee on Alternative Dispute Resolution

American Psychological Association

Association of Family & Conciliation Courts

Association of Family & Conciliation Courts — California Chapter

British Columbia Judges Committee on Family Law

California State Bar, Family Law Section, Custody & Visitation Committee

Canadian Federal Government — Department of Justice, Policy &

Planning Center for Dispute Resolution, Denver, Colorado
Children's Judicial Resource Council
Colorado Bar, Family Law Section
Council on Accreditation of Services for Families and Children
Family Mediation Association
Family Mediation Center, Scottsdale, Arizona
Family Mediation Service of Ontario
Hennepin County Court Services
Legal Aid of Quebec
Los Angeles Conciliation Court
Maricopa County Conciliation Court
Mediation Association of Southern Arizona
Mediation Consortium of Washington State
Mediation Council of Illinois
Mediation Institute of California
Minnesota Council of Family Mediation
Montreal Conciliation Court
National Association of Social Workers
National Council on Family Relations
National Institute for Dispute Resolution
Northwest Mediation Service
Ontario Association for Family Mediation
Pima County Superior Court
Pinal County Conciliation Court
San Diego County Superior Court Family Services Society of Professionals in Dispute Resolution
South Florida Council on Divorce Mediation
Southern California Mediation Network
State Bar of California — Legal Specialization Committee Wisconsin Association of Family & Divorce Mediators

Appendix 10D

Family Mediation Canada
Code of Professional Conduct

Reproduced with the permission of Family Mediation Canada.

Article 1: Application and Enforcement

1. Membership in Family Mediation Canada requires explicit agreement to abide by:
   (a)   this Code of Professional Conduct; and
   (b)   the disciplinary procedures and sanctions adopted from time to time by the Standards and Ethics Committee and the Board of Directors of Family Mediation Canada.

2. The following rules are intended to govern the relations of family mediators with their clients, their professional colleagues, and the general public so that all will benefit from high standards of practice in family mediation. Members of Family Mediation Canada shall observe the spirit as well as the letter of provisions in this Code.

3. It is the obligation of family mediators to report and to encourage their clients to report, in writing, real or apparent breaches of this Code forthwith to the Chairperson of the Standards and Ethics Committee and/or to the President of Family Mediation Canada and/or to the President of their provincial or territorial association.

4. Members shall make this Code available to clients or the public upon request.

Article 2: Types of Mediation and Their Meaning

1. For the purposes of this Code, "family mediation" is defined as a non-adversarial, cooperative decision-making process in which a qualified and impartial third party, "the mediator", attempts to help family members resolve their disputes by agreement. The resolution is to be voluntary and based upon sufficient information and advice for each party.

2. The "closed mediation" process is intended to be confidential.

3. The "open mediation" process may result in the mediator preparing a report and/or making recommendations.

Article 3: Goal of Process and Role of Participants

1. The goal of family mediation is a fair and workable agreement, not a settlement at any cost.

2. The primary responsibility for the resolution of a dispute rests with the parties. At no time shall a mediator coerce the participants into agreement or make a substantive decision for any participant.

3. The mediator's role is that of a facilitator, i.e. to assist the parties to reach an informed and voluntary agreement that is consistent with the needs of their children.

Article 4: Integrity

1. Mediators shall avoid any activity that could create a conflict of interest. They shall not become involved in relationships with clients which might impair their professional judgment or in any way increase the risk of exploiting clients, such as, but not limited to, mediating disputes involving close friends, relatives, colleagues, supervisors or students. It is a violation of this Code to engage in sexual intimacies with a participant in the mediation process.

Article 5: Competence

1. Family mediators shall perform their services in a conscientious, diligent and efficient manner in accordance with this Code.

2. It is the obligation of a member acting as a family mediator to ensure that he or she is qualified to deal with the specific issues involved. Mediators shall acquire substantive knowledge and procedural skills as defined by the Education Committee and adopted by the Board of Directors of Family Mediation Canada.

3. While family mediators have a diversity of education and training the obligation to refrain from rendering services outside the limits of a mediator's qualifications and capabilities remains.

4. Family mediators shall engage in continuing education to ensure that their mediation skills are current and effective.

Article 6: Inter-Professional Relations

1. A mediator shall respect the complementary relationships among mediation, legal, mental health and other social services. He or she should promote cooperation with other professionals and encourage clients to use other professional resources when appropriate.

2. Where more than one mediator is participating in a particular case, each has the responsibility to keep the other(s) informed of developments in the mediation process essential to a cooperative effort.

Article 7: Confidentiality

1. A mediator shall not voluntarily disclose to anyone who is not a party to the mediation any information obtained through the mediation process except:

    (a)   non-identifying information for research or educational purposes; or

    (b)   with the written consent of the parties to the mediation contract; or

    (c)   when ordered to do so by a judicial authority with jurisdiction to compel such disclosure, or required to do so by legislation or other law; or

    (d)   when the information discloses an actual or potential threat to human life or safety.

2. Any information so divulged shall be limited to what is absolutely necessary to accomplish such purposes.

3. While closed mediation imposes the intention and duty of confidentiality on a mediator, it cannot confer privilege, and the mediator shall advise the parties that the intended confidentiality cannot be guaranteed unless legislative privilege exists.

4. Clients shall be informed, at the outset, of these and other limitations to confidentiality.

5. A mediator shall maintain confidentiality of clients' files and shall ensure that office staff do so as well in the storage and disposal of such records.

Article 8: Impartiality

1. A mediator has a duty to act with impartiality in relation to the participants. Impartiality means freedom from favouritism or bias either in word or in action.

2. Notwithstanding impartiality, a mediator has a duty to restrain parents from coming to arrangements that are perceived by the mediator not to be in the best interests of the children involved, and to withdraw from the mediation if this proves not to be possible.

3. The perception by one or both of the parties that the mediator is partial does not in itself require the mediator to withdraw, but in such circumstances, the mediator shall remind both parties of their right to terminate the mediation.

4. A mediator shall disclose to the participants any biases he or she may have relating to the issues to be mediated and any circumstances which might constitute or cause a conflict of interest, real or perceived, to arise.

Such disclosure shall be made as soon as the mediator recognizes the potential or any bias becoming operative or any conflict of interest arising.

5. A mediator shall refrain from mediating in cases where there has been any significant prior involvement between the mediator and one of the participants, unless every other participant expressly consents to the mediation proceeding after there has been full disclosure of such prior involvement. In this case, the role of the mediator should be carefully distinguished from the earlier relationship.

6. A lawyer-mediator, or any partner or associate of such lawyer-mediator, shall not represent either party during or after the mediation process in any related legal matters arising out of the issues discussed in the mediation.

Article 9: Ensuring Fair Negotiations

1. A mediator shall endeavour to ensure that the participants reach agreement freely, voluntarily, without undue influence, and on the basis of informed consent.

2. A mediator shall ensure that each party has had an opportunity to understand the implications and ramifications of available options. In the event that a party needs either additional information or assistance in order for the negotiations to proceed in a fair and orderly manner or for an agreement to be reached, the mediator shall refer the individual to appropriate resources.

3. A mediator shall explore whether the participants are capable of engaging in the mediation process. If a mediator believes that the parties are unable or unwilling to meaningfully participate in the process or that a reasonable agreement is unlikely, the mediator may suspend or terminate mediation and should encourage the parties to seek appropriate professional help.

4. The mediator has a duty to ensure balanced negotiations and shall not permit manipulative or intimidating negotiating techniques. While mediation must be impartial towards the participants, impartiality does not imply neutrality on the issue of fairness. If such negative tactics cannot be eliminated, the mediator has a duty to terminate mediation.

5. It is a fundamental principle of mediation that competent and informed parties can reach an agreement which may not correspond to legal guidelines contained in the relevant statutes or case law or that does not correspond with general community expectations and standards. Although the mediator's role is that of a facilitator and the primary responsibility for the resolution of a dispute rests with the parties, if the mediator finds an agreement or any part of it to be inherently unfair, he or she is expected to indicate his or her nonconcurrence to the parties.

Article 10: Information, Disclosure and Advice

1. It is the duty of a mediator to actively encourage the participants to make decisions based upon sufficient information, knowledge and advice.

2. Where financial or property issues are involved, the mediator shall obtain an undertaking from the parties to make frank and full disclosure of their financial and related circumstances at the appropriate time in the mediation process. The mediator will assist the parties and their advisors to achieve such disclosure. A mediator has an ongoing obligation to advise both parties to obtain legal and other professional advice and assistance in this respect.

3. Every family mediator has an ongoing obligation to advise participants of the desirability and availability of independent legal advice. While neutral legal information may be made available to the parties, each should be encouraged to obtain legal advice.

Article 11: Agreement to Mediate

1. The mediator shall explain the mediation process clearly to the parties before agreeing to mediate their dispute. In particular, the mediator should at the outset:

   (a)　define and explain mediation, both closed and open, and distinguish it from reconciliation counselling, therapy, assessment, advocacy, adjudication and arbitration;

   (b)　discuss the appropriateness of mediation for the parties in light of their particular circumstances, the benefits and risks of mediation, and the other alternatives open to the parties;

   (c)　discuss the differences between closed and open mediation and the implications of each, and if the mediator practices both types, require the parties to choose between closed and open mediation;

   (d)　advise the parties that either of them or the mediator has the right to suspend or terminate the process at any time;

   (e)　make explicit the costs of mediation and reach an agreement with the parties regarding payment of these costs;

   (f)　advise the parties of the role of legal advice in accordance with Article 10 of this Code. If the mediator is also a lawyer, he or she shall inform the parties that he or she cannot represent either or both of them in any related legal action;

   (g)　discuss with the parties the mediator's specific procedures and practices, such as when:

      (i)　separate sessions may be held;

      (ii)　there are to be separate communications with the parties or their counsel; and

      (iii)　other persons are to be involved in the mediation; and

(h)   recommend that the agreement to mediate be written and signed by the parties and the mediator.

Article 12: Termination of Mediation

1. It is the duty of a mediator to suspend or terminate mediation whenever continuation of the process is likely to harm or prejudice one or more of the participants, such as when mediation is being misused to:
(a)   develop a status quo with respect to the custody of the children; or
(b)   to dissipate or conceal assets.

2. A mediator shall suspend or terminate mediation when its usefulness is exhausted.

3. When a mediator believes that an agreement being reached is unreasonable, he or she shall so advise the parties and shall consider withdrawing from the mediation.

4. Mediators have a duty not to withdraw their services except for good cause and upon reasonable notice to the parties.

Article 13: Public Statements and Promotional Activities

1. The purpose of public statements concerning family mediation should be to:
(a)   educate the public generally about the process; and
(b)   present the process of mediation objectively as one of several methods of dispute resolution in order to help the public make informed judgments and choices.

2. Public communications shall not mislead the public, misrepresent facts, or contain any:.
(a)   false, fraudulent, misleading or unfair statements;
(b)   statements likely to mislead or deceive by making only a partial disclosure of relevant facts; or
(c)   statements intended or likely to create false or unjustified expectations of favourable results.

3. When advertising professional services, mediators should restrict themselves to matters which educate and inform the public. These could include the following information to describe the mediator and the services offered: name, address, telephone number, office hours, relevant academic degree(s), relevant training and experience in mediation, appropriate professional affiliations and membership status, advantages of the mediation process, and any additional relevant or important consumer information.

4. Public communications shall not falsely imply that membership in Family Mediation Canada or a provincial or territorial family mediation association constitutes certification as a mediator.

5. Mediators should promote the advancement of mediation by encouraging and/or participating in research, publishing and other forms of professional and public education.

6. Mediators are encouraged to provide some mediation services to the community for no or nominal charge.

7. Mediators should generally promote a cooperative approach to problem-solving and the welfare of the family as a whole, especially children.

Article 14: Charges for Services

1. At the outset, the mediator shall explain the fees to be charged for mediation and any related costs. He or she shall obtain agreement from the parties as to how the fees are to be shared and the method of payment.

2. No commissions, rebates or similar forms of remuneration shall be given or received for referral of clients for mediation services.

3. It is inappropriate for a mediator to base fees on the outcome of the mediation process.

4. When a retainer has been collected before mediation services were rendered, any unearned fees should be promptly returned to the clients upon the termination of mediation.

November 8, 1986

Index